CIVIL RELIGION IN ISRAEL

CIVIL RELIGION IN ISRAEL

Traditional Judaism and Political Culture in the Jewish State

Charles S. Liebman and Eliezer Don-Yehiya

UNIVERSITY OF CALIFORNIA PRESS
Berkeley, Los Angeles, London

DS112
L65
1983

University of California Press
Berkeley and Los Angeles, California

University of California Press, Ltd.
London, England

Copyright © 1983 by The Regents of the University of California

Library of Congress Cataloging in Publication Data

Liebman, Charles S.
    Civil religion in Israel.

    Bibliography: p. 277
    Includes index.
    1. Civil religion—Israel.   2. Israel—Politics and
government.   3. Israel—Civilization.   4. Zionism—
Israel.   I. Don-Yehiya, Eliezer.   II. Title.
DS112.L65   1983   306'.2'095694   82-17427
ISBN 0-520-04817-2

Printed in the United States of America

1 2 3 4 5 6 7 8 9

For Sara and Drora

Contents

Preface

Our study is concerned with the impact of Judaism on the
political culture of the modern Jewish settlement in the Land of
Israel—that is, from the period of the *yishuv* (the prestate
Zionist settlement) until today.

Political culture is such a popular term among political scien-
tists that it is sometimes used indiscriminately. We prefer to
follow Almond and Powell in defining it as "the pattern of . . .
attitudes and orientations toward politics among the members
of a political system" (*Comparative Politics*, p. 50). Our focus is
on civil religion. A good part of the first chapter is spent
explaining what we mean by civil religion. Our shorthand
definition is the ceremonials, myths, and creeds which legitimate the social order, unite the population, and mobilize the
society's members in pursuit of its dominant political goals.
Civil religion is that which is most holy and sacred in the
political culture. It forges its adherents into a moral community. The yishuv and Israel have had more than one civil
religion. Our special interest is the extent to which each civil
religion has appropriated ceremonials, myths, and creeds of the
Jewish religious tradition—consciously or unconsciously, directly or indirectly, in unchanged or distorted form.

Political systems differ from one another in the role played
by civil religions in their political cultures. From its inception,
modern Jewish society in the Land of Israel has been marked by
the prominent role civil religion has played in its culture and
politics. Hence the study of civil religion in Israel is necessarily
concerned with an important, if not the most important, component of Israeli political culture.

Our study will show that civil religion has declined in importance in the last few years. This in itself is perhaps the most important statement one can make about the changing nature of Israeli political culture.

The first chapter defines terms and explains the setting for the development of Israeli civil religion. Chapters two through six describe the various civil religions from the period of the yishuv until today. Chapter seven is concerned with the different responses of religious Jews to the civil religion—in theory and practice. The final chapter represents our summary and conclusions.

The study is very much a joint effort, the product of a continual interchange of ideas between us. The book does not include a single major idea for which one of us can claim exclusive credit.

Research began in 1975 under a grant from the Israel Foundations Trustees of the Ford Foundation, to whom we want to express our gratitude. We were assisted by a typing grant from the Book Committee of Bar-Ilan University. Sections of the study, in revised form, have appeared in *Midstream*, *The Journal of Church and State*, *Kivunim* (in Hebrew), *The Jerusalem Quarterly*, and *Modern Judaism*.

1 Traditional Religion and Civil Religion: Defining Terms

This is a study of civil religion in Israel. While the term *civil religion* has been used with increasing frequency in recent years, there is no consensus on its definition. This is hardly surprising, since scholars disagree even about the meaning of *religion*. Because our special concern with civil religion in Israel will be to specify its interrelationship with Judaism—the dominant religion of the society—we cannot avoid grappling with the problem of definition, even if we cannot resolve it completely. But readers who are satisfied with the shorthand definition offered in the preface may choose to skip this section and begin with our discussion of the identification of civil religion in the middle of the chapter.

TRADITIONAL RELIGION

For the sake of clarity, we will occasionally refer to religion as *traditional religion* in order to distinguish it from civil religion. There is a vast literature concerned with the definition of traditional religion.[1] We conceive of it as a system of symbols which provides ultimate meaning through reference to a transcendent power.

Let us begin with the term *ultimate meaning*.[2] This refers to meaning about the most important questions that confront man. Man seeks meaning.[3] That is, he seeks a sense of purpose; an understanding of who he is, of his role in life; an assurance that what he does and what he experiences transcend the immediate and the sensory. He seeks an order in the universe, of which his life (and death) are a part.

1

Family relations illustrate how religion can provide the ultimate meaning sought by man. The traditional concept of
family embraces a variety of obligatory relationships based on
an assurance that the family is rooted in the very nature of life,
that it complies somehow with the order of the universe. Religion relates to family by legitimating its ultimate meaning,
rooting it in ultimate reality.[4] It does so by prescribing behavior
in law with its source in a transcendent authority, by binding
family members together with ritual, celebrated together, and
by conveying in myth the image and importance of the family.

The family crisis we are experiencing today results in part
from the breakdown of the meaning of family provided by
religion. Family relationships cease to have meaning in a world
where life or activity or experience do not interrelate in some
meaningful, ordered pattern; where relationships are not
grounded in some ultimate sense of rightness; and where nothing is left but a utilitarian measuring stick of personal satisfaction. Without religious legitimation, one's obligations to the
family arise only from personal decisions made for selfish
advantage.

Culture is the system of inherited conceptions of meaning,
expressed in symbols by which men communicate, perpetuate,
and develop their knowledge of and attitudes toward life.
Symbols are the vehicles of cultural expression. They stand for
patterns of meaning but, unlike signs, they also shape these
patterns because symbols are perceived as part of the reality
they signify.

Both signs and symbols stand for something. They are shorthand for a set of ideas or feelings or both. But signs are simply
denotative and artificial. Symbols, on the other hand, do not
come into being as a result of man's creative imagination but
"appear to be built into man's experience as such."[5] Unlike
signs, symbols do not deal with "the observable and measurable
aspects of human experience, but attempt to get beyond the
empirical to meaning and value."[6] Symbolic language uses
sensory images to speak of that which transcends them. The
symbols, in turn, filter man's perception of the world in which
he lives.

Traditional religion is concerned with ultimate reality,
which is assumed to be beyond our immediate, everyday sensory experiences. Religion therefore utilizes symbolic lan-

guage. It portrays "ultimate reality and the manner in which the meaningful life is to be lived in relation to it"[7] by rooting our cultural conceptions in the general order of the universe. This is what makes the symbols of religion especially significant, that is, sacred. But precisely because religion is expressed symbolically it shapes our conceptions of meaning as it legitimates them. To return to the example of family, religion legitimates family relations by assuring us that family is part of the general order of the universe. Thus, for example, the Biblical story of Adam and Eve, as a mythic symbol, or the Passover Seder, as a ritual symbol, serve these roles, among others. These religious symbols not only legitimate the family but they convey models for particular types of family relationships.

The term *transcendent power* is the most problematic in our definition of traditional religion. It represents an equivocation between the terms *transcendent reality* and *supernatural power*, neither of which is quite satisfactory. Transcendent reality, like ultimate reality, suggests there is a reality that is a central concern of religion, the existence of which has implications for the way man conducts, or ought to conduct, his life; and for the way in which society is, or ought to be, organized. This reality, if only by virtue of its existence, imposes obligations. Because of its transcendence, this reality cannot be directly and immediately known by man through empirical observation.

Every religion is concerned with transcendent reality. But the same is true, at least by implication, of other meaning systems such as liberalism, communism, fascism, or nationalism. The distinguishing characteristic of religion, at least to Western man, is that at the heart of transcendent reality is a supernatural power—God—who not only exists, exercises influence, and imposes obligations by virtue of his being but is an active force in the universe. Hence one might infer the term supernatural power should be substituted for transcendent reality. But that would leave us with the problem of Buddhism for which the transcendent reality is not a supernatural power in the sense we have described it here. Consequently we chose the more equivocal transcendent power. What we want to suggest by the term *power* is the centrality of the transcendent in the core conception of reality as the religionist understands it. In communism, fascism, or other forms of civil religion, one can infer the notion of a transcendent reality. It is there by implication, particularly as a source of ultimate authority. But adherents of these ideologies and those who articulate them place no stress on this notion. Indeed, they may even take pains to avoid confronting the fact that transcendence is built into their ideological formulations. The adherents and articulators of traditional religion, by contrast, tend to emphasize their specific formulation of transcendent reality and source of authority, that is, God, even when alternative formulations are equally available and otherwise convenient.

CIVIL RELIGION

Civil religion embodies characteristics of traditional religion—it projects a meaning system, expressed with symbols—but at its core stands a corporate entity rather than a transcendent power, even if it also refers to transcendent reality or even a supernatural power.[8]

This does not mean that traditional religion has no concern with collectivities. Quite the contrary. Some traditional religions were also born with a central focus on collectivities rather than individuals. The salvation or redemption Judaism envisions is a national, collective redemption, not an individual, personal one. Jewish religion defines a Jew by birth rather than belief or rite. Within the religion itself there is a conception of the Jewish people which is independent of faith, belief, or ritual. And concern with this people continues to play a vital role in Jewish religious formulations.

Traditional Judaism thus has some characteristics of a civil religion. (This is a feature Judaism shared with other religions in traditional societies. T. Dunbar Moodie, using a definition of civil religion not very different from ours, points out that "any distinction between personal and civil religion in traditional societies is purely analytic."[9]) As we shall see, it is this civil religious characteristic of Judaism which renders the relationship of religious Jews to Israel's civil religion so problematic. However, at least since the destruction of the first temple in the sixth century B.C.E., Judaism also has been concerned with the individual and has conceived of the individual Jew as distinct from the Jewish collectivity. This changed emphasis was made possible by Judaism's assigning, from its outset, a central role to the concept of a supernatural power, that is, God. The notion of God as an active force in the universe, rewarding virtue and punishing evil, bears within it the seeds for the privatization of traditional religion, since it is the individual who relates to God. From its outset, then, Judaism has been a traditional, not a civil, religion.

We shall treat civil religion in functional terms—as a symbol system that provides sacred legitimation of the social order,[10] a definition recalling the functionalists' view of traditional religion.[11] But this is only one function of traditional religion. More significantly, it is a function that the observer, not the religionist, assigns to religion. Therein lies a critical difference between traditional religion and civil religion.

By placing God at the center of its meaning system, traditional religion gains the ability to address a variety of problems and individual quests without losing its ability to address the problems or meaning of collective existence and social organization. Because it places the collectivity at the center of its meaning system, civil religion can only order the environment and shape experiences for those whose personal identities are merged with their common, communal identity. Civil religion's success is measured by its ability to accomplish this fusion, but, clearly, it is likely to succeed only under a limited set of circumstances; generally it will succeed only partially. In other words, the transfer of ultimate authority from God to society (and the consequently secondary role assigned to problems of individual existence) means civil religion can neither provide the individual with the ultimate meaning nor evoke from him the intensity of commitment which traditional religion can.

The objective of civil religion is the santification of the society in which it functions. We will focus our study on what we believe to be the three main expressions in the attainment of this objective: (1) integration (uniting the society by involving its members in a set of common ceremonies and myths, which are themselves integrative and in turn express a sense of a common past, a common condition, and a common destiny on the part of the participants); (2) legitimation (transmitting the sense of an inherent justness or rightness in the nature of the social order and in the goals pursued by the society); and (3) mobilization (galvanizing the efforts and energies of society's members on behalf of socially approved tasks and responsibilities).

THE STRUCTURE OF CIVIL RELIGION

Structurally, civil religion, like traditional religion, comprises beliefs and practices, each of which deserves separate treatment. We will also consider the organization of civil religion.

Beliefs

Beliefs may be sensed or expressed cognitively as a set of assertions about the nature of the society, the individual's obligations to society, the relationship of the society to other societies and the significance of the society. Rokeach calls these descriptive or existential beliefs.[12] These elements of belief can also be expressed in the form of myths rather than cognitive assertions. In either case the term belief subsumes both images of reality and judgments about what is desirable or undesirable—what Rokeach calls prescriptive or proscriptive beliefs.[13]

Many of the beliefs of civil religion, like those of traditional religion, are directed toward the transcendent and the nonempirical. However, as we noted, the authority or source for the beliefs is less likely to be anchored in the transcendent. The beliefs of civil religion, like those of traditional religion, are grounded in their adherents' sense of rightness and wrongness. The ultimate authority for both is nonempirical; whether it is more likely to be sensed as instrumental and utilitarian by the adherent of civil religion is an interesting empirical question. Durkheim observed that the distinguishing character of religious beliefs is their obligatory nature.[14] Religious man senses his obligation to believe—an obligation which may be imposed coercively but finds its greatest force in the inner or moral obligation of the adherent to believe. Religious man may feel that he has arrived at his beliefs independently of the religious system, but he is aware that he must believe even if his own mind or conscience rebels. Indeed, religious belief involves imposing that which one ought to believe on that which one might otherwise believe, in the absence of religious obligation.

In their essence, civil religious beliefs may be identical to religious beliefs. The central prescriptive belief (value) of Israeli civil religion is the belief in Israel as a Jewish state. Not all Israelis, not even all Jewish Israelis believe it. Among some of those who do, it is as meaningful and important as any other belief to which they adhere. It goes to the very essence of their identity. For others, it is a belief which evokes various shades of commitment reflected both in varying interpretations and in varying attitudes toward nonbelievers. But even among many of civil religion's most devout believers, we sense that the moral obligation to believe is not quite as overwhelming as it is for the devout religionist.

Civil or political myths bear marked resemblance to religious myths. By labeling a story a myth we do not mean it is false. Myth "objectifies and organizes human hopes and fears and metamorphosizes them into persistent and durable works."[15] A myth is a story that evokes strong sentiments, and transmits and reinforces basic societal values.

Civil-religious or political myths tend to be far more circumscribed than religious myths. They are more clearly rooted in human history, their function is more obvious and they relate to a much narrower field of concern than do religious myths.[16] Furthermore, as we shall see, the historical specificity of political myths is likely to limit the period during which they can continue to evoke strong emotional resonance.[17] In chapters that follow we discuss three central political myths of Israeli civil religion—the Trumpeldor—Tel-Ḥai myth, the Masada myth and the Holocaust myth. Each occupied the central stage in Israeli civil religion in different periods and each was appropriate to a different stage of the belief system of the civil religion. Yet one wonders about the significance of political myths which can rise and decline in importance over such a short span of time. Indeed, as we shall see, not only does the importance of its myths change over time but the importance of civil religion in general changes. Perhaps this impermanence stems from the explicit centrality of society in the structure of civil religion. This ties civil religion to social change far more directly than traditional religion is tied to it.

This distinctive characteristic of political myth, that is, its changeability, is related to a second feature found in at least some political myths which may not be found in religious myths. It seems to us that many of the political myths we have studied serve a cathartic function. The recital of a myth like dreams in Freud's formulation expresses in diguised form ambivalences, contradictions and dilemmas which neither the

individual nor the society can confront directly.[18] This is true of
central political myths of Zionism. The dilemma or ambivalence within Zionism is its relationship to the Jewish tradition.
If Zionism is the heir to the Jewish tradition then by that
definition it inherits a history and culture of passivity, self-
abnegation, humility, and a host of traits which Zionism seeks
to negate. But if Zionism constitutes a revolt against the tradition, what is the basis of its legitimate right to speak on behalf of
all Jews, to affirm the claims of Jewish history to the Land of
Israel? For that matter, where are its roots and what is the
source of its culture?

This theme, as we shall see, recurs in a variety of different
semiconcealed formulations in a number of central political
myths. These myths do not appear or disappear overnight. But
they do gain or lose much of their force or resonance as the
particular forms of the dilemmas, contradictions, and ambivalences to which they relate rise or fall in significance.

Practices

The traditional framework of religious practices is religious
ritual. Rituals or rites are distinguishable from practices. The
latter implement sacred values but unlike rituals are not in and
of themselves symbolic expressions of the values. The term
ritual, like *myth*, has been appropriated by students of political
and social behavior.[19]

There are a number of definitions of ritual resembling each
other to a great extent. Susanne Langer defines ritual as "the
formalization of overt behavior in the presence of sacred symbols."[20] Bocock, stressing the physical aspect, defines ritual as
"the symbolic use of bodily movement and gesture in a social
situation to express and articulate meaning."[21] Lukes redefines
Langer's sacred symbols as objects of thoughts and feelings of
special significance, emerging with a virtually identical definition: "rule-governed activity of symbolic character which
draws the attention of its participants to objects of thought and
feeling which they hold to be of special significance."[22]

It is worth repeating that, at least in our terms, *sacred* or *holy*
symbols mean symbols of special significance. These symbols
tend to be more special, more sacred, as they intensify the
individual's relationship to the ultimate conditions of existence.

Bocock distinguishes civil from religious ritual in three respects.[23] First, the symbols of religious ritual refer to the holy, those of civic ritual to the group and the secular world, although we would add the group may assume all the characteristics of the holy. This is particularly true when the group is conceived as an historical entity. A symbol such as Yad Vashem, the symbol of the Holocaust, which plays a critical role in Israeli civil religion, assumes a sanctity not only because it symbolizes six million Jews who died but because it symbolizes the Jewish people and culture of the Diaspora whose suffering and death legitimize the Jewish right to Israel.

Second, participants in religious rituals are expected to be deeply involved in the meaning of the ritual whereas in civic ritual, according to Bocock, no deep understanding of the inner meaning of the ritual is cultivated and there is no stress on subjective awareness. The difference, however, may be one of degree, at most. We will refer below to the two-minute sirens that summon Israelis to observe the memory of Jewish heroes and martyrs. All activity ceases when the sirens sound on memorial holidays, and everyone stands at attention. It is our impression that the ritual of standing silently at attention fulfills the definition of a religious ritual.

Finally, Bocock distinguishes between civic and religious rituals in terms of their impact on the rest of the participants' lives. He notes that civic rituals carry very few implications for other areas of life—a distinction that is not quite valid for all civil rituals. In Zionist-socialism, the civil religion of the political elite in the prestate period, dancing was of special importance. It served purposes of social integration, certainly, and it reaffirmed a variety of Zionist-socialist values including egalitarianism, simplicity, and intense commitment.[24] It is difficult to believe that participation had no implications for the rest of the participants' lives or that failure to participate would not have aroused a sense of guilt. Nonetheless, it seems to us that of Bocock's three distinctions this one has the greatest moment. Perhaps the explanation is that the civil ritual lacks the implications of traditional religious ritual because the participant himself does not believe that the authority for the civil ritual is transcendent. The referent of the ritual, the symbol of the ritual, may be transcendent, but not the authority that commands its performance.

At the same time, we emphasize that, like traditional religion, civil religion makes demands, imposes obligations, and evokes total involvement of the person; this distinguishes it from a political point of view or even an ideology.

Organization

In those societies in which traditional religions freely coexist within an independent national political system, the organization of the civil religion tends to be diffuse. The civil authorities who prescribe its practices seek to incorporate folk custom rather than to initiate or impose totally new rituals. Rules tend to be broad and flexible rather than detailed and specific. Nor are those responsible for determining ceremonial procedures generally of especially high status in the political system. In fact, this may be the feature most clearly distinguishing civil from traditional religion. The elaboration of the hierarchy and authority in civil religion does not compare with that in traditional religion, perhaps because the state and its leaders constitute the institutions and elite of the civil religion. This reduces competition between civil and traditional religions and permits the civil religion to benefit from the legitimating functions of the traditional religion. Indeed, the virtual identity of political and civil religious institutions is an important difference between traditional and civil religion. However, where the political elite views traditional religion in a negative light, as an opposition to the social order, a more specific and detailed civil religious organization is likely to develop. Although little attention has been paid to the subject, this seems to have been the case in postrevolutionary France, Nazi Germany, and Communist Russia.[25]

THE IDENTIFICATION OF CIVIL RELIGION

There are two theoretical problems in measuring civil religion.[26] First, what are the criteria by which one establishes the presence of a civil religion? Second, once one establishes its presence, what proportion of the collectivity addressed by the civil religion must adhere to it, with what intensity of commitment, in order to classify it as effective?

We are not prepared at this stage to answer these questions. Our study really relies on our sense—shared by those to whom we have spoken, observers of and participants in Israeli society—that civil religion (as we have defined it) is present and engages, with varying degrees of commitment, the adherence of the vast majority of Israelis. In the material that follows we do allude to survey data which demonstrates that large numbers of Jews adhere to the principles of the civil religion. The survey was conducted in late 1975 among 2,000 Israeli Jews who represented a random sample of the population aged eighteen and above.[27] But our survey does not prove the existence of an integrated symbol system, nor does it tell us anything about levels of commitment. Apart from the survey we analyze the symbols themselves, their nature, the frequency of their occurrence, and the contexts in which they are used. But we are sensitive to the inadequacy of our measures of civil religion. We can only offer, as apology, the pioneering nature of this study.

It is obvious to us, even from comparing Israeli civil religion in different periods, that different civil religions can be distinguished by their varied religious intensity, that is, by the relative emphasis each, compared to the others, places on the sacred dimension of its beliefs and practices and on the demanding nature of the obligations it imposes. In this regard, Israeli civil religion is less religiously intense than traditional Judaism, and the most recent civil religion is less religiously intense than the earliest. We return to this last point in our final chapter.

Our definition of civil religion implies that there can be societies without a civil religion. We leave open the question whether a society can function without an overarching integrative symbol system.[28] But even if every society requires an integrative symbol system, it need not be a civil religion as we have defined it. Civil religion implies an element of consensus or, to use Durkheim's formulation, a consciousness of "moral unity" and a need for representation of that moral unity by sacred symbols. This element seems to us to be absent in most Western societies. Furthermore, even if we assume that individuals do require some symbol system that provides ultimate meaning by reference to the collectivity, and even if we further assume that traditional religion cannot satisfy this need because of religious pluralism or increased differentiation in society and the separation of religious institutions from the significant economic, political, and cultural institutions, it still does not follow that a single civil religion will emerge. Perhaps there will be a variety of civil religions serving to sanctify different subgroups within the larger society.

This point of view seems to be implied in the consociational model of politics. The theory behind the model posits that certain societies are characterized by a division of power among fairly homogenous groups who differ sharply from one another with respect to religion, language, ethnicity, and social class. In consociational societies these major bases of social cleavage do not overlap but are additive. Group members consequently share little in common with members of other groups, and the potential for social conflict is enormous. Political stability in such societies is maintained because each group is dominated by its own elite; the elites, recognizing the threat the cleavages represent, seek an accommodation on a pragmatic basis. As far as the masses are concerned, however, there is no consensus on basic societal values. Hence there is no need for a civil religion to integrate, legitimate, and mobilize the entire society. Presumably, each group is integrated, legitimated, and mobilized by its particular traditional (or civil) religion. The elites simply attempt to prevent the civil religions of the separate groups from working entirely at cross purposes.[29]

ISRAEL'S CIVIL RELIGION

Out study is concerned with the civil religion of Israel. We feel justified in speaking of one civil religion because we perceive one supported by, and transmitted in part through, the instrumentalities of the state, one commanding the adherence of the vast majority of citizens. The very nature of the civil religion excludes the Arabs who comprise roughly seventeen percent of the population of Israel proper, that is, excluding the population of the West Bank and the Gaza Strip. We briefly discuss the various modes of Arab integration into Israeli society in chapter five, but these have not included assimilating Arabs into Israel's civil religion.

Obviously, living in a Jewish state poses very special kinds of identity problems for non-Jews. But only in the last decade have Israeli non-Jews voiced objections to the Jewish nature of

Israeli society and to this date the objections are still phrased delicately. However liberal and libertarian the laws of Israel may be with respect to freedom of religion and equal rights for non-Jews, the latter represent a political minority, since the majority of the population not only define themselves as Jewish but view their Jewishness as a matter of political relevance. In fact within Israel the generic term for non-Jews is "the minorities," a term that includes primarily Muslim Arabs but also Christians who are mostly Arabs, and Druse, Bahai, Circassians, and Samaritans.

Among Israeli Jews, the terms Israeli and Jew are synonymous. Israelis call their state Jewish as do others, friends as well as enemies. The term *Jewish state* denotes far more to Israelis than the fact that a majority of its population is Jewish. Ninety-three percent of the Jewish population believes that Israel ought to be a Jewish state. Now Jewish state undoubtedly means different things to different people, but to the vast majority of the population it means a state which is predominantly Jewish (83 percent), which lives in accordance with the values of Judaism (64 percent), and whose public image is in accord with the Jewish tradition (62 percent). Seventy-seven percent feel that there ought to be some relationship between religion and state in Israel. In other words, Jewishness contains religious overtones for the vast majority of Israeli Jews, and they seek a reflection of this content in the conduct of the state. Being Jewish is the ascriptive characteristic most Israelis share. Virtually every Israeli Jew celebrates some aspect of the religious tradition.[30] This is also the characteristic which Israel's enemies emphasize. Therefore, it is only natural that a system of symbols will develop which expresses as it reinforces the tie between the Jewish tradition and what most Jews believe Israel ought to be. This is the common core of the varieties of Israeli civil religion in the different periods we will discuss.

The reality of a Catholic France or a Christian America may indeed be a thing of the past. The point is debatable.[31] In the United States and many countries of Western Europe the majority of the population and its political elite no longer associate religious affiliation and national identity. But two points should be made in this connection. First, even in France or the United States, a *Catholic* Frenchman or a *Christian* American refers to a member of an ascribed community, not to a person who necessarily subscribes to certain religious beliefs and practices. Second, that which may be true in the United States and Western Europe is not true in many other societies in which the majority of the population is identified with one particular religion. Certainly in those areas from which the great majority of Israeli Jews trace their immediate origins, North Africa and Eastern Europe, there is a sense of the identity of national and religious affiliation. Bernard Lewis notes that as Arab regimes come closer to the masses, "even if their verbiage is left-wing and ideological, they become more Islamic," since Islam is "the most effective form of consensus in Muslim countries."[32] Indeed, religion even more than language dictates national identification. Lewis notes that in Turkey non-Muslim citizens of the ostensibly secular republic do not call themselves Turks, nor are they called Turks by their neighbors. The exchange of population between Greece and Turkey

> was not a repatriation of Greeks to Greece and of Turks to Turkey but a deportation of Christian Turks from Turkey to Greece and a deportation of Muslim Greeks from Greece to Turkey. It was only after their arrival in their putative homelands that most of them began to learn their presumptive mother tongues.[33]

The same is true in Eastern Europe. A study of the Uniate Church in the Ukraine finds that residents of Poland were defined as Ukrainians as long as they remained Uniates even though they spoke Polish. Similarly, families in the Ukraine who might not even know Polish were considered Poles as long as they remained Roman Catholics.[34]

It would be a mistake to understand religion simply as a set of beliefs and practices. It is a matter of birth, family association, and acknowledgement of the individual's relation (by childhood memories if by nothing else) to the beliefs and practices of one religion and not another. The matter is complex and need not detain us here. But is is important to note that whereas Islam in North Africa and the Middle East and Christianity in Eastern Europe are certainly religions, they evoke a far more pervasive sense of identity than Western Christianity does from most of its adherents. The same is true of Judaism in Israel. It ought not to surprise us, therefore, that Jews who label themselves as atheists or totally nonreligious continue to call themselves Jews and insist that Israel must be a Jewish state.

The literature concerned with the debate over the essence of Judaism—whether it is a religion, a people, a nation, an ethnic group, a race, a civilization, etc.—is a voluminous one.[35] It is not our intention to review the literature although we touch upon the relations of modern Zionism to Judaism in the chapters that follow. At this point it is sufficient to note that no definition of Judaism, regardless of how secular or purely nationalistic, denies the historical association of Judaism and religion. Hence, any ideological position that asserts Israel ought to be a Jewish state must accept symbols, myths, ceremonies, and historical associations that evoke religious associations.

Why then a civil religion? Why will traditional religion not suffice? There are a number of reasons. The first is that Judaism has evolved a meaning system which speaks both to the individual Jew (who shares the history and the fate of other Jews) and to a community of a very special sort. Judaism's energies have been directed to the creation of a symbol system and a world view for the individual who is a member of a powerless minority, not a modern state. Reliance on God as savior and redeemer stands in conflict to modern values of national self-redemption.

By way of illustration, Passover and Ḥanukkah (the Feast of Lights) are among the most widely celebrated Jewish holidays. Both have explicit national historical referents. Passover commemorates the Jewish exodus from Egypt. Ḥanukkah commemorates the Maccabean or Hasmonean revolt and the attainment of cultic freedom and a large measure of Jewish sovereignty in the second temple period. Both these holidays, one might expect, would serve as important components in Israeli civil religion providing mythic-ritual symbols reminding Israelis of their heroic past, their long history, their ability to overcome past vicissitudes. The problem is that the holidays have assumed a fairly specific meaning in the Jewish tradition and subsymbols have developed or have been interpreted in accordance with this meaning. One central theme in the traditional meaning of the holidays was that success or victory was due entirely to God's miraculous intervention on behalf of the Jews and not to any action of the Jews themselves—not even of their leaders. As the traditional *haggada* (plural, *haggadot*) that Jews recite at the inception of Passover states: "And the Lord brought us forth from Egypt, not by means of an angel, nor by means of a seraph, nor by means of a messenger: but the Most Holy, blessed be He, Himself, in His glory." The meaning of Hanukkah is conveyed in the prayer which Jews are instructed to repeat three times a day and following every meal during the holiday: "Then didst thou in thine abundant mercy rise up for them in the time of their trouble . . . thou delivered the strong into the hands of the weak, the many into the hands of the few . . . the arrogant into the hands of them that occupied themselves with thy Torah." What, according to the traditional liturgy, did the Jews themselves do? "After this, thy children came into the inner sanctuary of thy house, cleansed thy Temple . . . kindled lights . . . and appointed these eight days of Hanukkah." The symbols and values, expressed in traditional forms, conflict with the needs and values of the modern state. This does not mean that Judaism cannot undergo change, that it cannot be rendered suitable to function as a civil religion; but this would require a reformulation which many of its own religious authorities resist.[36]

The second reason the idea of Israel as a Jewish state must rely on a civil religion is that God is the ultimate source of authority and focus of commitment in traditional Judaism, not the state, not the Jewish collectivity. The potential for conflict here threatens the stability of the state unless state leaders are to assume the authority to interpret the religious tradition, that is, unless Israel is to become a theocracy.

The third reason is that the Jewish people are a transnational group. To render traditional Judaism into the civil religion of Israel would be to create two religions, since Judaism in its civil transformation could not serve the needs of Diaspora Jews.

Finally, traditional Judaism's overall symbol system is attractive to, but doesn't command obedience from, a majority of Jews. Traditional Judaism expresses itself primarily through a system of law which the vast majority of Israeli Jews do not feel obligated to observe and a series of myths which many, if not most, do not find credible.[37] Hence, traditional Judaism alone cannot serve to integrate, legitimate, and mobilize contemporary Israeli society, not even the Jewish majority.

We have observed that Israeli society needs a civil religion rooted in the religious tradition but not synonymous with that tradition. This poses different problems for religious Jews than it does for nonreligious Jews. The religious sector comprises roughly fifteen percent of the total population. A minority of religious Jews interpret the tradition as antithetical to the state. This leads them to challenge the very legitimacy of the state. This position is associated with the group best known in the west as *Neturei Karta* (Guardians of the City). Neturei Karta is the more activist and extremist element of a much larger community in Israel, the *Edah Haredit* (The Pious Community), numbering a few thousand families centered in Jerusalem with a subcenter in B'nei B'rak and isolated adherents in a few other communities.[38] To the Neturei Karta and those who share its ideology, the establishment of Israel was an act of rebellion against God. Jews, they believe, are enjoined to wait for God to reestablish a Jewish state. Zionism is the great heresy of modern Judaism. In fact the Holocaust, the murder of six million Jews by the Nazis, was God's punishment for the Zionist heresy, inflicted on the Jewish people for abandoning their true religion and substituting secular nationalism. Any display of loyalty to Israel or recognition of its legitimacy is contrary to Jewish law.

Most religious Jews in Israel affirm both Israeliness and Jewishness as components of their identity. Jewishness to them is synonymous with the Jewish religion. Among this group, the inherently secular nature of the state and early Zionism and the antireligious propensities of the Zionist founders raise serious problems. One group of religious Jews, whose orientation is best reflected by Agudat Israel (the smaller of the two religious political parties), tends to minimize the importance of Israel as a component in their identity. A second group, whose ideological forefather was Rav Kook and is best represented today among religious ultranationalists (for example, Gush Emunim), has sought the transformation and transvaluation of traditional Zionist and Israeli symbols in religious terms. Although most religious Jews belong somewhere between these two camps, those who occupy this middle ground lack a clear ideological formulation.

What religious Jews cannot accept is a conscious reformulation of the religious tradition to make it more acceptable to the majority of Israelis or more compatible with the needs of the state. Nevertheless, many of them, because their commitment to Israel emerges out of their religious conceptions, do not feel the need for a civil religion; they suspect it constitutes a substitute for the tradition. At the same time, they welcome efforts to link Israel and Judaism. This explains why religious Jews in Israel stand outside the civil religion although, especially in recent years, they have made important contributions to its formulation. In chapter seven we discuss the variety of attitudes among religious Jews toward the civil religion.

For the nonreligious the affirmation of both Israeliness and the tradition poses other problems. What does the tradition mean? How can the tradition be integrated into the civil religion such that it remains true to itself on the one hand and serves the needs and values of a modern state on the other?

Just as a minority of religious Jews, sensitive to the conflict between the tradition and the needs of a modern state, have opted for the tradition rather than seeking a reconciliation, so a minority of nonreligious Jews have opted to reject the tradition. Such a position, which dissociates Jewishness and Israeliness, is that of the Canaanites.[39] The term Canaanite was popularized in the late 1940s and early 1950s. The position was most clearly articulated by a group of then young, relatively talented Israeli writers. It was shared by a substantial number of Israelis, particularly among the native born. It is difficult to know how many Israelis held this position, but some observers once felt that Canaanism, at least in modified form, would ultimately dominate Israeli society.[40]

The Canaanites believe that life in Israel bears no relationship to Jewish life in the Diaspora. In Israel, according to the Canaanites, a new Hebrew nation is evolving. This nation comprises both Jews and Arabs and obliterates all past affiliations. Linking this new people with Jewish history or world Jewry only serves to distort the development of the nation. The Canaanites find Judaism inadequate as a source from which the symbols for their new society can be drawn. Instead they seek a symbol system associated with the land and the ancient peoples who occupied the land (including but not limited to the early Hebrew settlers). The effort to dissociate the Hebrew settlers from subsequent Jewish history in general and the Jewish religion in particular engages the Canaanites in some rather intricate historical juggling, but our purpose is not to take issue with any of the viewpoints we present. The Canaanites' numbers have dwindled since the 1950s to the point where today they are virtually nonexistent. They sought a symbol system for the emergent Hebrew, as distinct from Jewish, society which also would provide personal meaning.

It is difficult to measure how many Israelis accept any version of the position, be it radically religious or radically secular, which dissociates Jewishness and Israeliness. Six percent of our respondents did not feel that Israel should be a Jewish state. Among this 6 percent, only 2 (0.1 percent of the total sample) identified themselves as religious. This understates the presence within the population of a Neturei-Karta-type ideology, since its adherents are likely to decline to be interviewed. The remainder of the 6 percent represents the number of Israeli Jews in sympathy with even the mildest variant of a Canaanite-type position. Bearing in mind that the religious sector accounts for roughly 15 percent of the total, this leaves us with about 80 percent of the sample who favor a Jewish state but don't believe that religion and Jewishness are coterminous. It is among this part of the population that Israeliness and the tradition must be reconciled.

If the tradition is to be reconciled with the needs of a state and with the belief and behavioral pattern of the nonreligious majority, its symbols must be reformulated through a process of transformation and transvaluation. By transformation we mean retaining certain structurally recognizable features of the symbol but changing other aspects of its form. For example, the ritual of reading from the haggada can be transformed by rewriting parts of the haggada. Transvaluation means retaining the form of the symbol but interpreting it to have a meaning other than the traditional meaning. Declaring the Passover a holiday that celebrates Jewish self-liberation would be an example of transvaluation. Generally, reformulated symbols are both transformed and transvalued, although, as we shall see, one variety of civil religion is characterized by transvaluation but not transformation.

We distinguish three primary strategies or approaches in the reformulation of symbols: confrontation, dissolution, and reinterpretation. These three strategies differ in the degree to which they are consciously or unconsciously pursued and accepted. Along with specific symbols and their value referents, these three strategies will serve as the distinguishing features of the varieties of Israeli civil religion to be described in the chapters that follow. However, these strategies are not mutually exclusive. They characterize one variety or another of the civil religion, but aspects of one strategy are present in a civil religion characterized by another strategy. We will find that different varieties of civil religion, each with an appropriate strategy of transformation and transvaluation, dominated Israeli political culture in different periods. But there always have been those who interpreted the civil religion or reconciled the tradition and their commitment to Israel in accordance with a strategy dominant in another period.

Confrontation

In the first strategy or approach, the civil religion self-consciously confronts, to some degree rejecting, the tradition. But it forms its symbols out of this rejection. The link to the tradition is maintained by the very seriousness accorded to traditional symbols that are deliberately changed in order to adapt them to new needs and values.

This approach is particularly suited to culturally sophisticated people among whom the tradition is too deeply embedded to be ignored. They cannot ignore the tradition, but they reject many of its symbols and their referents.

It is not easy to sustain a confrontation strategy in a pluralistic, democratic polity in which a considerable part of the population is traditionalist. A civil religion based exclusively on such a strategy is likely to be a divisive, rather than an integrative, force in society. Hence over the long run this approach can be maintained only as one variant in a civil religion that also makes room for other approaches.

Dissolution

The second strategy, which we call dissolution, maintains that the tradition is composed of a variety of strands reflecting different sets of symbols and values. Some of these are affirmed, while others are ignored rather than confronted and rejected. Selectivity, it is argued, is quite legitimate within the context of the tradition itself. In fact, some proponents of this approach claim that the part of the tradition they affirm is really more legitimate, authentic, or essential than the part they ignore.

This strategy is associated with a system of beliefs and symbols which aspires to become the common civil religion of the whole polity. Such a civil religion tends to stress the importance of that which unites the nation, such as the state and its institutions.

Reinterpretation

The third strategy transvalues but does not transform traditional symbols. The civil religion associated with this approach is characterized by the penetration of traditional symbols throughout the culture and their reinterpretation such that new values may be imposed upon them. All religious development is characterized by reinterpretation and imposition of new values. The distinction is really the degree to which traditional symbols are reinterpreted to meet contemporary needs. Reinterpretation can also mean the conceptualization of contemporary events in the format of traditional symbols, a process that forges stronger links between tradition and society.

This is the least self-conscious of the three strategies and is closest, in structure as well as content, to traditional religion. The attitude toward the tradition is very positive. Were the adherents of the reinterpretation approach to admit to their transvaluation of traditional symbols they would transform them into arbitrary signs devoid of meaning and defeat the very purpose they seek to achieve: legitimating their values by linking them to the tradition. The reinterpretation approach is encouraged by a decline in the influence of modern secular belief systems and a decline in their capacity to legitimate societal institutions and values.

THE CASE OF ISRAEL

The confrontation strategy was associated with Zionist-socialism, the dominant civil religion of the *yishuv*, the modern Jewish settlement in the Land of Israel in the prestate period. But Zionist-socialism involved more than confrontation. As we shall see in chapter two, the Zionist-socialists also sought to affirm at least part of the tradition. They did so by adopting a dissolution or reinterpretation approach, that is, selecting secularist-nationalist elements from within the tradition and dissociating them from their religious context.

How much sympathy does such a position evoke today? How many Jews in Israel subscribe to the radically secular position that Israel ought to be a Jewish state but that being Jewish today has nothing to do with religion? Eighteen percent of our sample felt that whereas Israel should be a Jewish state this did not mean that the state should be conducted in accordance with the religious tradition. Nineteen percent of the sample had the opinion that there should be total separation of religion and state. The two figures suggest that a little less than 20 percent of the present population subscribes to classical Zionist-socialist values dissociating Judaism from the religious tradition.

When Zionist-socialism was the dominant civil religion of the yishuv significant segments of the Jewish population were excluded from participation. Cleavages were so deep that we feel justified in talking about a number of civil religions coexisting among the different subcommunities of the yishuv. (One subcommunity, the *old yishuv*, whose roots go back to the late eighteenth century, did not share in any version of the civil religion. It is treated in chapter seven.)[41] In chapter three we discuss revisionism, the major alternative to Zionist-socialism in the yishuv period.

Since the establishment of Israel in 1948 Israeli civil religion has become more inclusive. Indeed the very existence of different subcommunities prior to 1948 impressed upon the political elite, Ben Gurion in particular, the necessity for an integrated symbol system. As Masuri noted in his studies of emerging states in Africa, nationalism, which he defines as a more assertive or defensive degree of national consciousness, may arise from external insecurity (a continuing problem for Israel) but also from internal insecurity resulting from a population's heterogeneity. Heterogeneity multiplies the number of conflicts and "the need for devices which would help the resolution of those conflicts."[42] Obviously, a single civil religion is one such device. But we are not suggesting that Israel has a civil religion because there is a functional necessity for such a religion. If the functional necessities of societies dictated the presence of civil religion, then the Lebanese and the Northern Irish would have developed a national identity and a civil religion, and thus avoided civil war. We suggest that if any one factor accounts for the development of Israeli civil religion and its particular character, it is the continued Jewish identity of the vast majority of the population, the desire of most Israelis to express that identity symbolically and transmit it to their children, and their inability to find in traditional Judaism an adequate expression and vehicle for their Jewish identity.

Ben Gurion's sensitivity to the need for a unifying symbol system that would serve the needs of the entire Jewish population led him to the dissolution strategy, which characterized statism, the dominant civil religion from 1948 until the late 1950s. Chapter four is devoted to a description of statism. Dissolution was also the characteristic strategy of revisionism; although as we shall see, the values and symbols of statism and revisionism were not the same.

Statism failed to evoke the continuing commitment of a majority of the population for reasons elaborated in later chapters. In chapters five and six we describe the new civil religion which has succeeded statism with its strategy of reinterpretation. This strategy is especially suited to the new majority in Israel—immigrants or the children of immigrants from Muslim countries—a population which is traditional in orientation, respectful of religion, but neither punctilious in religious observance nor especially knowledgeable about the basis of the tradition or the distinction between custom and religious law.

We are not suggesting that the civil religion has successfully overcome basic divisions in Israeli society. One cannot help but observe that deep divisions still separate groups within the Jewish sector of Israeli society. Nevertheless, there is today only one civil religion in Israel to which the vast majority of the population adheres with varying degrees of commitment. And we argue that the civil religion, at the very least, has made an important contribution to preventing even deeper divisions.

Most treatments of religion and politics in Israel stress the divisive function of religion.[43] They note the existence of political parties which reflect differences in religious outlook. They stress the fact that the population is divided over such issues as permitting or prohibiting civil marriage and divorce, permitting or prohibiting public transportation on the Sabbath, or providing or denying public recognition to non-Orthodox interpretations of Judaism. These studies concern themselves with the distribution of opinion among the population and within the parties. They examine the mechanisms with which the religious parties, representing a small minority of the population, succeed or fail to impose religious legislation on the entire population or to defend the particular interests of the religious camp.

Such studies obviously proceed from a traditional definition of religion. Religious Jews are those who subscribe to the basic tenets and practices of Jewish orthodoxy. Moreover, such studies assume that politics is concerned exclusively with group conflict. There is much to be said for the importance of these studies. Indeed we shall also discuss such conflict. But, taken by themselves, they provide an unbalanced image of the role of traditional Judaism in Israeli political life. We have taken a very different view of religion and politics in Israel. In accordance with our view the major focus of attention should be first of all the civil religion of Israeli society—the system of sacred symbols, that is, the beliefs and practices which integrate the society, legitimate the social order, and mobilize the population in social efforts while transmitting the central values and worldview that dominate the society. Civil religion by definition fulfills a political function not adequately accounted for by focusing on group conflict.

No single volume could adequately describe Israeli civil religion today, much less trace its historical evolution. We attempt a summary description but our primary focus is on the role of traditional Judaism in Israeli civil religion in the past and present. This focus is entirely appropriate since, as we have suggested, the core value or belief of Israeli civil religion is Israel as a Jewish state. At the same time we are attentive to the variety of meanings with which traditional Judaism has been invested as we describe the evolution of civil religion from the prestate period to the present.

2 Zionist-Socialism

THE BACKGROUND TO ZIONIST CIVIL RELIGION

The movement to emancipate Jews in the eighteenth and nineteenth centuries imposed both internal and external pressures on Jews to renounce their distinctive collective identity.[1] The secularization process which intensified during this period ended the traditional consensus on the compelling authority of the *halakha* (Jewish law, literally the Jewish way) in public, as well as private, life and on the identity of religion and Jewish nationality. Postemancipation Judaism witnessed the emergence of a range of approaches to the questions of religion, nationality, and state.[2]

Those who favored religious reform sought to harmonize the Jewish religion with conceptions and values embedded in the sociopolitical systems of Western Europe. Their modification of conventional religious practices and reinterpretation of traditional Jewish values included the elimination of Judaism's distinctive national features. Jewish nationalists, represented primarily by secular Zionism, sought substitutes for religious symbols which would mobilize and integrate the community and legitimate their particular vision of the Jewish condition and the Jewish future. Both nationalists and reformers secularized the Jewish messianic conception, transforming it into a vision of sociopolitical redemption to be realized by natural rather than supernatural means. The difference between the two was that the reformers stressed redemption of the individual and all mankind, not of one people in one territory. The reformers assumed the integration of the Jews in their respective countries of residence. In contrast, the nationalists stressed

25

the redemption of the Jewish people as a national entity. In Zionist terminology redemption could be affected only with the return of the Jews to their own land and the restoration of their political independence.

Zionism claimed that its goal was the normalization of Jewish existence, but the concept of normalization meant different things to different Zionist groups. Furthermore, some only paid lip service to the concept.

The political Zionists, those whose Zionist aspirations meant nothing more than the achievement of an autonomous commonwealth of Jews, probably took the notion of normalization most seriously.[3] On the whole, they also gave least consideration to the nature of the society or commonwealth they hoped to establish. But political Zionism, which eschewed settlement of the land and the slow, evolutionary development of an economic and political infrastructure in the Land of Israel (Palestine), opting instead for bold tactics at the international level, was necessarily weakest within the yishuv. After all, the settlers had no choice but to articulate their own social, economic, and political goals and a sense of how the enterprise that engaged their very existence was connected to Judaism, the Jewish past, and the Jewish future. They could hardly postpone consideration of such questions until they had achieved the ultimate political goals of the Zionist movement.

The indigenous labor movement was firmly committed to building a base within the Land of Israel and from its inception projected a vision beyond the normalization of Jewish existence. This was not true of all its leaders, nor even of all its major cultural heroes. But, even for those who were the exception, normalization itself was a vision generating an ideology and a symbol system that reflected the abnormal Jewish condition they sought to overcome. This group sought to detach itself from traditional Jewish culture, but by defining its values as the negation of the Jewish tradition and Jewish culture it retained a paradoxical association. Its adherents denied that there was anything inherently unique in the Jewish people or its culture that merited cultivation in a Jewish national homeland. Redemption, so basic to mainstream Zionist thought, was presented as the aspiration to free Jews from their unnatural way of life and normalize their national existence. The myths and symbols inherent in the national historic tradition were of no significance to this group in the legitimation of their efforts.

Their goal was to introduce revolutionary changes in the Jewish way of life, to encourage the emergence of a new Jewish people, free and independent in its own territory, liberated from the burdens of the religious tradition which had been shaped by abnormal Jewish life in exile.[4]

Haim Yosef Brenner (1881–1921), the foremost literary figure of the second aliya (immigration; literally: "going up") was representative of this tendency. He denied that Judaism was defined by specific patterns of life or values, or that the Jewish people had any special mission.[5] He refused to recognize secular nationalism as a legitimate transformation of the Jewish tradition and eschewed "any ideology offering itself as an equivalent to religious belief."[6] The same attitude characterized other renowned writers and poets of that period, such as Micha Josef Berdyczewski (1865–1921), Haim Hazaz (1898–1976) and Saul Tchernichowsky (1875–1943). Like Brenner, they opposed any religion, traditional or secular, which offered its followers a comprehensive interpretation of the meaning and purpose of existence and demanded from them devotion to, and sacrifice on behalf of, a religious, national, or social ideal.[7] This does not mean that these writers had no values and symbols to replace those they rejected. But these were primarily oriented to problems of individual, rather than collective or social, existence. Most of the yishuv, by contrast, objected to an interpretation of Zionism which limited its goals to the normalization of Jewish existence.

Zionism, like other modern Jewish movements, arose from the breakdown of the religious tradition and represented an effort to devise a new basis of Jewish identity and unity.[8] But Judaism, like all traditional religions, was also concerned with questions of ultimate existence and, like other religions, represented a system of personal meaning for its adherents. Hence for some Jews the weakening of faith meant not only a crisis of Jewish identity but also the necessity of coping with ultimate existential problems without any assistance from traditional religion.

Zionism's task was broader than that of other late nineteenth century national movements. Others strove for national liberation of peoples settled in their own lands and possessed of national cultures and national consciousness. They could afford to be less concerned with the building of a new society, a preoccupation of the Zionist enterprise.[9] Indeed, Zionist efforts in this respect remind one more of post-World War II efforts at nation building in postcolonial societies, although there are differences in this case as well.

Zionism, therefore, had a special need for values and symbols of a sanctified character which would attract Jews to its ranks, integrate them into its new society, and mobilize them in the pursuit of Zionist goals. Our concern is confined to efforts made within the yishuv itself. The old and new yishuv existed fairly independently of one another. This was less true, of course, of religious Jews among the Zionist settlers.[10] Our discussion of the civil religions of the yishuv focuses on the later period (the 1930s and the 1940s) though much of our description and analysis is appropriate to the earlier period of Zionist immigration as well. Indeed, it is the second aliya (1904–1914) which is the formative period of Zionist-socialism.

THE CIVIL RELIGIONS OF THE YISHUV

The yishuv was united in its commitment to Zionism, to settlement of Jews in the Land of Israel, to a renaissance of Jewish culture, and to the formation of an autonomous Jewish society. This commitment was expressed through and reinforced by a symbol system such that one could talk of the civil religion of the yishuv. However, the yishuv was divided into four ideological camps, though none was entirely homogeneous. (The term *camp* was used within the yishuv itself as we use it here.) Thus we prefer to talk about a plurality of civil religions.

The most cohesive and powerful of the camps was the labor movement. As we hope to demonstrate, one can speak meaningfully about the civil religion of the labor movement, which we call Zionist-socialism. The labor movement was divided into two wings—left and right—which split over loyalty to the values and symbols of socialism and over attitudes toward traditional Judaism. Each wing, and sometimes each subgroup within each wing, maintained its own institutional framework, but both wings were united by a common loyalty to the Histadrut (the General Federation of Workers, with its elaborate set of economic, cultural, social, political, and welfare enterprises) and by a common ideological and symbol system.

A second community, the religious camp, was also divided into two wings—Zionist and non-Zionist—the latter generally known as the *haredi* (pious) community, which was really part of the old yishuv. Unlike the labor movement, the religious camp lacked umbrella institutions. On the other hand, both its wings sought legitimacy from the symbols of traditional Judaism and their interpretation of the religious tradition. The overriding importance of religious law and custom to all the adherents of this camp provided bonds and mutual interrelationships, which mitigated in many ways the deep social, political, cultural, and ideological divisions between them.

The third, revisionist camp, suffered from the fewest internal divisions, although, as we shall see, it was not without dissidents and splinter organizations. The revisionists were the last camp to build an institutional network. Their activity in this regard was marked by frequent indecision and hindered by strong opposition from without. Therefore, revisionism never developed the social and economic base the other camps developed to reinforce their symbol systems.

These three camps were, to a great extent, communities of believers with distinctive symbol systems. The fourth camp, generally referred to as the civil (*ezrahi*) camp, was the most nebulous in its ideological and symbolic formulation.[11] It never developed a coherent civil religion and will not concern us. Its political approach tended to be pragmatic and moderate; its institutions were the least cohesive; its ideology was the least articulate. Its adherents at different times moved in and out of the other camps of the yishuv.

The secular religions of Zionist-socialism and revisionism were designed to serve as functional equivalents of traditional religion. They formed systems of values and symbols the purposes of which included integrating their own adherents, legitimating their claim to hegemony over the whole yishuv, rendering their very existence significant, imbuing their members with a sense of mission, and mobilizing them to serve their objectives. Both civil religions drew selectively from the religious tradition's values and symbols, detaching them from their original context and suiting them to new and different cultural-ideological systems.

In the remainder of this chapter we will confine our discussion to Zionist-socialism. Chapter three will treat revisionism.

We will postpone a discussion of the religious camp to chapter seven, where we will explore it as part of a broader concern— the response of religious Jewry to Zionist civil religions.

ZIONIST-SOCIALISM: THE CIVIL RELIGION OF THE LABOR MOVEMENT

Zionist-socialism was a religious surrogate. It provided meaning and purpose to individual existence by mobilizing the individual in the collective effort to establish in the Land of Israel an ideal society based on social equality, social justice, and productive labor. The vision of this society was ostensibly founded on values present in Judaism itself, and many of the symbols that conveyed these values were derived from the Jewish tradition. But the radical secularism of the movement led it to absorb the symbols and values of the tradition selectively and to reformulate the tradition in its own spirit. The strategy characterizing the reformulation was confrontation. Reformulated symbols and new values were projected as the converse of the tradition, sometimes subtly, often explicitly. Zionist-socialism did not rely exclusively upon traditional Judaism for its symbols. It drew extensively from the internationalist socialist movement, particularly to reinforce values of class consciousness. Finally, some of its unique elements— such as its conception of *halutziut* (pioneering), which emerged from the fusion of Zionism and socialism—led to the creation of unique symbols.

THE VALUES OF ZIONIST-SOCIALISM AND LINGUISTIC SYMBOLS

Ḥalutziut

The *ḥalutz* (pioneer) was portrayed as the bearer of the national mission, paving the way for national redemption. The pioneer was part of an elite, but an elite defined by special obligations and responsibilities, not a privileged elite. The term ḥalutz had two meanings in the Zionist-socialist vocabulary. In its inclusive meaning, anybody who settled in the Land of Israel and led a productive life participated in the enterprise of national redemption, and hence was a ḥalutz. In its more exclusive sense, the real pioneers, or the pioneering elite, were those who literally settled the land, who engaged in agricultural labor in the framework of the kibbutz, who led a collective, communal, egalitarian life.

The term *ḥalutz* originated in the Bible.[12] Ḥalutzim led the Israelite camp. They were the first to heed the call to war. But the biblical pioneer acted "before the Lord," that is, in God's name. The Zionist-socialist ḥalutz undertook a purely national mission. His authority did not derive from any supernatural source; he relied exclusively on his own strength to realize his goals. The Zionist-socialist conception of the halutz was inspired by the ideals and climate of opinion permeating the revolutionary movements in Russia. Pioneering came to suggest renewal and change. The pioneer was the harbinger of the Jew of the future. Kibbutz publications frequently quoted Brenner on this point. "These individual Hebrews are few but they are alive. They are a new type among the children of Israel."[13]

Labor

The *Haskala* (the Jewish *enlightenment* movement of the nineteenth century) had emphasized the importance of "productive labor" and the necessity to normalize "the Jewish economic structure."[14] Zionist-socialism went a step further. Labor became an intrinsic value, the basis of national redemption and personal fulfillment. This concept of labor owed much to certain nineteenth-century European ideas expressed in various socialist doctrines.[15] It was particularly functional for an emerging voluntary society, which was highly dependent on the commitment of its members to effect its goals.

Labor is not merely the performance of a task. It is a quasi-ritualistic act, *holy work* requiring total and absolute devotion and unconditional commitment. "Labor demands the whole of a person. It exhausts all one's energy and gives but little reward."[16] The powerful religious dimension in the conception of labor was acknowledged in the very term *religion of labor*, which was associated in particular with the message of A.D. (Aharon David) Gordon (1856–1922), one of the eminent spiritual leaders of the labor movement. Gordon's teaching, like his personality and way of life, reflected the religious, almost mystical, value he attributed to productive labor, especially labor that furthered national aims. In one article Gordon responded to the argument that Jewish employers were justified in hiring Arabs rather than Jews because hiring Arabs was cheaper and more efficient. Gordon asked:

> Would a religious Jew be willing to desecrate the Sabbath on the basis of such arguments? He would say: "Religion is a different matter." It is. Religion is not toying with ideals. Religion knows how to impose duties, to assert its rightful place and to be intrinsically important. . . . Is national life, which so crucially depends on the yishuv, valuable enough to require the same effort made by the religious Jew on behalf of religion?[17]

Echoing the biblical verse that demands the people of Israel choose between worship of God and paganism,[18] Gordon noted that those who live in the Land must choose between productive labor, working with one's hands, which is true and real life, and parasitic life, which is *exilic* even in the Land of Israel.

The religious dimension in the Zionist-socialist attitude toward labor had direct political implications. The demand to unite the different labor parties was based on the *unity of believers* in the religion of labor, which required political unity regardless of whatever differences might exist. "We all direct ourselves to one God. We all want labor and a life of labor and hence, we all must live together."[19]

Redeeming the Land

The primacy Zionist-socialism gave to agricultural labor stemmed from the bond between man and nature and the redemption of the nation and its homeland, which found their most forceful symbolization in *working the land*. This was the antithesis of the "exilic" way of life. The return to nature was appropriate to a people returning to its own land. In an article published in the major organ of Mapai (the dominant political party within the labor movement) the ideal of the land was described as "a sense of duty, persistence, endurance, love for the permanent, the real and the firmly rooted."[20] In the Mapai writer's opinion one source of anti-Semitism was that Diaspora Jews had no land of their own and alienated themselves from the land.

A recurrent metaphor in the Zionist-socialist literature was the plant that returns to the soil of the homeland, strikes roots, and blossoms anew. Others were the son returning to his mother and lovers reuniting after long separation. Interestingly, many of the metaphors can be found in biblical proverbs and rabbinical homilies. But in the traditional sources the relationship between the Jews and their land derived its sanctity from God, or was actualized because of God. The reverence Zionist-socialism manifested toward the land, nature, and physical communion between man and nature is far more evocative of paganism than of Judaism.[21]

Land or soil, the symbol of the concrete and the physical in Zionist-socialism, was grasped as the antithesis of the exaggerated spirituality that characterized traditional Judaism. The enemy, in symbolic terms, was the sky—representing religious men of spirit—of the exile and all that this entailed.[22]

The cult of the land in Zionist-socialism symbolized the tendency to transfer the focus of sanctity from the heavens to the earth. In one of the first settlement camps the cry was to remove all the obstacles between the settlers and the land: "The land and only the land will be the holy of holies for the Hebrew soul."[23]

A particularly rich source of material on the sanctification of Zionist-socialist values are the Passover haggadot published by various kibbutzim. (The haggada, as we noted in chapter one, is the classic text recited at the festive meal that inaugurates the Passover holiday. The custom of reading the haggada is deeply ingrained in Jewish culture.) Zionist-socialists transformed the traditional haggada in conformance with their own ideology. Not atypical of kibbutz haggadot of the 1930s and 1940s is the passage in one haggada which includes an invocation to the land by its "few sons" who vow to treat it with filial loyalty. "And we shall cross the stormy seas until we reach you and cling to you. In our blood and toil we shall redeem you until you are entirely ours."[24]

Asceticism and Equality

Zionist-socialism in general and the kibbutz movement in particular ascribed great ethical meaning to a modest, ascetic way of life. Yonina Talmon-Gerber argued that the ideology of the kibbutz life, like the Protestant ethic, combined asceticism with a positive and active orientation toward the universe.[25] Unlike Protestantism, she maintained, the kibbutz ideology was completely secular.[26] This is only partially true. No one claimed supernatural sanction for the value of asceticism. On the other hand, asceticism was revered not as an instrumental ideal but as rooted in a transcendent structure of right and wrong. Talmon herself noted that working for the advancement of the kibbutz became, in part, "a secular worship of God—a sort of holy work—the devotion to work through frugality became a ritualistic and symbolic expression of loyalty to values."[27] In addition "voluntary poverty" established the moral supremacy of the workers' elite and their claim to hegemony in the Zionist movement and the yishuv.[28] Associated with the value of asceticism among Zionist-socialists were the values of equality and mutual cooperation.

Military Heroism

Although some Zionist-socialist circles held pacifist views and were reluctant to idealize the values of military heroism and prowess[29] the concerted Arab efforts against the yishuv, those of 1920–1921, 1929, and 1936–1939 in particular, weakened these circles. Increasingly, Zionist-socialists attributed the role of military defender to the pioneer. He was both a worker and a soldier. The increased tension between the yishuv and the British authorities served to further enhance the value of military heroism, and World War II and the Holocaust confirmed this trend. But the value of military heroism only reached its peak after the establishment of the state, and we will deal with this in greater detail in chapter four.

Nationalism and Class Consciousness

A characteristic of civil religion we have noted is that the collective replaces God. It is the collective that is sanctified, that legitimates, that requires fulfillment of its needs. In Zionist-socialism the sanctified collective is generally the Jewish nation, but not always. Passover haggadot of the kibbutzim, for example, are concerned with a specifically Jewish holiday. Therefore, they stress values and motifs related to Judaism. But socialist and working class motifs also appear, even in some of the haggadot. For example, the exodus from Egypt is presented as a symbol of the struggle for liberation of oppressed classes all over the world.[30] Class motifs stand out more strikingly, however, in symbols and rituals drawn from non-Jewish sources. One party within the labor movement, Hapoel Hatzair, whose leadership included A. D. Gordon, resisted the use of such symbols. It even refused to identify itself as socialist because of its objections to conceptions of class consciousness and to the materialism it charged was embedded in classical socialism.[31] However, the differences between Hapoel Hatzair and Ahdut Haavodah, the largest of the labor Zionist parties, were gradually overcome. The 1930 merger of the two resulted in the establishment of Mapai, the dominant party of the yishuv and the State of Israel until 1977. In that merger, Ahdut Haavodah's conception of socialism emerged triumphant.[32]

Preserving the unity of the working class was a sacred value in Zionist-socialism. The struggle against the religious Zionists and the revisionists derived in large measure from the support these groups gave to workers outside the Histadrut. Indeed, even the opposition to institutionalized religion was based in part upon the notion of the Zionist-socialist elite that religion competed with class for feelings of loyalty and solidarity.

But class consciousness leads to class struggle, which surely impairs national unity. The ideological solution was *constructivism*, which was supposed to resolve the conflict between these two sacred values. Constructivism meant substituting for violent revolution the influence exerted by exemplary behavior of the labor movement and by the political control of the *society of workers*. Zionist-socialism did not quite surrender the conception of class conflict, but replaced armed struggle with constructive activity and political struggle. Constructivism prevented an overt confrontation between the labor Zionists and other camps of the yishuv. Nevertheless, the labor movement was criticized for creating segregated economic, cultural, and educational institutions, which critics charged impaired national unity. The Zionist-socialist response was that class loyalty and national loyalty, far from being mutually exclusive, are in fact complementary. Both, they claimed, served the interests of the entire yishuv and strengthened each other. Such arguments reflected the conviction that the Jewish working class in the Land of Israel had a special national mission requiring it to organize itself in a separate framework promoting its unique way of life.

Despite such arguments, conflict between national and class orientations troubled the labor movement itself. In some circles, the international working-class and socialist ideology were endowed with a degree of sanctity equal to that of the Jewish people and Zionism.

Zionist-Socialism and Traditional Judaism[33]

We have already had occasion to observe how Zionist-socialism utilized symbols of traditional religion, transforming them and transvaluing them to suit its purposes. But while it acknowledged (at least by implication) the resonance of the traditional symbols for the Jewish people, Zionist-socialism rejected any political role for traditional religion. A few dissidents argued that traditional religion was a basic component in national integration, but a more typical point of view affirmed that Jewish nationalism would formulate its own value system and shed the forms of traditional Judaism—even though religion had once served "as a barrier against national disasters."[34]

This attitude was influenced in part by currents that prevailed in both Jewish and non-Jewish working-class circles in Russia and Poland. Zionist-socialist leaders in Eastern Europe represented the war against religion as one of their primary aims. A manifesto to Jewish Youth composed by Nachman Syrkin (1868–1924), first ideologist and leader of Zionist-socialism, stated that: "Zionist Socialism sees, in the applied Jewish religion, which is not a religion but a tragedy, the major impediment confronting the Jewish nation on the road to culture, science, freedom."[35]

By contrast religion to the settlers in the Land of Israel was not an obstacle to the realization of their vision. They saw themselves forming a new society where there was no powerful religious establishment with which to contend. Nostalgia and longing for the homes from which they came, intensified by their bitter loneliness,[36] also served to mitigate their antagonism to the religious tradition. Finally, the Zionist-socialists' recognition of the necessity for political cooperation with the religious Zionists was both a result of diminished antagonism toward, and cause for further restraint from attacks on, religion.

None of this, however, led to a disavowal of a militant secularist ideology. Furthermore, the meaning which Zionist-socialism attributed to two of its most important symbols, *exile* and *redemption*, evoked continued antagonism to traditional Judaism.

Exile and Redemption

Exile, in the Zionist lexicon, implied a way of life devoid of any redeeming quality. An exilic Jew was one characterized by exilic Jewish traits: cowardice, dependency, excessive spirituality, nonproductive labor, flawed social relationships, egoism, vulgarity, coarseness, weakness, separation from nature and art, lack of pride, and conservatism. Without question, this caricature of world Jewry bears the imprint of anti-Semitic stereotypes, although its roots can be found in the haskala literature as well. The haskala, however, sought to reform the Jew whereas the Zionist-socialists believed that Jews who remained outside the Land of Israel were beyond the hope of redemption. (They were not alone in this view, and some were more radical than others.)

The anti-exilic attitude, *negation of the Diaspora* as it came to be called, was also expressed in the selective use of traditional Jewish symbols by the Zionist-socialists, utilizing a dissolution strategy. Those symbols associated with the temple periods, when the Jews lived in their own land, carried greater legitimacy and were more readily invoked than symbols associated with the 2,000-year period of Jewish exile which followed the destruction of the second temple in 70 C.E. A central place in the Zionist-socialist educational system was accorded to the Bible and symbols of biblical origin. The attitude Zionist-socialists exhibited toward rabbinical, as distinct from biblical, symbols and to *halakha* (rabbinical law and rabbinical interpretation of biblical law) was generally negative.[37]

Redemption, meaning attainment of both individual and national freedom by individual and collective effort of the Jewish people, stood in juxtaposition to exilic Judaism.

Ber Borochov (1881–1917), foremost theoretician of Zionist-socialism, writing about the Passover holiday, praised the wicked son of the traditional *haggada* text because he wanted no part of the freedom given by God. The wicked son, said Borochov, insisted upon attaining freedom by himself. The "wicked ones," he argued, who in our generation insist on attaining freedom with their own hands are creating "the foundation for the construction of new Jewish life."[38]

The traditional story of Ḥanukkah recounts how, after the Jews recaptured the temple, they found a container with sufficient oil to keep the sacred candelabrum lit for only one day. But the oil lasted for eight days, enough time to produce new oil. A popular Ḥanukkah song of the yishuv compared the ḥalutzim favorably to the Jews of yore because "no miracle occurred to us, we found no container of oil." A kibbutz *haggada* proclaims, in a parody of the traditional text, "every generation must be its own redeemer that it may be redeemed."³⁹ And redemption includes freedom from the tradition itself. According to another *haggada*, "we, the generation of free men, will celebrate our holiday without the spirit of enslavement to the tradition."⁴⁰

Zionist-socialism conscientiously excised God from its symbol system. Nation and Land were frequently substituted for God, but sometimes the working class or even all humanity became the source of values and obligations, the focus for feelings of identity and loyalty—the objects of ritual and ceremony. Typical in this regard is the transformation of biblical verses deeply embedded in folk usage. For example, the traditional phrase, "who can retell the glories of God" was transformed into the opening phrase of one of the most popular of all Ḥanukkah songs: "Who can retell the glories of Israel." Even the most sacred of all passages—"Hear O Israel, The Lord our God, the Lord is One"—was transformed in one kibbutz haggada: "Hear O Israel, Israel is our destiny, Israel is one."⁴¹

Linguistic Secularization

The type of transformation referred to here seems to exemplify a process which various scholars have identified as linguistic secularization: the use of words, idioms, and phrases derived from religious sources but detached from their original meaning to serve secular purposes.⁴² Yet there is more to this phenomenon. When adherents of civil religion transform sacred idioms and phrases they are sacralizing the values and concepts they seek to express with these transformed symbols. In other words, a process of sacralization, as well as secularization, is taking place. This is evident in the frequent use Zionist-socialism made of such traditional religious terms as *kedusha* (holiness), *mitzva* (commandment), *Torah* (on its many sacred meanings, see below), *brit* (covenant), and *korban* (sacrifice).

It is almost impossible to convey in English, especially to anyone unfamiliar with traditional Hebrew, the elaborate and intricate usage of traditional Jewish terminology in Zionist-socialism. We have already noted some examples. Here are some more: "Where are the holy ones? . . . All Israel is holy."[43] "Let us sanctify and bless the pioneers of the nation."[44] This is part of a longer statement transforming the traditional Friday evening ceremony called *Kidush* (sanctification). "May the Hebrew man be glorified and sanctified."[45] This is part of a transformative text of the traditional prayer for the dead, which was sometimes changed to read: "May the working man be glorified and sanctified." It was traditional among the kibbutzim to contribute part of their earnings to the Jewish National Fund and the ritual presentation of the contribution was referred to as the "sanctification [of the agricultural produce] to the redemption of the land."[46]

Not only did Zionist-socialists make extensive use of mitzva, they even utilized the notion of *taryag mitzvot* (613 commandments incumbent on Jews). For example: "There is a limit to compromise. The Histadrut has 613 commandments that it observes."[47] Another example: "The 614th commandment imposed on every boy and girl."[48]

In traditional religious language, Torah may refer to the Pentateuch, to the entire Bible, to both the written and oral law, and in broadest terms to the entire rabbinical corpus. In the Zionist-socialist vocabulary it meant the ideology of Zionist-socialism. In a parody of the introduction to the most popular of all Mishnaic tracts, *Pirkei Avot*, Zalman Shazar, who was to become Israel's third president, wrote:

> Syrkin received the Torah from Hess [Moses Hess, 1812–1875, a German socialist, one of the precursors of Zionism and the father of Zionist-Socialism] and passed it on to Berl [Berl Katznelson, 1887–1944, the leading Zionist-Socialist ideologue of his period] and Berl created with it the Great Assembly of the men of the second aliya.[49]

Zionist-socialism talked about a *new covenant* with the land and nature to replace the old covenant with the God of Israel. Kibbutz haggadot quoted Brenner: "Now we have arisen to throw off the yoke of exile and to make for ourselves a new land and a new sky with a strong hand and faithful arm . . . and to renew our covenant with this land and with the plants that grow."[50]

Zionist-socialism also made frequent usage of the religious concept of sacrifice. But sacrifice was self-imposed rather than demanded by God. Moreover, the sacrifice was to the land, not to God. By virtue of sacrifices the ḥalutzim established a covenant of blood with the homeland which created an eternal bond.[51]

The example of Zionist-socialism demonstrated how traditional symbols may be used to express conceptions or values in opposition to the very tradition from which the symbols spring. Nevertheless, the reliance on symbols from traditional sources reflects a measure of attachment to those sources, even among those who were ostensibly most antagonistic.

Despite their differences, there were structural analogs between Zionist-socialism and traditional Judaism beyond a shared set of symbols. For example, the use of the term *commandment* by Zionist-socialism reflects its tendency, like traditional Judaism, to impose a system of detailed norms on individual and social behavior.[52]

MYTHS

The myth is a story that both expresses and reinforces beliefs and values about the relevant past, and hence about one's self and the present; it explains and gives meaning to reality; it acts as a guideline to the individual and the group; and it may be an agent for social catharsis, enabling societal dilemmas and ambivalences to be expressed in symbolic form. It serves to legitimate the social order and contributes to social integration and mobilization.

Civil religion may transform or transvalue traditional myths or create myths of its own. Zionist-socialism did both. The biblical story of the exodus from Egypt is an example of transvaluation of a traditional myth. In the biblical text God does virtually everything for a rather helpless, generally unsympathetic, ungrateful, and pathetic people who resist their own liberation, look back with longing to their own slavery, and are unworthy of entering the Land of Israel. (The religious tradition itself moderated the biblical story, but not in nearly as radical a fashion as the Zionist-socialists.) Various kibbutz haggadot represent the exodus as a story about a people who took their fate into their own hands, throwing off the yoke of their oppressors, and about a leader, Moses, who transformed a horde of slaves into a free and united people.

An example of transformation, as well as transvaluation, is the story of the Maccabean revolt in the second century B.C.E. which is commemorated on the holiday of Ḥanukkah. The religious tradition emphasizes the miracle of the flask of oil as the central motif of Ḥanukkah, generally deemphasizing the heroic deeds of the Maccabees. The special Ḥanukkah prayer mentions the Maccabees but praises God for the miracle of giving the strong and the many into the hands of the weak and the few. The Zionist mythology shared by Zionist-socialism tells a story of struggle for national freedom and political sovereignty won by the military prowess and courage of the Maccabees. The Zionist version ignores the fact that it was religious oppression, not national enslavement, that stirred the revolt.

Creative myths dealt with contemporary and historical events to which the Jewish tradition had not attached any special significance. A striking example is Masada.

The Masada Myth

Masada was the last Jewish stronghold to fall to the Romans three years after the destruction of the second temple in 70 C.E. The Jewish historian Flavius Josephus in his classic text, *The Jewish Wars*, recorded that the last survivors chose mass suicide rather than capture and subsequent enslavement by the Romans. Neither the fall of Masada nor the suicide (a violation of Jewish law) was endowed with symbolic significance in the Jewish tradition. The scene of the event—Mt. Masada in the Judean desert—became a quasi-sacred site serving as a focus for ceremonies, pilgrimages, and the development of a cult only in the later period of the yishuv.

It was primarily the ḥalutzim who transformed the events of Masada into a sacred story symbolizing the heroism, self-sacrifice, uncompromising struggle, unwillingness to yield, and ardent desire for freedom of the Jewish people. Masada also had symbolic meaning as a place. Its location in the heart of the desert symbolized the isolation of the Jewish people in the world and the isolation of the ḥalutzim among the Jews. Masada is located at the summit of a mountain whose ascent is hard and steep—an obvious symbol of the pioneering motif of aliya to the Land of Israel despite the hardship and legal prohibitions involved. The ascent also carries the broader meaning of persistent striving toward a goal despite all the obstacles. Masada was also the last refuge, the only alternative. There was no escape from Masada, no possibility of retreat; one was forced to defend it with body and spirit.

Those who created and nurtured the myth of Masada emphasized that everything must be done to ensure that "Masada will not fall again." This conclusion, formulated as a promise and an oath, was repeatedly affirmed by the yishuv; and the slogan spread to the Diaspora as well.

The phrase was coined by the Hebrew poet Yizhak Lamdan (1899–1954) in his epic poem *Masada*, first published in 1927.[53] The poem reflects the spirit of the halutzim of the 1920's,

> who had left behind them not only the memory of the brutal, senseless murder of defenseless Jews but also their shattered illusions about the possibility of establishing a free revolutionary society in Eastern Europe . . . [Masada] in Lamdan's poem symbolizes Erez Israel, the last stronghold of the destroyed Eastern European Jewish communities.[54]

The hero of the poem, the fugitive from Eastern Europe, is clearly identified with the halutz, the emissary of the people striving to return to their land. "I was sent by my people and will endure any hardship for them."[55] The God of Masada is "the God of the few who are brave," but they are the "divine inspiration of the people."[56]

The Masada myth also expresses a societal dilemma. The dilemma did not stem from the fact that Masada's defenders all died. (Many, perhaps most, central political myths are stories of defeat and death. The living generation, by identification with the heroes of the myth, turns death and defeat into life and victory. Moreover, death, since it purifies, is the ultimate form of atonement. Death legitimates the acts of those who die. Death is not a final defeat because it becomes a source of legitimation for those who identify with the fallen. The living succeed the dead, whose death legitimates the enterprise of the living.) The striking aspect of the Masada myth is not the death of the heroes, but their suicide. The suicide motif, we suggest, is a paradoxical resolution of the dilemma expressed in the myth. While the suicide was viewed as a problematic aspect of the myth in the 1960s, it did not trouble Zionist-socialism. We cannot dismiss the possibility that suicide had particular meaning to the ḥalutzim, among whom, oppressed as they were by terrible loneliness and fits of depression, suicide was not so uncommon as it had been in traditional Jewish society.[57]

The Masada myth expresses a dilemma particular to the yishuv—the limits of human will. Herzl had inspired the Zionist movement with his aphorism: "If you will it, it will be." A central tenet of Zionism was that Jewish failure in the past stemmed from lack of resoluteness, defiance, pride. Zionism would succeed because its adherents really wanted to succeed. By an act of will, they could cease to be objects of history and become its subjects. This article of faith was an important component of Zionist-socialism.[58] It was essential to those whose living conditions were difficult, to whom the possibility of improving those conditions seemed remote. It is easy to forget, in the wake of the creation of the State of Israel, that some settlements actually were abandoned, that the yishuv depended upon philanthropy from abroad because its own enterprises were not economically self-sufficient, that the independent efforts of the yishuv could be seen, in a certain light, as a failure. Did this mean that the settlers lacked will? Put another way, if they had all the will any people could have, and they still failed, did not this mean that an important article of Zionist-socialist faith was wrong? With hindsight, the whole dilemma seems absurd, Herzl's aphorism nonsense. But, in this earlier period, faith in the power of the will was too important to the mobilization of effort to be abandoned. The Masada myth expresses the contradiction between the will to succeed and failure. The suicide then becomes, not an act of despair, but an act of resolution: the final act of will, when will is no longer sufficient for victory over the enemy. Taking one's own life at least deprives the enemy of the symbols of his victory. True, one dies, but one's death is an act of one's own will.

We cannot prove our hypothesis. However, Masada lost some of its meaning in the early statehood period (see chapter five) when the problem of failure no longer posed the kind of dilemma it had for the yishuv. This is consistent with, if not confirmation of, our conjecture. Perhaps the reason the Masada myth declined in importance was that the first architects of the civil religion of Statehood were less concerned with the voluntary mobilization of individual effort. Perhaps the creation of the State and its early successes blinded them to their own limitations.

The Masada myth recaptured its resonance in the 1960s as a prefiguration of the Holocaust, but by that time, as we shall see, it had assumed a different meaning and the suicide motif had become troubling. Even in the period of the yishuv, however, the articulated interpretation of the myth never glorified suicide. Indeed, Lamdan's poem does not even mention it. Nor, we must stress, did the stories of Masada which circulated in that period overtly recognize the dilemma that we suggest the myth expresses. This is to be expected. The myth is a catharsis. One purpose of reciting the myth is to avoid confronting the stark reality of the dilemma.

The Myth of Tel Ḥai

The central political myth of Zionist-socialism was the story of the death of Yosef Trumpeldor (1880–1920) and seven comrades and the fall of Tel Ḥai and Kfar Giladi, two settlements in the Galilee in March (the eleventh of Adar according to the Jewish calendar) 1920.[59] Trumpeldor's last words, reported to have been "it is good to die for our country," were widely circulated and became an integral part of the myth.

Zionist-socialism transformed the story of Tel Ḥai into a symbol of the heroism and valor of the halutzim and an expression of the values of labor, agricultural settlement, courage, and defense. The myth was related in poems and stories and Tel Ḥai itself became the object of pilgrimages on the anniversary of the settlement's fall.

The mythologization began almost immediately after the historical event. Within a year of the fall of Tel Ḥai a prominent journalist of the period wrote: "Buds of a national myth are already appearing. These modest heroes, who worked towards the rebuilding of the land, are becoming folk legends. . . . Such is the power of our effort which opens the door to the creation of myths."[60]

In the myth of Tel Ḥai, Trumpeldor and his followers represent the pioneers and defenders who gave their lives to defend their land and in so doing, won for their people the sacred right to the land. The heroes of Tel Ḥai ". . . with their blood, bought . . . the hills of the Galilee for us." Their stand represented the decisive test of Zionist-socialism since "the test of every idea is whether those who believe in it are ready to give their lives for it."[61]

In the immediate aftermath, the fall of Tel Hai and the death of Trumpeldor and his followers was interpreted differently. The first response of the yishuv was guilt that it had not done enough to assist in the defense.[62] But as the myth evolved, the element of guilt was replaced by the frequently cited words of one of the defenders: "no settlement is to be deserted, nothing built is to be relinquished."[63]

Thus, the myth of Tel Hai served to legitimize basic values of Zionist-socialism, helped recruit people to its ranks, and rallied them to its goals by identifying with those who fought and died for those goals. The sacrifice of Trumpeldor and his followers established a new basis for the sanctification of the land and the right of the Jewish people to that land. Ben Gurion declared that "for this generation"—those to whom he referred as "the comrades of Trumpeldor"—"this land is more holy than for the tens of generations of Jews who believed in its historical and religious sanctity; for it has been sanctified by our sweat, our work, and our blood."[64]

Those who nurtured the myth emphasized that which was unique and new in the personalities and actions of their heroes. They were presented as the archetypes of the new Jew as opposed to the traditional Jew. The story of Tel Hai was the expression of the revolutionary change these heroes and others like them brought about in Jewish values and behavior. Trumpeldor was particularly suited for such a role. He was an agricultural laborer, a participant in a communal settlement, and a war hero. A folk hero, Trumpeldor was known for his courage even before his death. The first Jew to be appointed an officer in the Czarist army, he had lost an arm in the Russo-Japanese war. He was the antithesis of the Jew who would go to almost any lengths to avoid service in the Czarist army.

Comparison between the defenders of Tel Hai and classical Jewish martyrs led the Zionist-socialists to invidious distinctions.

The early martyrs all sought in return for their deeds . . . a place in the world-to-come—the personal pleasure which every religious Jew feels in giving his life. . . . This was not true of the martyrs of Tel Hai who did not sacrifice their lives for personal pleasure. . . . They were not concerned with whether or not they would earn pleasure in the next world. All that mattered to them was that the Jewish people should survive and the Land of Israel be rebuilt.[65]

Furthermore, unlike Jewish heroes of the past "Trumpeldor is not merely a victim, a passive hero; he is an active hero."[66] Finally, in what can only be described as the adoption of anti-Semitic stereotypes, one writer contrasts Trumpeldor with traditional Jews as follows: "He had not a trace of sickliness, nervousness, impulsiveness, disquietness—qualities which characterize the Diaspora Jew."[67]

The myth of Tel Hai also reflected a central dilemma of the yishuv in general and of Zionist-socialism in particular—the belief that one can live in peace with the Arabs despite the Arabs' competing claim to the Land. (Our discussion here is conjectural, but we believe our explanation is plausible). Once one thinks in archetypical terms, it is clear that blood and death confer legitimacy and that Trumpeldor's death has claimed the Land for his spiritual heirs. But the title would be more secure if the enemy who spilled his blood were the same one disputing the claim. Then there would be perfect symmetry. The death of Trumpeldor and his comrades in defense of their right to settle the Land would confer title, whereas those who killed Trumpeldor would lose their claim to that title. In the ideal legitimating myth, the enemy is particularly evil because his act delegitimates his title. But the Tel Hai myth is not the ideal legitimating myth because it does not firmly resolve who killed Trumpeldor and his comrades. Who spilled the blood? This expresses the Zionist-socialist dilemma: Zionist-socialism laid claim to the Land of Israel, sensed that Arabs made a similar claim but refused to either recognize the Arabs as enemies or to legitimate their claims. Zionist-socialism finally recognized the Arab as an enemy long after the Tel Hai myth had evolved. Then the murderers of Trumpeldor were specified as Arabs, but the myth itself began to lose its resonance. Until the mid-1930s Zionist-socialist leaders denied that Jews were engaged in a national conflict with the Arabs.[68] They believed the conflict arose because of the British, or the wealthy Arabs, or mistaken perceptions of the Arabs whose own best interests were actually served by Zionist efforts. But if the halutzim were not fighting the Arabs, then against whom were they defending Tel Hai? Against whom were they asserting their claim to the Land of Israel? It is on precisely this point that the original myth is vague. So are the historical sources. The myth of Tel Hai describes an archetypical enemy, who despite superior numbers must rely on cunning and deception to overcome the courageous defenders, who are defeated in the end only by their own innocence. Because the enemy is not identified with precision, because the enemy does not dispute Jewish rights to Tel Hai or Kfar Giladi, the myth lacks a certain symmetry. Thus it reflects the problematic relationship of the Zionists to the Arabs.

CEREMONIES AND SYMBOLS

The most successful myths are those associated with specific places around which ceremonials and rituals can be organized. Masada and Tel Hai are good examples. The statue of a roaring lion was erected at Tel Hai symbolizing the courage of the defenders and parades were held in the square in front of the statue. The eleventh of Adar was marked by pilgrimages to Tel Hai-Kfar Giladi, or, for those unable to get there, by pilgrimages to settlements closer to home.[69] Masada was the gathering site for youth movements who, following the quasiceremonial ascent to the summit, presented plays reciting the history of its defense.[70] The kibbutzim of the Emek (the Jezreel Valley) also gained symbolic significance as the location of a great pioneering enterprise.

Masada, Tel Hai and the Emek are natural symbols. But myths also give rise to artificial symbols, such as the statue of the lion erected at Tel Hai. Flags and uniforms are additional examples of artificial symbols. The artificial symbol represents a value, an idea, or an emotion, but, unlike the natural symbol, does not partake of any of these. The blue and white Zionist flag, unlike the kibbutzim of the Emek, does not constitute a part of the actual process by which socialism and Zionism are realized.

Ceremony, in contrast to myth, is always artificial. That is, it constitutes behavior which is denotative rather than behavior which engages the participant in the realization of goals or values. According to one of the halutzim of the second aliya:

> In those first years there was no need for special rituals, not on the Sabbath or other holidays. There was a festiveness in the very construction of the first cell of a new Hebrew society. There was something of the ritual in setting out at dawn to the furrows. . . . No ordinary agricultural labor was being performed . . . but the holy labor of monks.[71]

Ceremonial behavior may also serve as symbolic compensation for a failure or inability to personally realize values with which one is identified. Adherents of the labor movement in urban areas made pilgrimages to the settlements of the Emek on Passover. According to a sympathetic newspaper report, to many visitors from the cities the Emek represented a common focus of longing, a symbol of unfulfilled aspirations, of abandoned desires, of circumstances of life that were dislocated and distorted.

Ceremonial behavior possesses great social significance because it rallies the community around common goals and reaffirms ultimate values. In this case it also legitimated the political leadership of those who were members of kibbutzim and actually realized those values which the visitors from the cities merely affirmed symbolically.

FESTIVALS AND RITUALS

The leaders of labor Zionism recognized the importance of traditional ceremonies and holidays. According to Berl Katznelson, "The Jewish year is full of days whose depth of meaning is nowhere surpassed. Is it the interest of the Jewish labor movement to squander the forces latent in them?"[73]

Recourse to traditional holidays and to the customs and rituals associated with them was selective. Zionist-socialists widely ignored some holidays, such as Rosh Hashana and Yom Kippur, even though they held a central position in traditional Judaism. This probably stemmed from the purely religious elements, as distinct from national or agrarian elements, in the holiday which imposed difficulties in adapting these holidays to Zionist-socialist purposes. Holidays of secondary importance in traditional Judaism, such as Ḥanukkah, Tu Bishvat, or Lag Baomer assumed greater importance. Indeed, Ḥanukkah was transformed into one of the central holidays of the yishuv.

Traditional symbols and ceremonies were transvalued to conform with the values of Zionist-socialism and transformed by changes in the ritual. There are a number of elements common to the transformations. The celebrations were transferred from synagogue and home to more public forums. Political leaders played conspicuous roles in the holiday ceremonies. The celebrations became occasions for announcement of political positions on contemporary issues. And monetary contributions to labor movement projects were solicited at these gatherings.

The most striking feature common to all the transformed rituals was the involvement of all the participants in song and dance, which became a functional equivalent of public prayer. Dance was particularly important in ḥalutz culture. Descriptions of the pioneering life note the spirited dancing that followed a hard day's work. The literature of Zionist-socialism elaborated and perhaps even exaggerated the importance of the dance: "Without the hora the State of Israel would not have arisen."[74]

Dance plays a major role in the rituals and ceremonies of many religions, traditional and civil. It expresses and evokes feelings of unity and solidarity. It can arouse a sense of devotion and elevation. Dance, especially when spirited and prolonged, symbolizes the ability to withstand hardship. The dance enables the participant "to draw strength for life from the faith within us"[75] according to one girl who explained why it was not cynical to dance while the Jewish people were persecuted in Europe.

The transformation and transvaluation of the holidays occurred over a long period. The early tendency was to refrain from providing a well-defined festive expression to the traditional holidays.[76] Over the course of time, even the most secular circles came to recognize the need for celebrating these days in some manner.

Passover

The nationalist and socialist elements of Passover were recognized from the earliest period of Zionist-socialism. According to Borochov, the story of Passover demonstrates that "we are incapable of being slaves."[77] Katznelson represents Passover as a striking example of a traditional holiday which should be preserved and nurtured by the labor movement: "I know of no other single ancient memory . . . which serves as a better symbol of our present and our future than the memory of the exodus from Egypt."[78]

The *seder* (plural: *sedarim*) is the festive meal traditionally eaten in a family setting that inaugurates the holiday. The haggada is the text read at the seder. As we noted the kibbutzim

produced new haggadot considerably different from the traditional one. At first, they were satirical parodies of the traditional seder.[79] Only later did the kibbutzim introduce their own
sedarim of a serious nature with haggadot that were adapted to
the values and way of life of the labor movement in the Land of
Israel.

The new haggadot lacked a uniform format. Those of the
ideologically moderate kibbutzim emphasized the nationalist,
agricultural, and natural aspects of Passover (the holiday of
spring). The more leftist kibbutzim stressed motifs of class
and revolution. Texts changed from year to year reflecting
changing social and political conditions or shifting ideological
perspectives.[80]

Kibbutz sedarim were also characterized by new or revived
rituals. The most prominent was the reaping of the *omer* (barley
offering), an effort to revive a ceremonial from the temple period
of Jewish history. The celebrations began with a ceremony devoted to the harvesting of the first crops. Afterward, girls from
the kibbutz, with bundles of grain on their heads, would present
a pageant of song and dance.[81] The central portion of the seder
was the recitation of the haggada. Following the meal, all the
participants would dance. Many guests, including leaders of
the labor movement, participated in these sedarim and in
sedarim for the workers that were organized in the cities.[82]

Shavuot (the Festival of Weeks)

The focus of the traditional holiday was the giving of the
Torah at Mt. Sinai. Zionist-socialists sought to "revive" the
biblical motif—offering the *bikkurim* (first fruits). In the Talmud and the Jewish religious tradition of the last two thousand
years, *Shavuot* is *the time of the giving of the Torah* and the
traditional prayers and rituals give little emphasis to the agricultural origins of the holiday implied in the verse from the Torah,
"thou shalt observe the feast of weeks, of the first fruits of the
wheat harvest."[83] In Zionist-socialism Shavuot was represented
as a holiday of nature and agriculture. The new rituals also
expressed the nationalist motif in the ceremonial redemption of
the land. The focus of the celebrations was the bringing of the
bikkurim. The first fruits of the agricultural produce were
dedicated to the Jewish National Fund. They were brought in a

festive procession by representatives of the different agricultural sectors of the settlement. The produce was borne in decorated baskets and presented to a representative of the Jewish National Fund. Portions of the Torah, once recited when Jews brought the bikkurim to the Temple, were read. The bikkurim were then declared redeemed, symbolic of the "full redemption of the Jewish people and its homeland." The representative of the Jewish National Fund would then combine the seven traditional fruits of the Land of Israel, hold them in his hand, and say: "They are the symbol of the House of Israel. One by one, the children of Israel will be gathered from the lands of dispersion and will become a single unit and a great people."[84] The ceremony was accompanied by song and dance and recitation from both traditional and modern Hebrew sources.

These ceremonies were also introduced into schools, where the children, when presenting the bikkurim to the Jewish National Fund representative, said: "We have brought of the first fruits of our land *as an offering* for the redemption of Israel" (instead of *as a holy offering*).[85]

Zionist-socialists represented their rituals as more authentic than those of traditional Judaism: "Our holidays, which arose out of the land of Israel, were impoverished in the Diaspora. . . . It is therefore our duty today, having returned to Zion . . . to renew and revive the celebration of these holidays. Indeed, the holidays of nature which had grown alien to us . . . are now striking roots in our homeland."[86] Shavuot in particular offered a striking opportunity to both reject the religious tradition (the giving of the Torah) and affirm continuity with what the Zionist-socialists claimed was the origin of the holiday (a harvest festival).

Hanukkah

While the labor movement, particularly the kibbutzim, initiated the revival of Passover and Shavuot, Hanukkah had already been transformed into a national holiday by the Zionist movement, as we noted earlier. Zionists of all types participated in the Hanukkah ceremonies. Participation included lighting the candles, eating special foods, giving speeches, singing songs, and marching in parades.[87] A failed attempt was

made to introduce a socialist motif by describing the wars of the
Maccabees as a popular uprising of the lower classes against
exploitation by the upper classes.[88]

Passover and Shavuot occupied a central place in the Jewish
tradition, and those who had a certain attachment to that tradition resisted radical innovations in the rituals associated with
them. The ceremonies we described were confined principally
to the kibbutzim or to settlements with high concentrations of
strongly committed Zionist-socialists. The majority of the
yishuv, for example, shrank from initiating changes in the
traditional format of the Passover seder, which assumed a certain sanctity even for many otherwise nonreligious Jews.
Ḥanukkah held a less prominent place in the religious tradition.
Furthermore, the laws pertaining to its observance were not,
for the most part, as exacting and strict as the laws pertaining
to other holidays. Hence, even those with a positive attitude toward the religious tradition could alter, without violating their sense of propriety, the customs related to Ḥanukkah transforming it from a traditional religious holiday into a
national holiday.

Zionist literature and the ceremonies conducted in honor of
Ḥanukkah ignored the religious meaning of the Maccabean
revolt and of Ḥanukkah itself. The Maccabees were presented
not as fighters for religious freedom but as patriots rebelling
against national subjugation. The miracle of the flask of oil had
no place in the Zionist interpretation of the holiday. Indeed,
Zionists pointed to its central place in the traditional holiday as
an illustration of the passivity of exilic Jewry. The new theme of
Ḥanukkah was self-redemption; the active struggle for national
liberation without reliance on outside powers, natural or supernatural.[89] The ḥalutzim were presented as the new Maccabees,
or descendants of the Maccabees, and those who opposed them
were *Hellenists*. (The term *Hellenist* was often used in the
internal struggles of the yishuv. It was usually used to describe
anti-Zionist circles, notably the Communists, but it sometimes
also was applied to the Zionist left, especially during the period
in which the Zionist left tended to identify with the Soviet
Union.)

The heroic tales of the Maccabees were in effect transformed
into a revived national myth, providing symbols of identification and solidarity, granting meaning to the Zionist enterprise,
and spurring the community to action. This myth was pro-

moted in public ceremonies held in honor of Ḥanukkah. Events such as the "kindling of the candles with great festivity, lectures and speeches held in synagogues, cultural centers, schools, and kindergartens on the freedom fight of the Maccabees," according to Ben-zion Dinur, were intended "to teach the people . . . how its heroes acted, how a people can act if it has faith, if it has confidence, if it is ready for self-sacrifice . . . if it perseveres in its work. . . . Ḥanukkah became 'the holiday of the Maccabees,' the Maccabees became the symbol of the generation, and Ḥanukkah the holiday of the generation."[90]

The new Ḥanukkah celebrations included such traditional elements as kindling of the candles. But instead of the miracle of the flask of oil, the candles symbolized the light of redemption. In place of the traditional blessings, political songs, speeches, and proclamations accompanied the kindling of the candles. Among the most striking of the new Ḥanukkah rituals were the pilgrimages to the birthplace of the Maccabees, Modiin. A torch was lit there and carried by runners to settlements throughout the land. The participants were told that "the torch is being lit here and carried by runners who are the great-grandchildren of the Maccabees . . . not only in order to kindle the Ḥanukkah candles but also to kindle the hearts of the Jewish youth, and to give them the signal for national unity and action."[91]

Sukkot (The Festival of Booths)

While the transformation and transvaluation of ceremonies and rituals was particularly striking in the cases of Passover, Shavuot, and Ḥanukkah, other traditional holidays, such as Sukkot or Rosh Hashana and Yom Kippur, were more often ignored than remolded.

Within the kibbutzim attempts were made to celebrate Sukkot as an agricultural holiday and to infuse national elements into its celebration. In some kibbutzim a *sukkah* (a hut or a booth) was erected in the center of the settlement. The sukkah was interpreted as a "symbol of the wandering of the Jews in the deserts of the world," and members of the kibbutz would gather nearby for a ceremony in which the children brought gifts for the Jewish National Fund from the produce of the kibbutz. From the roof of the sukkah, someone would call out: "The tabernacle of David will be rebuilt," a phrase that was then repeated by all present. In addition, those verses of the Bible which deal with the *promised land* and the blessings for its fertility were read.[92] Sukkot and the holiday which immediately follows it, Shmini Atzeret-Simḥat Torah, were also celebrated in some kibbutzim as the "holiday of water." In the early days of the kibbutz, Sukkot was marked by a festive ceremony of drawing water from a well. In the cities, Sukkot served as an occasion for national ceremonies, such as handing over the flag of Jerusalem to the school that had excelled throughout the year in Zionist activity.[93] However, these ceremonies never won general acceptance in the yishuv or even within the kibbutz movement itself.[94]

Tisha B'av (The Ninth Day of Av)

Tisha B'av raised in an especially keen fashion the problematical relationship of Zionist-socialists to the most sacred of all Jewish places—the *western (wailing) wall*; all that remains of the first and second temples. The western wall has special associations with Tisha B'av, which commemorates the destruction of both temples, and traditional Jews gathered there on that day. The western wall was a reminder of the period of Jewish statehood and a symbol of the heroic war the Jewish rebels waged against the Romans—a symbol with which Zionist-socialists could identify. But the weeping, fasting, and lamentations associated with Tisha B'av conflicted with Zionist-socialist values, as did resignation, passivity, and awaiting divine salvation, which the wall also symbolized. An early leader and heroic figure of the labor movement, Rachel Yanait Ben-Zvi (1886–1978), wife of the second president of the state, related that, when she approached the wall, "a desire to cry out to the wall in protest against the weeping arose within me . . . to cry out against the unfortunate verdict of fate: no longer will we live in the land of destruction, we will rebuild the ruins and regenerate our land."[95]

In a play presented to children who had survived the Holocaust, one group of Zionist-socialist youth leaders portrayed Jews mourning the destruction of the temple, while a second group portrayed halutzim who declared, "the house of Israel will be rebuilt with bricks, not with prayers and mourning."[96]

The Sabbath

The Sabbath also proved problematic for Zionist-socialism. All agreed that the Sabbath should be the weekly day of rest and leaders of the labor movement recognized its social importance. However, some worked for reasons of collective convenience or economic efficiency. Various attempts were made to endow the Sabbath with a festive character through celebrations of one form or another, or festive dress and meals, particularly in the kibbutzim. Zionist-socialism succeeded in retaining the sense of the Sabbath as a special day, perhaps because it was so deeply embedded in the tradition, perhaps because it was uniformly accepted as a day of rest, but it did not succeed in imparting its own flavor to the day or in recapturing the dimension of holiness which characterizes the day in the religious tradition.[97]

NEW HOLIDAYS

Until the establishment of the state, no new holidays, in the fullest sense of the word, were created by the yishuv. However, several days of remembrance were inaugurated, the most prominent of which was Tel Hai Day (celebrated on the eleventh of Adar) marking the revival of heroism and pioneering in Israel. Less successful efforts were made to mark off other days: Balfour Declaration Day on November 2, the death of Herzl on the twentieth of Tamuz, or Histadrut Day during Hanukkah. The only holiday that had no roots in the Jewish tradition or Zionism was May Day.

May Day

Ber Borochov believed May Day proved that man could free himself from his dependence on divine powers and still endow his life with meaning and content. The liberation from religion, he felt, must be complete

> not only in our daily lives, not only in the realm of pure science, but also in our great longings and ideals. . . . In abolishing religious belief . . . we did not strip man of his higher feelings . . .

and we did not impoverish the meaning of beauty. . . . We found within ourselves enough inspiration to create new celebrations, to form new ideals.[98]

Proletarian holidays express the change that has occurred in man's relation to the divine, according to Borochov, for they undermine the distinction "between heavenly and mundane, between sacred and secular" on which the traditional holidays are based.[99]

Borochov implies that socialism provides an alternative to traditional religion. Socialism is

> a total world view that provides a solution for the most profound gropings and quests of man's spirit . . . and the foremost advantage and strength of socialism lies in the fact that it puts an end to all religious quests. For, through human, worldly means, it fulfills all those spiritual needs whose fulfillment religious faith sought to find in God.[100]

Borochov notes that the bourgeoisie also substitutes secular celebrations such as independence days for religious reliance on the divine. But unlike socialism, the bourgeoisie has no substitute for traditional religion's sense of hope or a goal toward which one can struggle. Hence, he claimed, only socialism can successfully abolish religion, and May Day is the beginning of just such an effort.[101]

Unlike the Jewish holidays Zionist-socialism had to reconstruct, May Day had a ready-made format. The central symbols and rituals of the holiday—the red flag, the parades, the slogans and proclamations, the singing of the "International"—all were drawn from May Day celebrations in other countries. However, the labor Zionists added nationalist symbols. The blue and white Zionist flag was displayed together with the red flag, national slogans were added to class slogans, and both the national and labor Zionist anthems were sung together with the "International."[102]

May Day was a controversial holiday from the very outset. Hapoel Hatzair opposed its celebration, which it termed an "alien graft" that had no place among the holidays of Israel. Following its merger with Ahdut Haavoda in 1930, May Day became the holiday of the entire Labor Movement. But the civil and religious camps were most uncomfortable with May Day celebrations and the revisionists bitterly denounced them. Whereas the revived holidays of Zionist-socialism led to a national integration of most sectors of the yishuv, May Day served to integrate the Zionist-socialist subcommunity alone.

The major feature of the May Day celebration was its mass nature. The huge parade demonstrated the strength of the labor movement and encouraged its supporters to take an active part in the achievement of its goals.

The most direct forms of political mobilization are speeches and declarations. However, when the goal is to attract a wider public, visual symbols and ceremonies, or simple and comprehensive slogans are more effective. Speeches did indeed occupy an important place in May Day rallies. However, these rallies also included programs of entertainment—song and dance, readings, dramatizations and gymnastic exercises. The gatherings opened with the hoisting of flags and the singing of appropriate songs, and included ceremonies evoking the memory of the fathers of the labor Zionist movement and of those who had fallen in the struggles of the international labor movement.

As a factor in political consolidation and mobilization, parades are even more effective than gatherings. The display of power is most evident in a parade, which also provides the supporters of a movement with an opportunity for active participation. Tens of thousands of people participated in May Day parades, which were held in most cities and towns throughout Israel to express the solidarity of the working class. Ironically, various labor parties often held separate parades because they disagreed on the wording of slogans.

The hegemony of the labor movement in the yishuv was reflected in the virtually total cessation of the economy on May Day. The only newspapers to appear were those published by the religious or revisionist camps. In the major cities, public transportation shut down for part of the day. Schools under labor movement auspices were closed and in many other educational institutions the absence of many teachers and students made regular classes impossible.

Yet May Day never played the role Borochov ascribed to it. Despite the social and political significance of the holiday it never assumed the kind of existential personal meaning that would allow it to substitute for traditional religious holidays, and the Zionist-socialist elite never really sought to infuse it with such meaning. They devoted greater cultural-creative effort to the transformation and transvaluation of the traditional holidays. As we shall see in chapter four, the significance of

May Day dissipated very quickly once the elite lost interest in the holiday—an indication of how faint were the echoes it evoked among the rank and file of the labor movement.

SUMMARY

The settlers who constituted the adherents of Zionist-socialism were too intimately associated with the religious tradition, too familiar with its broad outlines, yet also too estranged from its basic values to either ignore it or unconsciously transform it. The labor Zionist goal included the creation of a new type of Jew and a new society. The image of the ideal Jew and the ideal society was an inverted image of the traditional Jew and traditional Jewish society. For example, labor Zionism's attitude toward non-Jews and other nations was more universalist than the dominant civil religion of any other period. Zionist-socialism deliberately rejected the particularism and ethnocentrism that characterizes the Jewish tradition. That rejection expressed itself in a strategy of confrontation in which Zionist-socialist values and symbols were deliberately contrasted to those of the tradition. We found this in the celebration of holidays and myths as well as the projection of explicit values. Strategies of dissolution and reinterpretation were less central, although they were also employed. Confrontation, therefore, was Zionist-socialism's characteristic strategy but not its exclusive one.

3 Revisionist Zionism As a Civil Religion

Revisionism, both the ideology and the movement, was founded and led by Vladimir (Ze'ev) Jabotinsky (1880–1940).[1] The Union of Zionists-Revisionists, established in 1925, was the major opposition party to Chaim Weizmann's leadership within the World Zionist Organization (WZO). In 1935 the main body of revisionists seceded from the WZO and established the New Zionist Organization. They rejoined the WZO after World War II. Throughout these twenty years the revisionist and labor Zionist camps each viewed the other as its major political antagonist.

The conflict between the revisionists and the labor movement stemmed from their struggle for power, but their mutual enmity was heightened by the zealous devotion of each group to its own symbol system and the antipathy of each for the symbols of its antagonist. The sacred is that which is set apart. A symbol may be sacred by virtue of its purity, but also by virtue of its impurity. Holy wars are waged because that which one religion regards as holy is an object of antipathy to another. This is true among civil religions as well.

Revisionist leaders and thinkers were more explicit than their rivals in acknowledging the religious dimension of their world view. Jabotinsky described his Zionist activity as "the work of one of the builders of a new temple to a single God whose name is—the people of Israel."[2] One of the ideologists of Betar (the autonomous revisionist youth movement) argued that the difference between Betar and other Zionists was not that the others did not want a Jewish state but that it was not for them, as it was for Betar, "a question of conscience . . . the religion of their lives."[3]

Revisionism was an all-embracing ideal which provided meaning and purpose for the lives of its devotees. According to his biographer, a young man once said to Jabotinsky: "Our life is dull and our hearts are empty, for there is no God in our midst. Give us a God, sir, worthy of dedication and sacrifice, and you will see what we can do." Jabotinsky, according to the biographer, himself a revisionist leader, "met that request."[4]

VALUES OF REVISIONISM

Jewish Statehood

The first commandment of the revisionists' civil religion was Jewish Statehood. Revisionists located themselves in the Herzlian political Zionist tradition. Hence, Zionism meant the effort to restore Jewish political sovereignty through political-diplomatic activity. However, unlike the early political Zionists, the Jewish state envisaged by the revisionists was not simply an instrument to solve the problem of Jewish suffering and oppression in the Diaspora, but an intrinsically sacred value: "It is not the notion of statehood alone that Jabotinsky endeavoured to imbue in the youth of Betar, but *Malkhut Yisrael*—the Kingship of Israel, with all the historic, spiritual, and poetic connotations that the term implied."[5]

The Monistic Principle

The restoration of Jewish statehood was considered an important goal by many labor Zionists, but they also subscribed to other values and goals, most of which were related in some way to socialism. The revisionists vigorously opposed the fusion of Zionism with any other ideology, and the infusion of symbols which the entire nation could not share. Jabotinsky defined the revisionist position as Zionist monism, "the belief in the integral Zionist ideal, as opposed to any synthetic concoction of Zionist and other ideologies."[6] What the Jewish people requires, Jabotinsky declared, is "a youth in whose temple there is but one religion."[7] According to another revisionist leader: "Every ideal has only one jealous and vengeful God, who does not tolerate the presence of other gods. . . . The golden calf and the cherubs above the holy ark cannot exist side by side."[8] Monism meant the subordination of all values and interests to the Zionist idea and to the national interest. In line with this were the revisionist demands to outlaw strikes and lockouts, and to introduce compulsory arbitration in labor disputes.

The Revisionist View of Labor and Ḥalutziut

Monism was reflected in the revisionist attitude toward labor and pioneering which, as we saw, occupied a central place in Zionist-socialism. To the revisionists, however, labor was simply an instrument for the realization of Zionist goals, secondary in importance to diplomatic and military efforts. Agricultural labor was one source of employment but hardly an ideal way of life. The revisionists opposed Zionist immigration policy which granted the farmers and workers clear priority over the urban middle class.[9]

The revisionists redefined ḥalutziut. They denied that it was expressed by one class or one form of settlement. Ḥalutziut was applicable to any form of activity that reflected self-sacrifice and dedication to the Zionist ideal. According to Jabotinsky, the ḥalutz is not tied to a particular trade or occupation, and is free from any obligation, except to the national ideal. He must devote all his effort, loyalty, and dedication to that ideal.[10] With regard to Zionist-socialist conceptions of ḥalutziut, Jabotinsky asserted: "The word ḥalutz has acquired a new composition: one tenth idealism and nine-tenths business. . . . No one is required to be a ḥalutz . . . but a ḥalutz is only someone who is prepared to make sacrifices without keeping accounts . . . and without demanding a return for his sacrifices."[11]

The revisionists opposed the establishment of separate economic, social, and cultural organizations by the labor movement which, they claimed, divided the yishuv. Furthermore, they charged, such activity led the Zionist-socialists to prefer their material and group interests over national ideals. Uri Zvi Greenberg, whose poetry reflected his revisionist commitments, wrote: "A man becomes both socialist and proprietor and says, I have built a house, I have planted a garden, and that is enough."[12]

One important consequence of this attitude was the late development of revisionist enterprises, and the relative weakness of their institutional base compared to that of the labor Zionists, or even the religious camp. The revisionists were finally forced to adopt the methods of their rivals forming *communities of believers* in opposition to those of the labor movement, but the delay was critical. They never seriously rivaled the *constructive activity* of Zionist-socialism.

Militarism and Heroism

Among the tasks which revisionism imposed on the ḥalutz, the military-security role was central. When he was elected the head of Betar in 1931, Jabotinsky declared: "The only substance of true ḥalutziut is the subjugation of the individual and the class to the absolute rule of the idea of the state. For this purpose, every member of Betar must be ready for call-up as a worker and as a soldier."[13]

Among Zionist-socialists, labor constituted a central value of intrinsic merit, whereas military prowess was a necessity imposed by special conditions of the yishuv. The labor camp viewed displays of militarism with disfavor. Revisionism, while it never elevated armed conflict to the level of an ideal,[14] regarded armed force as a symbol of national sovereignty, an expression of self-liberation, and a means of securing the right of Jews to the Land of Israel.

This approach was reflected in Jabotinsky's efforts to establish the Jewish Legion during World War I and in his struggle to preserve the Legion after the British decision to disband it. Jabotinsky did not measure the value of the Legion by its actual contribution to the British war effort in the Middle East.

> The British army could have liberated the Land of Israel without us as well. . . . However it liberated the Land of Israel with us. . . . The very fact of the Legion's military activity has a moral value. War is bad; but we paid for the recognition of our right to the Land of Israel with war . . . that is to say, with human sacrifice.[15]

Betar was established as the sucessor to the disbanded Legion. Its hierarchical structure, the names given to its units, the ranks within the organization, and its ceremonies, all reflected its admiration of militarism.[16]

Militarism found vivid expression in the quasimilitary uniforms of Betar. The brown uniforms, similar in color to those of the Nazis, provided the labor movement with evidence that Betar and the revisionists were fascists. The parades and processions of uniformed members of Betar served as pretexts for violent attacks by workers on members of Betar.[17] Following the attack on a Betar parade in 1933 Jabotinsky said, "Jewish blood has been sprayed on the brown shirts in the Land of Israel; moreover by Jewish hands. The color has been sanctified."[18] Militarism was expressed in Jabotinsky's call to Jewish youth

> to learn a new alphabet of military training. . . . The alphabet is simple. . . . Our youth should learn to fight . . . The recognition that a people in our situation must know the new alphabet, the psychology of fighting, the longing to fight—all these are important. . . . This is a healthy instinct of a people in a situation such as ours . . . What is better: to conquer the land with arms and with sacrifice or is it better that the Englishman should do the sordid work . . . and then allow us, tranquil and clear, to come and settle on it?[19]

The historian of the IZL (the Irgun Zvai Leumi, the larger of the two underground organizations identified with revisionism), indicates that these statements were made "in the heyday of Jewish pacifism and aversion for anything having to do with military education" and were intended as a counterweight to this tendency.[20] Jabotinsky noted the positive characteristics of army life: order, simplicity, courage, ceremony, and equality between rich and poor. War was to be condemned but not military life, he said. Of special importance was army discipline, an expression of national unity and a precondition to national existence. The revisionist leader was particularly impressed by the capacity "of the masses to sense and even to act in certain moments as one unit, with one will."[21]

Most revisionists accepted Jabotinsky's views on militarism. Some did not. One small group opposed the excessive emphasis on militarism. It feared increasing tensions with labor Zionism and was inclined to accept Zionist-socialist definitions of halutziut.[22] A second minority called itself Brit Habiryonim (The *Biryonim*, literally *terrorists*, were zealots who fought both

the Romans and Jewish moderates in the first century c.e.). Brit
Habiryonim was more radical. It stressed the monistic and
militaristic elements of revisionism, and portrayed labor
Zionists as traitors to the national cause. The leaders of Brit
Habiryonim, Abba Aḥimeir (1898–1962), Yehoshua Yevin
(1891–1970), and the poet Uri Zvi Greenberg (1894–1981),
came to revisionism from the ranks of Labor Zionism. Like the
labor Zionist leaders, they were influenced by the climate of the
revolutionary movements in Russia—particularly by the
revolutionary fervor, the self-sacrifice, the fanatic loyalty, and
the absolute dedication which characterized the Russian communists. According to Aḥimeir:

> The youth were attracted to non-Zionist socialism because it
> proclaimed revolutionary means for the achievement of its goals.
> The best of the youth went to the Bund [the anti-Zionist revolu-
> tionary Jewish socialist movement] and to communism because
> they promised a life of heroism, dedication, war, prison, exe-
> cution; and not prattle, small talk and a cloistered life. . . . The
> Zionist youth was not educated to sacrifice. That is why the
> creators of revolutionary Zionism were so isolated.[23]

Aḥimeir called for discipline and obedience to the leader. He
associated this value with religion in general and Judaism in
particular. "Judaism did not stand for freedom of speech but for
discipline," and this trait is characteristic of all religion.

> In an atheistic society, people demand "freedom." A religious
> society, that is a society centered around a single (religious) idea,
> does not require that . . . which is known as freedom. . . . A
> healthy, harmonious religious society is not aware of a lack of
> freedom (so to speak), just as a healthy man is not aware of the air
> which surrounds him. . . . A truly religious people does not favor
> unrestricted freedom of speech.[24]

In place of liberal conceptions of freedom Aḥimeir substituted the principle of the leader who knows what is really best
for the people. Acknowledging his debt to fascist ideology,
Aḥimeir asserted that it is the leader's role to define the national
goals and outline the ways of achieving them; his orders must be
obeyed without question.[25]
   A majority of revisionists rejected Aḥimeir's ideology. While
Jabotinsky's attitude was ambivalent, he took exception to the
radical militarism of Brit Habiryonim.[26] Indeed, despite his

own emphasis on military education, Jabotinsky regarded political action, not armed force, as the primary means to achieve the goals of Zionism.[27]

The Shift from Politics to Armed Struggle

Arab hostility and Zionist disappointment with British policy in the years 1936–1939 led to increased reliance by the revisionists on military, as distinct from political, force. Menachem Begin, elected leader of Betar in Poland in 1938, declared that under present conditions the goals of Zionism could no longer be realized by building; the only alternative was conquest.[28]

The new orientation was most evident in the activities of the IZL and a second small underground organization that grew out of the ranks of the revisionist movement—Lehi. *Lehi* was an acronym for Lohamei Herut Yisrael, Fighters for the Freedom of Israel, known in the West as the Stern Gang after its leader Avraham (Yair) Stern (1907–1942). Lehi cultivated the *cult of power* in the manner of Brit Habiryonim. Lehi's ideological platform, written by Stern, linked the right of the Jewish people to the Land of Israel with its military conquest of the country. Glorifying military might, he affirmed that "the sword and the book were given together from heaven."[29] His platform spoke of "the conquest of the homeland by force from the hand of aliens," and "the solution of the problem of aliens through transfers of population."[30]

The Integrity of the Land of Israel

The two underground organizations shared with each other and with the parent revisionist movement the goal of renewing Jewish political sovereignty over all the Land of Israel within its historical borders. This included both sides of the Jordan River. The right of the Jewish people to the entire Land was defined as sacred and absolute. The revisionists never accepted the British decision to sever the east bank of the Jordan from the territory in which the Balfour Declaration had envisaged a "Jewish national home." In the poem that served as Betar's anthem, Jabotinsky declared: "There are two banks to the Jordan; the first is ours and the second too." Paraphrasing the traditional Jewish oath,

"If I forget thee, O Jerusalem, let my right hand forget its cunning," the revisionist leader said, "Let my traitorous right hand forget its cunning if I forget the left bank of the Jordan." The symbol of the IZL was a rifle superimposed on an outline of the borders of the Land of Israel and the slogan, *Only Thus*.

Revisionism used the Bible to legitimate Jewish claims to the Land of Israel within its historical borders. Our special interest is in determining the extent to which the religious tradition really played a role in defining the political goals of revisionism. This question is related to the broader and more fundamental problem of the relationship between revisionist civil religion and traditional Judaism.

The Relationship of Revisionism to Traditional Judaism

Notwithstanding its style and symbols, Revisionism was an essentially secular movement, particularly in its early years. By that we mean two things. First, most of its leaders defined themselves as secular Jews, and second, their vision of the Jewish state was not a state to be governed by religious law. Revisionists, however, struggled with the problem of the place of the religious tradition in its ideology, and the role of religion in the future Jewish state. In one respect, this was true of all Zionist parties. As we have seen, even Zionist-socialism linked itself to the Jewish tradition. But the revisionists were more disposed to affirm the religious tradition than were the other nonreligious parties, especially their archenemy, the labor Zionist movement. There are a number of explanations for this. First, whereas the Zionist-socialists could draw upon an alternative symbol system, that is socialism, to meet the spiritual needs of their followers, revisionist commitment to monism precluded this.

Second, the universalist-humanist element played a more prominent role in Zionist-socialist ideology than it did in that of the revisionists, who were more concerned with emphasizing that which was specific and unique to Judaism. The revisionists viewed this universalism as the value system of foreign ideologies and cultures.[31] But since they were not satisfied with confining their national identity to conceptions of territory and political sovereignty, they fell back on traditional Judaism as a source for values, conceptions, and symbols with which they could formulate and express their national-cultural identity.

Thirdly, the revisionists attracted a number of religious Jews to their ranks and established a special organizational framework for them. [32] Institutional opportunism, internal pressures, and also perhaps personal confrontation with religious Jews, influenced them to adopt a more favorable attitude toward traditional Judaism than the one adopted by the Zionist-socialists.

Finally, there was an antireligious *zeitgeist* in nineteenth and early twentieth century socialism that affected Zionist-socialists independently of their relationship to the Jewish tradition. The militant antisocialism of the revisionists may have had the opposite effect and resulted in a more positive attitude toward religion.

Related to this last explanation is the basic difference in the approaches of the two movements to the authoritative element in religion. Labor Zionists reinterpreted the traditional conception of redemption to mean, among other things, liberation from dependence on God. The revisionists, as we have seen, emphasized the need for leadership and discipline in society. In general they were influenced by the tradition of romantic nationalism which accorded great importance to religion as an authentic expression of the national spirit, and as a factor in preserving the unity and uniqueness of the people. However, it took some time for Jabotinsky and his followers to appreciate the deep bond between nationality and the Jewish religion.

Until the 1930s, revisionist leaders had little sympathy with traditional religion and objected to its integration into Zionist ideology. None of them came from religious or traditional backgrounds, nor did they "feel that there was any organic connection between Zionism and religion, least of all in the revisionist concept of an all-embracing national movement." [33] According to Isaac Remba, Jabotinsky's initial hostility to the Jewish religion was an outcome of his feeling of strangeness with traditional Jews of Eastern Europe. The "manifestation of surrender" in their behavior aroused an "instinctive aversion to the traditional Jewish way of life . . . from which he would later free himself only with considerable effort." [34]

Jabotinsky's aversion to the image of the *ghetto Jew* is evident in his 1905 article on Herzl. He attributes Herzl's attraction and charm to his non-Jewish qualities. According to Jabotinsky, Zionists sought to project a *new Jew* in the image of the biblical Hebrew. But since under conditions of exile it was difficult to find such a model, the Zionists described the new Jew as possessing the opposite characteristics of the ghetto Jew, to whom Jabotinsky refers with the anti-Semitic appellation *zhid*.

Jabotinsky explains the Jews' adoration for Herzl by stating that in his appearance and personality he represented a contrast to the "ghetto Jew—zhid." Herzl thus became the symbol and model of the new Hebrew. It is difficult to imagine a less attractive image of the ghetto Jew than the one conceived by Jabotinsky.[35]

As far as Jabotinsky was concerned, the religious commandments were a means to preserve the nation in the Diaspora in the absence of a territory of their own. Once the Zionist vision of the Jewish state was realized, it would be possible to forego most of them.[36]

Jabotinsky's position reflected the view that national preservation was the ultimate value to which all others were subordinate. "Not religion, but national uniqueness . . . is the sacred treasure which our people has so stubbornly preserved and continues to preserve."[37] Religion had preserved Jewish uniqueness by "artificial segregative factors" that would not be necessary once "natural segregation by means of national territory" was achieved. This achievement would lead to "the clipping of the physical and spiritual sidecurls" Jews had grown in the Diaspora.[38]

This approach did not involve wholesale rejection of the Jewish tradition. Even leaders of the radical wing, who were generally more antagonistic to traditional Judaism, did not totally reject the tradition. Their strategy was one of dissolution, which was adopted by the revisionist movement in general. Aḥimeir and Yevin differentiated two fundamental approaches in traditional Judaism. What they called the positive approach stood for political activism, aspired to national liberation, and accorded great importance to factors such as territory, army, and state. The negative approach was that which preached spiritualism, accorded little importance to territorial-political factors, and adopted a passive and resigned attitude toward the Diaspora and foreign rule.

These two opposing approaches, according to Aḥimeir and Yevin, were associated with different periods in Jewish history. The positive approach prevailed during periods of Jewish sovereignty, the negative approach during exile. The periods of

Jewish statehood, the first and the second temple periods, were preferred because only a people living in its own land and sovereign state could create an original culture expressing its particular national qualities.[39] According to Yevin, conditions in the Diaspora did not allow for national cultural creativity since "the spiritual assets of humanity were created by sovereign peoples," whereas "subjugated peoples created nothing." Hence, "the only remedy for the Jewish body and spirit" was Jewish national revival.[40]

Ahimeir argued that one could distinguish between secular and theological elements in all historical cultures. The secular elements are expressed in nationalism and political activism; the theological elements in spirituality and political passivity. According to Ahimeir, the Bible, more than any other product of Jewish tradition, is characterized by secular elements whereas the Talmud and the later rabbinic tradition express purely theological elements.[41]

Jabotinsky, Ahimeir, Yevin, and other revisionist leaders subsequently modified their approach to adopt a much more positive attitude toward traditional religion. But this did not mean that most revisionist leaders became religious Jews who observed the laws of traditional Judaism.

Jabotinsky remained a secularist in private life, but he espoused a policy of alliance between religion and state. When the revisionists seceded from the WZO in 1935, Jabotinsky supported a "religious clause" in the New Zionist Organization's platform "which would demonstrate the bond between national Judaism and the tradition handed down at Mount Sinai."[42] The clause, which was adopted, affirmed the principle of "implementing in Jewish life the sacred treasures of the Jewish tradition."[43] Jabotinsky noted the negative effects of church-state separation in Europe and observed that the state must be concerned with whether or not there will be churches or synagogues. "It is of concern to the State," he said, "whether religious holidays can be celebrated . . . and whether the voices of the prophets can still remain a living force in the life of the society."[44]

This positive attitude toward the tradition led the revisionists to support the integration of religious practices in the public life of the Zionist movement and the yishuv. Observance of the Sabbath and Jewish dietary laws were always mandatory in the agricultural training farm of Betar, but a general decision was later adopted to prohibit the desecration of the Sabbath in all Betar activities.

In summary, the revisionists affirmed, not religion per se but the nationalist values inherent in respecting the religious commandments. They voiced the opinion that an offense committed against religion was like one committed against the nation because "religion for us is very closely related to the nation."[45]

It is difficult to establish what caused the change in attitude by Jabotinsky and his supporters. Or perhaps we should say instead, it is difficult to explain their initial hostility to religion.

As one might anticipate, the revisionist affirmation of religion also entailed a process of selection and reinterpretation. To some extent this process characterizes all religious development; it is to be found even among the most traditionally religious segments of the population. The secular Zionists are distinguished only by their self-conscious selection and interpretation, and by their acknowledged use of religious symbols to serve what they construed as higher values. For example, Jabotinsky could describe religious faith as " . . . an army in active service, in the service of liberation."[46]

The self-conscious usage of the tradition is evident in Jabotinsky's attempt to formulate a broad revisionist world view that would rest on Jewish sources and would define the appropriate character of the Jewish state and the principles of its social and political regime. Jabotinsky advocated a reliance on the sources of traditional Judaism as a basis for social ideas. Much of what he considered most sacred in the Torah was, he acknowledged, a system of ethics. He asked: "Why implant them under the label of religion?" His answer was: "It is sounder to treat these ethical fundamentals as connected with superhuman mystery, and this is not only out of 'courtesy.' The Bible is indeed our primary source, so why should we hide it? . . . and why have we to be ashamed of quoting the Torah? . . . I go much further. . . . We need religious pathos as such. . . . I would be happy if it were possible to create a generation of believers."[47]

An important factor in the revisionists' initial hostility to religion stemmed from their negation of the Diaspora, a point of view they shared with the Zionist-socialists. The revisionists' negative attitude toward any manifestations of passivity or dependence, perceived as characteristics of Diaspora Jewry, resulted in the tendency to impugn the traditional Jewish way of life which had manifested these characteristics. The revisionists reserved a particular measure of animus to what they called *galut mentality* (the mentality of exile) which they associated with surrender and cowardice. The change in the attitude of revisionist leaders toward traditional religion effected no change in their negation of the Diaspora. Instead, the religious tradition was released from responsibility for creating and fostering the negative characteristics of galut. Instead, the "compromising" and "defeatist" policies of the labor Zionist leaders were presented as the products of a galut mentality from which they had not succeeded in freeing themselves.[48]

The Dissenters

As we noted, not all ultranationalists welcomed the change in the revisionists' position regarding traditional religion. There were those whose opposition stemmed from their own monistic conception and their single-minded devotion to the nationalist idea. During the debate on the religious clause at the 1935 New Zionist Organization congress some revisionists argued that all efforts should be directed to establishing the Jewish state without defining the nature of that state. One delegate declared, "I am in favor of the principle of the State of Israel, and nothing else concerns me," to which Jabotinsky responded, "I want a Jewish state that will be Jewish."[49]

Others expressed fundamental opposition to the traditional Jewish religion. They demanded the total secularization of Jewish nationalism and its dissociation from any tie to the Jewish tradition. Some went so far as to view the Jewish society in the Land of Israel as a new nation unconnected in any way to historical Judaism. They maintained that Jewish nationalism must base itself on concrete elements of territory, state, and language, not on a Jewish cultural tradition. In its most radical form this approach was expressed by the Canaanites mentioned in the first chapter, whose founders came from the ranks of the revisionist movement.[50]

The Canaanites were never a very large group, but their influence at one time was substantial, partly because so many among their small number were writers and artists. The Canaanites organized in 1942, declaring themselves the representatives of a new nation united on a territorial-political-linguistic basis, completely dissociated from historical Judaism and from Jews living outside the Land of Israel. The Canaanites wanted a single, Hebrew-speaking state that would include all the inhabitants of the area between the Euphrates and the Nile, united by their common tie to the ancient Canaanite culture.

The two foremost leaders of the Canaanite movement first expressed their position within the framework of the revisionist movement. The poet Yonathan Ratosh published a series of articles in the revisionist paper *Hayarden*, demanding that the principle of "the sovereignty of the people of Israel over the Land of Israel" be immediately realized.[51] Ratosh's articles gave early expression to the political maximalism of the Canaanite movement, which he subsequently founded and led. The other aspect of Canaanism, the rejection of religion and historical Judaism, found early expression in the remarks of Adaya Gurevitch (Gur) in the debate over the religious question at the founding congress of the New Zionist Organization. Gurevitch, who later became an ideologist of the Canaanite movement, maintained that he did not consider himself a member of the religion of Moses. "The Hebrew people existed for two thousand years before the Jewish religion. . . . I am not a Jew from Yavne but a Hebrew from Samaria."[52]

At a certain stage, the views of Yevin and Aḥimeir were not far removed from Canaanism. They shared Gurevitch's opposition to the Jews of Yavne, as well as Ratosh's demand for a takeover by force of the government in all of Palestine. Most of the writers Aḥimeir defined as the spiritual forerunners of Betar were the same ones the literary critic Baruch Kurzweil identified as the spiritual fathers of Canaanism.[53]

However, as we noted, Aḥimeir's attitude toward traditional Judaism changed. Furthermore, he never advocated the complete dissociation of Jewish nationalism from religion. The Canaanites completely rejected Judaism, both as a religion and a cultural tradition, distinguishing it sharply from what they called Hebrew nationalism.

Nationalism, carried to the extreme, may conflict with any religious or moral system not prepared to recognize state and territory as sacred values. The Canaanites maintained that traditional Judaism was incompatible with modern nationalism, since Judaism was a religious community, not a national one.

According to the Canaanites, the Jewish religion led to delegitimation and disintegration on the national and political plane. It constituted a serious obstacle to the formation and consolidation of the new Hebrew nation. Therefore, separation of religion and state was insufficient; the Canaanites sought to uproot the Jewish religion. They also conducted a vigorous propaganda campaign against Zionism because of its link with Judaism and the Jewish people.

The Canaanites represented the most radical expression of a broader phenomenon that Yaacov Shavit describes as the ideology of Israeli or Palestinian nationalism, whose common denominator was the desire to sever, or at least weaken, the link between the Jews of Israel and the Diaspora. This is a negation of Zionism and those who held such views had no place in the revisionist movement. In fact, those who actually joined the Canaanites did dissociate themselves from revisionism, but quasi-Canaanite views continued to be expressed within the revisionist camp and the two underground organizations, IZL and Lehi.

The IZL's Committee for National Liberation, which operated in the United States, expressed Canaanite leanings. The Committee's 1944 platform distinguished between Diaspora Jews who were members of the Jewish religious community and the political citizens of the Hebrew nation. American Jews, the platform stated, do not belong to the Hebrew nation, but are an integral part of the American people. They are Americans of Jewish origin.[54] The IZL itself did not accept the ideology of the committee, and the revisionists denounced it as contrary to revisionist ideology.[55]

Canaanite views also found advocates among some Lehi partisans who believed that the starting point and the driving force of the struggle in the Land of Israel was not the solution to the Jewish problem but the desire to liberate the Land from foreign rule.[56] One finds expressions of admiration for those born and raised in the Land of Israel "whose ties to their homeland were not founded on the longing of thousands of years, on pogroms. . . . But who sought a life of freedom and honor on national soil . . . and hated the foreigner who ruled the Land and sought to cast off his yoke . . . because he was not a Hebrew."[57] Both underground groups overcame the Canaanite tendencies among them. Jews of strong traditional, if not religious, propensities fulfilled central roles in their leadership.

Of the two outstanding leaders of the IZL, David Raziel was a religious Jew who observed the traditional laws and Menachem Begin had strong ties to the tradition.[58] Avraham Stern, the founder of Lehi, observed the Sabbath and religious dietary restrictions.[59] Many of the commanders and fighters of the underground movements also observed the religious laws.

MYTHS AND HEROES IN REVISIONISM

The revisionists eschewed traditional Jewish martyrdom which they discounted as passive. They glorified the active heroism of rebels and revolutionaries who risked their lives for the liberation of their people. "We do not need martyrs," wrote Ahimeir, "but heroes. Not Hebron [where Jews were murdered in 1929] but Tel Hai."[60]

The central myth of the revisionist movement was woven around the story of Tel Hai. The name Betar was an acronym for Brit Yosef Trumpeldor (the alliance of Trumpeldor). Betar members greeted one another with the words, Tel Hai. The revisionists were the first to organize pilgrimages to Tel Hai on the eleventh of Adar and to conduct ceremonies on that day in Betar branches throughout the country. At the parades and public gatherings, as well as in leaflets distributed on that day, the heroism of Trumpeldor and his companions was extolled, and their deeds presented as a source of inspiration for Jewish youth.[61]

The labor Zionists charged that it was an affront to name the revisionist youth movement after Trumpeldor when revisionism was foreign in spirit and in deed to Trumpeldor's ideology and way of life. The pilgrimages of the youth organizations to Tel Hai were occasions for violent clashes between Zionist-socialist youth groups and Betar. The treatment of Tel Hai illustrates how the same event can serve as the source for different myths. In the Zionist-socialists' version of the Tel Hai myth, heroism was interwoven with their conception of halutz-iut. In the revisionist version, Trumpeldor was a military hero who fought and gave his life for the liberation of his people. His halutziut included work and toil, but emphasis was on "halutz-iut of blood—the blood of the covenant of Brit Trumpeldor." It was this blood that distinguished it from the halutziut of Labor pioneers.[62]

According to the revisionists, the Zionist-socialists distorted Trumpeldor's image and misused the legend that developed around him. Jabotinsky wrote that among those who sang the praises of Trumpeldor "are the bitterest opponents to everything connected to the sword, the rifle, and the pistol. But Trumpeldor's name is associated, first and foremost, with these kinds of arms . . . in the collective memory of our nation Trumpeldor is first and foremost a soldier . . . a leader of Jews who bear arms . . . The legend of Trumpeldor . . . is the legend of a Jewish soldier, not a public official."[63] Jabotinsky noted that the admiration for Trumpeldor did not stem from his being a "holy person" who "fell as a sacrifice" in the hands of murderers. There have been thousands of such martyrs in our generation and none became a legend. Trumpeldor's significance stemmed from his "defense of the yishuv with arms." Evoking his memory helps "to implant in Jewish hearts the longing for strong hands." Jews, in particular, because they are *hefker* (literally, an object without an owner; hence, there for the taking) in the world, require such reminders. "That is why the nation so loves . . . Trumpeldor the soldier. Not his hammer, not his spade, not his plow, but really his sword. That is why Tel Hai the fortress is a thousand times more sacred than Tel Hai the collective settlement. In their eyes it is a symbol that, after all, one can escape being hefker."[64]

Whereas Zionist-socialists stressed Trumpeldor's role in the labor movement and in the establishment of the Histadrut, the revisionists emphasized his service as the first Jewish officer in the Russian army and his role alongside Jabotinsky in the organization of the Jewish Legion in World War I. Ahimeir stressed that Trumpeldor's conduct in the Russian army deserved special notice in light of the opposition to military service prevailing at that period among Russian Jewry. "In this atmosphere of desertion Trumpeldor appeared. . . . The outlook of the Trumpeldorists was a military one. A people of deserters is not deserving of rights."[65] Nevertheless, among a minority of revisionists the hero of Tel Hai was primarily a halutz-worker, one of the pioneers of cooperative agricultural settlements.[66]

When the IZL initiated its actions against the Arabs and the British, revisionists acquired new myths of heroism and sacrifice. The central figures were the underground fighters put to death by the British. Jabotinsky, referring to the first Jewish fighter executed by the British, wrote, "We will transform his scaffold into a tower, his grave into a temple, his memory into a civil religion."[67]

The revisionists also utilized myths taken from early Jewish history. Zionist-socialists extrolled the revolt of the Maccabees against Hellenistic rule. The revisionists gave special emphasis to the Jewish revolts against Rome and glorified the more radical and controversial rebels—the Zealots. In addition the revisionists expressed admiration for the leaders of Jewish messianic movements, such as David Alroy (leader of a twelfth-century movement in Kurdistan) and David Reuveni and Shlomo Molcho (leaders of a sixteenth-century pseudo-messianic movement).

THE SYMBOLIC DIMENSION IN REVISIONISM

The citations from Jabotinsky and other revisionist leaders indicate how rich their rhetoric was in symbols and metaphors taken from sacred Jewish sources. This expressed not only their link with the Jewish tradition but also the sense of holiness and total commitment the revisionists felt toward their own principles. Despite the importance attached to symbols and ceremonies, however, the revisionists never succeeded in establishing their own ceremonials and rituals, much less their own holidays. They lacked the comprehensive communal framework to socialize their adherents to transformed symbols and ceremonies in a meaningful manner. They emphasized symbols and ceremonies of an exhibitionist nature, such as uniforms, flags, and parades. But they had difficulty cultivating patterns of behavior one could define as a way of life, customs that, despite their ceremonial aspect, were not mere outward displays but an organic part of the lives of those who practiced them.

The fact that the revisionists were less symbolically inventive than their rivals can also be explained by their opposition to the explicit secularization of traditional Judaism. Since they also rejected symbols and ceremonies from foreign sources, there was nothing left from which they could forge their own distinct symbols.

Revisionists were especially forceful in rejecting Zionist-socialist symbols they branded as divisive. For example, they opposed the Histadrut's use of the red flag and its celebration of

May Day. The National Labor Federation, a workers' organization that was part of the Revisionist movement, designated the twentieth of Tammuz, the anniversary of Herzl's death, as Labor Day. (Their rationale was Herzl's vision of a seven-hour workday in the Jewish state.)

The intensity of the struggle the revisionists waged against ceremonies and symbols they viewed as divisive indicates the importance they attached to the symbolic dimension. In fact, we believe that, despite their failure to create their own integrated symbol system, the revisionists regarded symbols with even greater seriousness than did the Zionist-socialists. Jabotinsky said, "Almost three-fourths of true culture is made up of ritual and ceremony. Political law and freedom rise and fall through parliamentary ritual and procedure, and the life of social groups would sink into darkness without the primeval ceremonies of culture and custom."[68]

According to the historian Joseph Klausner, one of the intellectual leaders of revisionism, Jabotinsky

> was accused of according significance to external things—such as uniforms, flags, ceremonies, and slogans. . . . [But] his understanding was higher than that of his detractors . . . The philosophy of Israel, of which the belief in God and morality is the highest principle, recognizes the great value of deed and ceremony . . . in the education of the people. . . . There can be no national education without deeds, without ceremonies and symbols, without festive slogans and acts . . . if not, the heart withers and all becomes profane and materialistic.[69]

According to Jabotinsky, "Jews have a special need to be educated to ceremonials in the broadest meaning of the term . . . the clear and precise rules of how to stand, how to greet another, how to talk to a friend and to a commander. We, Jews, suffer from a lack of sensitivity to structural forms . . . the average Jew walks, dresses, eats, and relates to others without grace."[70]

Hadar

Jabotinsky's intense regard for ceremony found expression in the concept *hadar* (literally: splendor, majesty, glory, beauty) which he used to describe the pattern of behavior appropriate to the members of Betar. According to Jabotinsky, hadar "combines various conceptions, such as aesthetics, respect, self-esteem, politeness, faithfulness."[71] In a letter to members of Betar, he wrote: "Be tactful, be noble . . . learn to speak quietly. . . . You must shave every morning . . . every morning you must check whether your nails are clean."[72] Some revisionists saw in hadar a new way of life in contrast to that of traditional Jewry.[73] Jabotinsky himself spoke of the Betar member as the archetype of a new and unique race, but he also drew a parallel between the call for "princely manners" and the historical qualities of the Jewish people: "There is no aristocracy in the world equal to the Jews. There are no plebians among us." This is "an army in which each of its soldiers is a general at heart."[74] Hadar, at least in its outward manifestations, stood in marked contrast to Zionist-socialist values that denigrated "bourgeois etiquette."

Both revisionism and Zionist-socialism strove to create a new Hebrew, the antithesis of the exilic Jew, characterized by courage, commitment, and activism. But for Zionist-socialism the new Hebrew was a man of the soil, earthy, simple in dress and behavior, straightforward, indifferent to the consensus of bourgeois society.[75] In contrast to this image, which includes an element of roughness and vulgarity, the Revisionists cultivated the ideal of hadar in the image of the Western European gentleman, culturally polished and well mannered.

Sacred Sites

The revisionists accorded central significance to the western wall. A revisionist demonstration in front of the wall was one of the causes of the 1929 riots.[76] Revisionists later adopted the practice of blowing a *shofar* (ram's horn) in front of the western wall at the conclusion of Yom Kippur despite, or perhaps because of, the British ban against it.

Blowing the shofar is a religious ceremony, but the revisionists interpreted the shofar blowing at the western wall as a national rite. In an article by Aḥimeir, in which he writes that the wall is everything for him, he also refers to the changed meaning of the shofar blowing:

> There was a time that the shofar of the armies of Israel tumbled the walls of Jericho. After that came the exile and the shofar—symbol of the Israeli warrior—became a pure religious article. . . . But the shofar is returning now to the hands of the Segals and the New-

mans [two compatriots of Aḥimeir]. Their notes are not the notes that come from the house of study. They are the notes of the biryonim.[77]

The revisionist struggle gained sympathy within religious circles, but aroused resentment within the labor movement. Labor Zionists felt that this issue only aggravated relations with the Arabs and the British. Moshe Beilinson (1889–1936), a journalist and spokesman for Zionist-socialism, argued that "the value of the wall is great . . . [but] the central place in the revival of the people belongs to other values—immigration, land, and work."[78]

An important role in revisionist mythology was accorded to battle sites. Besides Tel Ḥai and Masada, the revisionists accorded special importance to Betar (a stronghold of Bar Kochba which along with Trumpeldor provided the revisionist youth movement with its name) and Yodefet (Jotapata—the stronghold of the Bar Kochba rebels in the Galilee). These sites filled the place in revisionist mythology which was filled in Zionist-socialist mythology by the Emek or Nahalal and Degania (two early agricultural settlements established during the period of the second and third aliyot, respectively). But the Zionist-socialists' historical sites were settlements as well. They were a living realization of Zionist-socialist values and in this way more meaningful than the sacred sites of the revisionists.

SUMMARY

Revisionism's greater sympathy for the religious tradition precluded adopting the confrontational strategy characteristic of Zionist-socialism. There are, however, aspects of confrontation in revisionism, for example, the invidious contrasting of the heroes of Tel-Ḥai to traditional Jewish martyrs. The revisionist movement's secularist elements, who were particularly influential before 1935, were not inclined toward a strategy of reinterpretation. Nevertheless, reinterpretation was also employed by revisionism. The association of hadar with the Jewish tradition is one example. More striking is the way in which the revisionists, particularly after 1935, embraced many traditional Jewish symbols, imbued them with a nationalist content, and integrated them into a revisionist value framework. But the characteristic strategy of revisionism was dissolution—defining a positive and a negative approach in the tradition, affirming the first, and ignoring the latter. The following chapters will demonstrate the striking parallels of revisionism's use of dissolution to the characteristic strategies of statism (dissolution) and of the new civil religion (reinterpretation).

4 The Civil Religion of Statism

THE DECLINE OF ZIONIST-SOCIALISM AND THE RISE OF STATISM

We have treated revisionism as a civil religion of the yishuv in some detail because, as we indicated, its followers constituted an important community of believers who offered an alternative ideology and symbol system to Zionist-socialism. But the attention devoted to revisionism should not mislead the reader about its importance compared to Zionist-socialism. First of all, Zionist-socialism represented the symbol system of the political and cultural elite. Second, the vast majority of the yishuv, while not quite dedicated to Zionist-socialism, did accept and participate in its major symbols, ceremonies, and myths. It is certainly fair to say that Zionist-socialism served as the point of reference for most of the yishuv. To examine the rise of a new dominant civil religion we must also look at the decline of Zionist-socialism.

The establishment of Israel and the mass immigration that directly followed are the two central events accounting for the decline of Zionist-socialism and the rise of statism. During the prestate period it was possible to cultivate the civil religion of one subgroup without hampering the basic unity of the Jewish population. The political leadership of the various camps interrelated through a complex network, compromising on some disputed issues and principles and ignoring many others. Avoiding decisions was possible in the absence of statehood and political sovereignty. Available resources, money, and jobs were distributed by the political leadership, using a *key*; according to a negotiated formula, each group received an allocation based roughly on its voting strength.[1] This arrangement

81

encouraged the pluralism that characterized the yishuv—what Val Lorwin has termed "segmented integration," the survival through cooperation and compromise of a variety of subcommunities of believers.[2] In addition all parties were united by certain national commitments discussed below.

The creation of Israel and the tripling of its population in three years led state leaders to feel that the country must be completely integrated; that the value-belief-symbol systems separating the various camps must be abolished and replaced by a unified symbol system uniting the entire Jewish population in support of the state and its institutions.

The yishuv lacked central political institutions that could evoke loyalty and commitment.

> With the establishment of the state, many functions and services— which had hitherto been performed by voluntary organizations— came under control of central state agencies and governmental ministries. The transfer of authority was accompanied by changes in social values. The establishment of a sovereign state, after so long a period of life in the Diaspora, placed an even greater emphasis on the state as the symbol of national survival.[3]

The more parochial institutions associated with the different camps of the yishuv performed instrumental functions and evoked sentiments of loyalty as well. Once Israel was established, these loyalties became intolerable to statists. Unconditional acceptance of state authority was incompatible, in their view, with the existence of independent foci of loyalty and identity.

Second, an important portion of the political elite believed the creation of a state made it necessary to adopt policies with respect to many of the issues on which the *yishuv* had avoided making a decision. The old system had been particularly appropriate to a voluntaristic society in which any group could opt out of the system—as extreme religious circles and, to some extent, the revisionists had done. But a state cannot allow that option. While a sovereign state can and must impose its authority on all its citizens, rather than do so by force, it seeks to institutionalize its authority by creating broad popular consensus around its values and symbols.

The old system, despite the existence of various communities of believers, relied on the sense that the symbols of all the civil religions pointed to a core of shared beliefs affirming certain values: the creation of a Jewish state in the Land of Israel, the qualitative distinction between life in the Diaspora and life in the Land of Israel, and the linkage between the new culture of the yishuv and the Jewish tradition.

In addition to the cooperative understanding among the various elites, and the shared referents of the different symbol systems, the prestate settlers were also united by the common economic, political, and security problems they confronted. Economic hardship, political struggle, threats to security, and war had produced in the yishuv a strong sense of cohesion not shared by the new immigrants. In socializing these immigrants to the values and symbols of one subculture or another there was a danger that they might miss the sense of underlying unity that had characterized the yishuv. Moreover, the new government believed that only the state could successfully socialize the new immigrants to Zionist values. Most new immigrants arrived identifying with Israel but not with any one of the subgroups. Many immigrants knew nothing at all about the different camps. But in order to build on the immigrants' identification with Israel and socialize them to the values of the state, an appropriate symbol system was required.

This was particularly true of the large group of immigrants from Muslim countries, products of a traditional Jewish culture. Since Zionist-socialism held no attraction for these immigrants but the labor movement could not ignore them without risking its political future, it sought to appeal to them with material benefits. As a result, the internal solidarity of the labor Zionist movement, in the past based on a shared commitment to an ideological-symbolic system, was undermined. It was replaced by a quasi-contractual relationship in which the individual exchanged votes and other forms of political support for services from the labor movement. The replacement of solidarity by this new relationship was a slow process. Efforts were made to socialize the immigrants to Zionist-socialism. Only gradually did it become evident that the new immigrants had exercised greater influence over the labor movement than vice versa. The immigrants had blurred the ideological differences between labor Zionism and its rivals, and turned it from a community of believers into a patron party.

The danger in the cultivation of subcommunal symbols and loyalties that originated in the *yishuv* period became apparent in the fierce battle over immigrants' education.[4] Each camp sought to maximize the number of children enrolled in its schools. The conflict involved pressures including threats of violence and even actual violence. It resulted in a series of political crises that threatened to disrupt the entire political system. Ben Gurion, the major architect of statism, led his followers in exploiting the crises and the consequent public discontent with unrestrained competition between different camps to propose and win approval of a national educational system.

The unified educational system caused a radical transformation in the status of Zionist-socialist education that had long-range consequences for the labor Zionist community of believers. Unlike religious education, preserved by the religious camp's maintenance of its own school system and much of its autonomy as a division in the Ministry of Education, Zionist-socialist education simply disappeared. The new national educational system became a major vehicle for the transmission of statist symbols and values. Paradoxically, the process strengthened Mapai, since, as the dominant party, it was identified by many Israelis, especially by new immigrants, with the state. At the same time, it further weakened the labor movement as an ideological camp.

THE DEFINITION OF STATISM

Statism affirms the centrality of state interests and the centralization of power at the expense of nongovernmental groups and institutions. In terms of symbols and style, statism reflects the effort to transform the state and its institutions into the central foci of loyalty and identification. Statism gives rise to values and symbols that point to the state, legitimate it, and mobilize the population to serve its goals. In its more extreme formulation statism cultivates an attitude of sanctity toward the state, affirming it as an ultimate value.

Our definition of statism as a civil religion refers to its symbols and style. In this respect it functions as a quasi-religion, a substitute for traditional religion. We are concerned with the policies and decisions of statist governments only as they relate to statism as a civil religion.

The civil and revisionist camps had supported the centralization or nationalization of governmental functions in the yishuv period. At that time the Zionist-socialists, from whose ranks the statist leaders later emerged, had been adamant proponents of the segmented system of providing such services as education, health, and employment exchanges. On one hand, despite differences in nuance, the operative principles of statism more closely resembled the platforms of the prestate revisionists and civil parties than those of the prestate Zionist-socialists. On the other hand, the continued enthusiasm of the General Zionists (the major part of the civil camp) and the revisionists for statism in the new state was mitigated by fear that Mapai was using statism to impose its particularist ideology and control on the nation. Our discussion of statism will focus on the ideology and symbols of the civil religion that emerged from the ranks of the labor movement, but we must bear in mind that the statists found allies, at least in principle, outside their own camp. Their severest opposition in fact came from within the labor camp itself.

Statism represented the State of Israel as the expression of the national Jewish spirit, the realization of the yearnings of the Jewish people for freedom and sovereignty in its own land, and the guarantor of national Jewish unity. This formulation recalls the central value of revisionism, but there is an important difference—revisionist symbols and values referred to a future state. The revisionists never attributed to the institutions of the yishuv or the World Zionist Organization the authority and significance they were willing to render to the sovereign Jewish state of which they dreamed. Statist symbols, in contrast, related to an existing system, not to a vision of the future.

THE VALUES OF STATISM

Redemption and Political Mobilization

The establishment of an independent Jewish state only a few years after the Holocaust evoked an outburst of enthusiasm from Jews both in the Diaspora and the Land of Israel. This enthusiasm served as a source of loyalty, identification, and even reverence toward the state and its institutions, forming the basis for consolidation of statist sentiments. Like traditional religion, the civil religion sought to recapture the spontaneous experience of the initial moment of revelation through symbol, cult, and ritual.

The military victory in the War of Independence and the mass immigration that followed the establishment of the state led to a perception among both religious and nonreligious Jews that the prophetic vision of the ingathering of the exiles and the victory of the few over the many was being realized. Hence, it is not surprising that the joy and enthusiasm evoked by the creation of Israel had the character of Messianic sentiments. In this context many believed the state to be the fulfillment of the traditional Jewish vision of redemption.

Ben Gurion expressed the belief that "we are living in the days of the Messiah."[5] Moshe Sharett (1894–1965), foreign minister and later prime minister, felt it necessary to emphasize that the Messianic vision had not been fully realized and therefore continued effort was required on behalf of the state.[6] Specifically, the goals that remained unfulfilled were: ingathering of the exiles, including their economic, social, and cultural integration;[7] the upbuilding of the Land of Israel and the economic development of its desolate regions;[8] and the establishment of an ideal society based on the highest moral principles—an example to all humanity.[9]

According to Ben Gurion, the Jewish redemption was related to the redemption of all humanity. The redemption of Israel depended primarily but, apparently, not entirely on the efforts of the Jews themselves. World redemption, in turn, depended on the realization of the Zionist dream, since only in their own land could Jews fulfill their mission to be a "light unto the nations."[10]

Ben Gurion's conception imparted a universalist and ethical meaning to the state. Rather than claiming that the state was the source of morality, he conceived of Israeli interests as subject to the judgment and authority of universal moral principles.[11] The state was an instrument to realize goals and visions, and an arena in which Jewish freedom and independence could be experienced and creatively encouraged—the antithesis of exile. At the same time, by attributing a universal moral meaning to the state, Ben Gurion strengthened the tendency to equate its very existence to the highest moral order. He himself proclaimed, "There is nothing more important, more precious and more sacred than the security of the state." If "all the great ideals of the world are placed on one side of the scale and Israel's security on the other," Ben Gurion would choose "without any hesitation the security of Israel."[12]

In addition, the conception of Israel as a light unto the nations implied an elitism that found expression not only in Israel's responsibilities to other nations but also in its self-image of moral and intellectual superiority.

Education and the State

Statism emphasized the educational task of the state in shaping the society and its national culture. The historian Ben-Zion Dinur (1894 – 1973) served as minister of education from 1951 – 1955. In presenting the law establishing a national educational system to the Knesset, he affirmed that the goals of the state were "to educate its citizens to full and total identification of every individual with the State . . . to create in the heart of each and every person the sense of direct identification with the Land."[13]

The Israeli army was also assigned an educational role. In addition to safeguarding the country's security the army was responsible for tasks in the fields of education, culture, settlement, and immigrant absorption.[14] The purpose in assigning these tasks to the army, beyond making use of available manpower, was to teach the soldiers to identify with the people and the state. According to Moshe Dayan:

> Care for the new immigrants had become not only a task of great importance, difficult though it was, but also a source of inspiration, human, Jewish, and pioneering, to all the troops who took part. This was what Zionism and brotherhood were all about. Even the most hardened soldiers were moved as they watched women soldiers tending the immigrant children, washing them, feeding them, administering the medicines that the army doctor had ordered, pacifying a crying baby, soothing an aged grandmother.[15]

The State of Israel and the Diaspora

Statism perceived Israel as the dominant partner in its relations with Diaspora Jewry. Avraham Avi-Hai terms Ben Gurion's attitude as Israelocentrism, which he defines to mean "that all which is done by Jews in Israel is central, vital, critical for the Jewish people and for Jewish history. The converse is also true; what is done by Jews in the Diaspora is . . . secondary."[16] Diaspora Jewry's role was to provide financial help and

assist Israel's public relations without exercising any influence
on policy.[17] Aliya, according to Ben Gurion, was the measure
of Zionist commitment. Those Jews who chose to live in the
Diaspora were not really Zionists. Hence, the state was superior to the World Zionist Organization,[18] which included Diaspora Jews among its leaders.

Diaspora Jewry played the role of antihero for Ben Gurion.
Diaspora Jews were foils for the true heroes of statism—those
who sacrificed themselves for the Zionist ideal—soldiers and
halutzim.

Ben Gurion felt there was a "deep and principled difference
between Jewish life in Israel and the Diaspora."[19] His feeling
was shared by broad circles, particularly young, native-born
Israelis. According to this view, Jews could not live a full Jewish
life, communal or cultural, outside Israel. At best they could
live in a cultural ghetto. Hence, Diaspora Jewry was "the dust
of man," since it could not experience full national-human
existence.[20]

Ben Gurion's approach was not new. It had roots in the
yishuv period, when mainstream Zionist-socialism and revisionism shared such beliefs. Nevertheless, in Ben Gurion's
version of statism, negation of the Diaspora received its most
radical formulation.

STATISM AND ZIONIST-SOCIALISM

Statism emerged out of the labor movement. It did not begin
by positing a radically new set of values but by arguing that
statehood provided Zionist-socialism the opportunity to extend
its influence over the entire society[21] and fulfill its vision.[22]

Even in the earliest period, Ben Gurion and his followers
stressed the unique aspects of Israeli socialism and warned
against imitating the ideology or structure of other socialist
states.[23] This reflected his concern about the increasing identification of the left-wing socialist party, Mapam, with the Soviet
Union. He compared Mapam to the Jewish Hellenizers of the
second temple period and other Jewish assimilationists.[24]

As time passed, statist spokesmen relied less and less on the
socialist rhetoric of class. National symbols moved increasingly
to the forefront. As an important example of this tendency, Ben

Gurion joined the General Zionists in opposing the flying of the red flag and the singing of working-class anthems in public schools.

While statism ostensibly continued to espouse many Zionist-socialist values, it really transvalued them. An important example is ḥalutziut. The National Educational Act defines one of the educational goals of the state as "preparation for ḥalutziut," but this was no longer the elitist and voluntaristic ḥalutziut Zionist-socialism had advocated in the yishuv. Statism introduced the notion of *Statist ḥalutziut*, involving mass participation in activities organized and directed by the state.[25] Ḥalutziut was now defined as engaging in any activity that strengthened the state, particularly in the fields of immigration and immigrant absorption, economic development, education, and culture. In 1949 Ben Gurion said, "ḥalutziut is not the property of a few . . . it is latent in the soul of every person . . . the pressure of historical needs and guided educational programs . . . are capable . . . of raising every person to the highest levels of courage and ḥalutziut."[26]

STATISM, TRADITIONAL JUDAISM, AND TRADITIONAL JEWRY

Despite Ben Gurion's reservations about the exilic aspects of the Jewish tradition, he was deeply committed to Judaism, as he was to the Jewish people. But he perceived the positive aspects of the tradition as having originated in the commonwealth periods when the Jews existed as a nation in their own land. The first temple or first commonwealth period extended from about 1200 B.C.E. to 586 B.C.E. and the second temple or second commonwealth period from 530 B.C.E. to 70 C.E. The aspects of the tradition that derived from these periods, according to Ben Gurion, had preserved the Jewish people during their exile.

Jewish survival was the result, first and foremost, of the belief in the primacy of the spirit. This belief, according to Ben Gurion, stemmed from the conception of man created in the image of God, hence, of the worth of each and every man. A second crucial tenet distinguishing Jews and contributing to their survival was belief in Messianic redemption—both national and universal, according to Ben Gurion. Thirdly, Jews survived because they were an isolated people, without cultural, ethnic, or religious ties to any other people. An important operative implication of this last belief was that the only ally on whom the State of Israel could rely completely and unconditionally was the Jewish people. Israel's attachment to world Jewry was "a central and determining factor in its policy."[27]

At the same time, statists emphasized the importance of cooperation between Israel and other nations. Indeed, they conceived the state as part of a world community of nations bound together by principles of morality and justice which had their source in the Jewish tradition.[28]

On the one hand, therefore, Ben Gurion's admiration of some aspects of the tradition was unbounded. On the other hand, he and other statists negated the cultural significance of that part of the tradition which originated in exile. However, the major portion of the religious tradition really originated in the exilic period. The statists were more extreme than the Zionist-socialists in their effort to represent the Zionist enterprise as a direct successor to the period of Jewish independence without any real relationship to the intervening 2,000 years of Jewish exile.

The result of the exile, according to Ben Gurion, had been to alienate the Jews from their own great cultural expression—the Bible. To understand the Bible one had to identify with the spirit of Jewish statism which informed the Book of Books. Postbiblical Judaism was apolitical, particularistic, prone to an exaggerated spiritualism and withdrawal. Hence, it neither understood nor properly appreciated the Bible or the biblical period with their rich harmony of spiritual, material, moral, political, Jewish, and universal values. Only the Jews of Israel who had returned to their Land and led an independent life could truly appreciate the Bible.[29]

Ben Gurion generally refrained from denigrating the rabbinical tradition, the product of the exilic period. However, his silence with respect to that literature, coupled with his reverence for the Bible and the biblical period, indicated his attitude very clearly. This break with the immediate past involved dangers of its own. Ben Gurion saw Canaanism as one response to the vacuum his own perception of Jewish tradition had inspired: "We are consciously divorcing ourselves from the recent past. This divorce is necessary, but it can also lead to degeneration."[30] His solution was the formation of an Israeli culture to which the youth would be socialized. The new culture would contain elements of continuity as well as change. It would draw upon both traditional Judaism and world culture. This task was critical, especially in view of Ben Gurion's perception that the new immigrants were "from a Jewish point of view, dust of man, without language, without tradition, without roots, without an orientation to the life of statehood, without the customs of an independent society."[31] These immigrants had to be remade in the image of the veteran, free Israeli culture. Immigration, Ben Gurion stressed, is not redemption but a necessary condition for redemption. Actual redemption takes place only in the process of immigrant absorption.

The effort to reformulate all Israeli culture in accordance with statist values required a certain ideological permissiveness. But the statist claim to encompass all citizens within its purview still brought it into conflict with the subcommunities that sought to retain their cultural autonomy. Besides the Zionist-socialists themselves, the subcommunity of religious Jews was also obviously threatened by statist hegemony.

Extreme statists perceived traditional religion as an alternative symbol system that competed with the state for absolute loyalty and allegiance. There were those who argued that "the life of a nation cannot be divided into secular and religious divisions; both cannot exist as separate authorities." The very existence of the rabbinate, for example, detracts from the state which "bears the myth and morality of Israel . . . with authority to teach the people and to judge them in all aspects of life."[32]

Traditional religion in this conception interfered with the absorption of the immigrants into Israeli culture and society. This was especially true of the masses of immigrants from Arab countries. Statists felt that these immigrants had to undergo a "cultural revolution." Their devotion to traditional Judaism was viewed as an impediment to their reeducation in the spirit of the new Israeli culture.

One of the motives of the program for a unified educational system in the immigrant camps was the statists' desire to prevent parents from enrolling their children in school under the auspices of the religious camp. Were religious schools for immigrants to be established, statists argued, these children would not be assimilated into the national culture.

The head of the unified school system in the immigrant camps, Nahum Levin, was a devout statist. Religious spokesmen charged him with violating the freedom of religious practice within the camps. He defended himself before an investigation committee of the Knesset by explaining the immigrants' need for a uniform educational program built around identification with the state and its institutions. They had to be provided with symbols that would unite them and deprived of symbols that would divide them.[33] Consequently, Levin prohibited religious study in the immigrant camps and sought to prevent even the entrance of religious teachers on a voluntary basis.[34]

The religious establishment in Israel and many immigrants themselves vigorously protested the effort to impose a totally secular education on immigrant children. The immigrant camp controversy between 1949 and 1952 served to moderate the extremist elements among the statists. The efforts to unite the country around statist symbols by denying the immigrants access to religious symbols only polarized the population and engendered bitterness against Mapai, which, as the dominant party, was held accountable for the conflict. As a result, Mapai adopted a new approach—it created a religious subsystem within the labor movement to compete with the religious camp in providing educational and religious services to the traditionalist immigrants. As an unanticipated consequence, labor Zionist antagonism to religious education and traditional religious values was moderated. But the tension between the statists and the religious parties was not moderated.

The statists, however, were forced to accept the existence of religious parties and even to invite their affiliation to the government coalition. The considerations were not simply arithmetical, that is, did not arise solely from the need for enough votes to form a ruling coalition. Mapai generally did not need the votes of the religious parties in the Knesset in order to form a government.[35] The major reason was the desire to avoid a *Kulturkampf*. As Ben Gurion phrased it, uncompromising conflict over the status of religion in Israel was "a national powderkeg."[36] In fact, Ben Gurion was more willing to acknowledge the legitimacy of religious-secular differences than he was to tolerate the institutionalization of other social and ideological subgroups.

THE LANGUAGE OF STATISM

Like Zionist-socialists and revisionists, statist spokesmen adopted biblical phrases and aphorisms to evoke a sense of the ceremonial, the festive, and the sacred. The statists in particular did so to express their identification with the bible and the biblical period.

The transformation of biblical phrases to make them accord with statist values was striking. Generally, some sacred object of statism—the nation, the land, the state or its institutions, especially the Israeli Defense Forces (IDF)—were substituted for the biblical reference to God. A huge banner carried by soldiers in a Haifa parade transformed the biblical phrase "Israel trust the Lord, He is your help and defender," to "Israel trust the IDF, it is your help and defender." One newspaper published a photograph of four Israeli planes under the headline "The guardian of Israel neither sleeps nor slumbers," a biblical phrase in which the guardian refers to God.[37] A banner in an army base read: "In the beginning the IDF created the soldier, and the IDF created the nation."[38]

Statists also used traditional terms, such as *commandment* or *covenant*, to express their loyalty and commitment to the state and its institutions. In an Independence Day pageant the players announced: "On Independence Day we assume the burden of the commandment of loyalty to our State."[39] The phrase *burden of the commandment* (Heb.: *ol mitzvot*) comes directly from the language of the rabbinical tradition. When Ben Gurion presented the first government to the Knesset he said that love for the State of Israel beats in the heart of every Jew, Zionist or non-Zionist, "except for that small group of violators of the covenant."[40]

The statists also reinterpreted biblical terms. For example, the word *komemiut* (literally: erect or upright) was redefined to mean sovereign and independent; the War of Independence was called the war of komemiut. *Kibbutz galuyot* (literally: ingathering of the exiles), a phrase with Messianic significance, now served to refer to the contemporary immigration of Jews to Israel from all parts of the Diaspora.

Israel's first foreign minister, Moshe Sharett, was a master of style who contributed much to the formation of statist termi-

nology. Ben Gurion himself placed great emphasis on language
and viewed himself as an arbiter in such matters. His admiration for the Bible found expression in this process. He argued
that the Bible was the authoritative source for rules governing
Hebrew syntax and usage.[41] Ben Gurion insisted that senior
army and government officials Hebraize their names and
sought to influence members of the government and Knesset to
do likewise. His preference was for biblical names. He even
insisted that streets surrounding the compound of government
offices have names of biblical origin.[42] Similarly, he argued that
medals awarded to IDF soldiers should bear only names of
biblical heroes.[43]

HEROES OF STATISM

Ben Gurion perceived the biblical heroes as ideal role
models, instruments to impress young Israelis that their roots
went back to biblical times, "the period of Jewish glory and
independence," and spiritual creativity which formed the
nation and accounted for its continued survival.[44] Indeed, the
heroes of later periods, the Maccabees or Bar Kochba, were
secondary to biblical heroes. Zionist mythology, he argued,
had glorified them in rebellion against the efforts of the rabbinic
tradition to blur their achievements.[45] But, unlike the Zionists,
the children of the land do not require heroes of protest. Instead, they need the educational heroes of the Bible, whose
original achievements are rooted in historical-literary sources,
whose national-cultural significance and authenticity are uni-
versally acknowledged. The biblical figure to whom Ben
Gurion was especially attracted was Joshua; one suspects that
he saw himself as a modern-day Joshua.[46]

Statism elevated the contemporary builders of Israel to
almost equal status with the biblical heroes. Indeed, the parallel
was often struck between biblical heroes of the first Jewish
commonwealth and heroes of the newly established state.
Hence, it is not surprising that Ben Gurion—who fulfilled the
central role in the creation of the state and the IDF and served as
first prime minister and minister of defense—thought of himself (and was considered by others) as the ideal hero-leader with
talents and capacities equivalent to those of the first great

leaders of the Jewish nation. This conception was strengthened by Ben Gurion's tendency to project himself as not only a statesman and soldier but also an educator and a man of the spirit—in the image of the biblical hero.

Ben Gurion never spoke of himself in these terms, but his followers described him as the ideal leader and the successor to the great leaders of the biblical period, possessed of their qualities. Moshe Dayan, for example, compared him to Moses.[47]

There is evidence that in the early years of statehood Ben Gurion was turning into the object of national cult. In welcoming him to Haifa, city officials called him "the prince of the nation."[48] The secretary general of Mapai, in a controversy with the opposition, declared, "You shall not take the name of Ben Gurion in vain."[49] In more extreme instances, particularly in the presence of new immigrants, adulation of Ben Gurion took on the overtones of Messianic ceremony. Immigrants kissed the soles of his feet, touched his clothing, brought sick children forward so that he might heal them with his touch, and called him the Messiah.[50] Ben Gurion's biographer related the following story about Ben Gurion's brief retirement in 1953. When the governmental secretary, Ze'ev Sharf, was asked why Ben Gurion retired to a small kibbutz in the Negev, Sharf responded, "The Messiah came, gathered the destitute of Israel, defeated all the nations around him, captured the land, built the temple, renewed the service of God—and after this he has to sit as a member of the coalition?"[51]

Statists shifted the mantle of modern hero from the shoulders of the halutzim to the IDF and the builders of the new state. As a result myths and heroes of the second and third aliyot declined in importance. But these myths and heroes also declined in significance because the statists now emphasized the role of the nineteenth-century settlers, calling them the true pioneers in agricultural settlement and economic production.[52]

However, one Zionist hero reached the peak of his authority in the statist period—Theodor (Binyamin Ze'ev) Herzl (1860–1904), founder of the World Zionist Organization and author of *The Jewish State*. Herzl's remains were transferred to Israel in 1949 amid an elaborate state ceremony and reinterred on a mountain in Jerusalem named for him—all in accordance with a special law adopted by the Knesset.[53] Mount Herzl became a sacred site and the date of his death, the twentieth of Tamuz, was declared State Day or IDF Day during the first years of statehood.

Speaker of the Knesset Joseph Sprinzak, speaking as acting president of the state, called Herzl "the prophet of Israel's freedom," who must be numbered among "the holy and the great builders of the eternity of Israel."[54] One of the founders of the Zionist labor movement wrote that Herzl Day was a "ray from the sunlight of freedom and redemption shining above our heads" because Herzl "felt the touch of the wing of the spirit of God and appeared with a supreme human aura."[55] Incredible spiritual and physical qualities were attributed to Herzl, all contributing to his transformation into a mythic hero of almost superhuman proportions.

The question is, why Herzl? One reason was that he had been admired by all the subcommunities of the yishuv. Zionist-socialists and revisionists both viewed themselves as his successors. Herzl, like the biblical heroes, was acceptable to all sectors of the society.

Another factor that may have contributed to Herzl's selection as national hero was his problematic relationship to the Jewish tradition. He was eminently suited to the image of the new Jew in contrast to the traditional, exilic Jew.[56] Ben Gurion noted that neither Herzl's assimilationist background nor his alienation from Jewish culture and tradition prevented his coming to the aid of his people.[57] The very language employed in his adulation was significant in this respect. He was compared in physical appearance to a "Roman God" or "a prince of Indian legend" or "a ruler of ancient lands."[58]

Statism also raised the *sabra* (the native-born Israeli) and the Israeli to the rank of hero. Special characteristics were ascribed to the generation that never knew exile, those who were born and raised as free men on the soil of the homeland. A number of literary critics and social observers have pointed to the cult or myth of the sabra as a characteristic expression of the new Israeli culture. Amnon Rubinstein has written with great penetration about this phenomenon.[59] The sabra in the early years of statehood was portrayed as the inverse image of the exilic Jew. Unlike the Diaspora Jew the sabra had no fear, no materialistic appetites, no obsequiousness. "He is a Hebrew and not a Jew and he is destined to bring an end to the humiliation of his parents. All that the Jews lack is in him: strength, health, physical labor . . . rootedness."[60]

It was appropriate for the sabra to sever himself from the Jewish tradition and Jewish customs of Diaspora Jewry. Indeed, Hebrew literature portrayed the sabra as lacking family ties, attachments, or loyalties, except to the collective nation. His mentor was not a father but the abstract collective.[61]

While the sabra was by definition native born, there was a tendency to ascribe his qualities also to those who had come to the country out of pioneering motivation, not because they lacked any alternative.

The mythologization of the sabra suited the statist values of negating the Diaspora and affirming the new Israeli rooted in the culture of his own state, but, as we have noted, statism never denied the Jewishness of Israeli society and culture. The ingathering of the exiles was one of its central tasks. Sabra was therefore not a racial category but a model. In order for the immigrants to realize their own potential, they had to acquire the sabra's characteristics and abandon values and customs brought from the Diaspora. With proper education and training, the new immigrants, youngsters in particular, could become sabras.

Youth had been an object of admiration in the yishuv as well. Like civil religions of other new states, statism admired and sought to harness the strength, energy, and enthusiasm of young people. Youth responds more readily to symbols and slogans of socio-cultural change, national integration, and political mobilization. The young are "prime objects of the regime's efforts to create a new culture."[62] In addition, statism, like many other civil religions, nurtured a youth cult because youth symbolizes motifs of courage, beauty, daring, and renewal—traits particularly admired by movements of national redemption.

According to Bar-Zohar, "Ben Gurion's belief in young people was enormous" and he was convinced that only lively young people were capable of executing the basic revolution in Jewish society.[63] This attitude contrasted with his contempt for the veteran party functionaries.

Israeli soldiers were exemplars of all the positive qualities statism attributed to young people and sabras. They were symbols of the new Jew. According to his biographer, Ben Gurion loved all the outward signs of military discipline and order. He saw the IDF as the expression of the normalization of the Jewish people,[64] but the IDF soldier was also the successor to the tradition of courage first revealed in the biblical period. According to Ben Gurion, the qualities of these new soldiers were no less heroic than those of their predecessors—the biblical warriors.[65] The IDF attained a special sanctity among the institutions of the state,[66] and those who criticized it were portrayed as profaning the holy.[67]

The combination of labor with defense, an important value to Zionist-socialism, assumed secondary importance in the statist period. The myths of the yishuv, including Tel-Ḥai and its heroes, declined in relation to the new myths and heroes associated with the establishment of the state, the War of Independence, and the ingathering of the exiles.

Ben Gurion hardly mentioned Tel-Ḥai or its heroes after 1949. Apparently, he saw them as particular to one subculture, whereas the statist heroes belonged to the entire nation and functioned as representatives of all the people. Furthermore, the heroes of Tel Ḥai, Trumpeldor in particular, were individualistic heroes. They acted on behalf of the collectivity but possessed their own private identities. The heroes of the War of Independence were "collective anonymous heroes."[68]

THE MYTHS OF STATISM

According to Ben Gurion, the four critical events in Jewish history were: the exodus from Egypt, the assembly at Mt. Sinai, the conquest of the Land of Israel by Joshua, and the establishment of the State of Israel.[69] The first three events are really stages in the transformation of the Jewish people into a sovereign nation in its own land. Hence, at least in one sense, the renewal of Jewish sovereignty through the establishment of Israel is equal to the combined importance of the first three events.[70] Furthermore, "with the establishment of the state the vision of Jewish redemption acquired a program and a practical basis . . . therefore, the state became a force that united and integrated the Jewish people in the Diaspora, as nothing else has ever before integrated and united them."[71] Ben Gurion also attributed universal significance to the event, since a large portion of the world's population has a spiritual attachment to the Land of Israel. The creation of Israel pointed to new possibilities that would change the destiny of all mankind.[72]

The central myth of statism was the establishment of Israel—the ultimate achievement of Jewish history—by a young generation possessed of qualities superior to those of any generation in Jewish history. The emphasis on achievement, victory, success, courage, confidence, power, and capacity are the characteristic elements of this myth. Hence, statism had little patience with, or capacity to absorb, different elements. Of greatest interest in this regard is statism's treatment of Masada and the Holocaust.

Masada

In the early years of statehood the importance of Masada declined. Masada was never included among the many historical events to which Ben Gurion alluded when he drew parallels between the establishment of Israel or the War of Independence and the Jewish past. True, youth movements continued climbing annually to the summit of Masada—indeed, the climb was adopted by the national military youth movement with which, in those years, all high school students were obliged to affiliate. But when we compare our own memories of the annual ascent to Masada in the early years of statehood with journalistic reports of the ascent during the thirties and early forties, we find a striking difference. The peak experience of the pilgrimage to Masada in the yishuv period was the pageant at the summit which dramatized the association of the historical Masada to the yishuv. One of us who participated in the 1951 ascent vividly remembers that the peak experience was the climb itself. The object was to get to the top. Once there, the youngsters ate and heard a very brief description of the historical event to which, in their exhaustion, they were hardly attentive. Nothing significant happened. After a rest they descended again and continued their hike around the Dead Sea.

Masada aroused the interest of archeologists in this period, but it was only in 1963 that large-scale excavations began under the direction of Yigal Yadin. In the wake of that excavation Masada once again became a central political myth.[73]

A number of explanations may account for the decline in Masada's importance. First, it was associated with the second commonwealth period, not the biblical period, which the statists most admired. A second explanation for statist reservations about Masada is connected to the event itself. The warriors of Masada were part of a band of zealots who engaged in sharp internal conflict. Their behavior was controversial in their own time and the object of criticism later as well. The myth of Masada, therefore, did not square with Statist tendencies to stress unity and that which was shared by the whole nation.

However, we feel that the prime cause for the deemphasis of Masada stemmed from the nature of statism as the civil religion of a new victorious state. Filled with self-confidence and a sense of their own power the statists were anxious to convince Israel's friends and antagonists at home and abroad that nothing lay beyond the new state's power. The story of Masada is one of not only courage but also defeat. Masada fell despite the brave effort of its defenders. Statism, unlike Zionist-socialism, had not yet tasted defeat. It had no need to account for a defeat that might occur despite courage and will. On the contrary, statism sought to deny that possibility.

There may be an additional, related explanation. The myth of Masada is a story of enmity and Jewish isolation, of a small band of warriors with their backs to the wall, without any alternative. Statism had difficulty absorbing a myth about a small band standing totally alone, surrounded by a hostile world. Young Israel aspired to join the family of nations with equal status and in mutual cooperation, and saw that goal within its grasp.

The Holocaust

The same factors that explain statism's reservations toward Masada also account for its treatment of the Holocaust. In the next chapter we rank the Holocaust as the central myth of Israel's present civil religion. But in the statist period, closer in time to the Holocaust, it received relatively little attention in myths and ceremonies sponsored by the state, or in speeches and articles by statist leaders.[74]

When we compare this silence with the comments of Amos Elon, a perceptive observer of Israeli society, we are overwhelmed by the contrast.

> The trauma of the Holocaust leaves an indelible mark on the national psychology, the tenor and content of public life, the conduct of foreign affairs, on politics, education, literature, and the arts. All over the country countless private and public monu-

ments to the grimmest phase in European history perpetuate a memory which lies in all its morbidity at the center of Israel's historic self-image. If, in Israeli eyes, the world at large has tended to forget too soon, Israelis hardly give themselves the chance. The traumatic memory is part of the rhythm and ritual of public life.[75]

Elon is of course commenting on Israeli culture in the poststatist period, but his observation serves to underscore the revolutionary change that has occurred in Israeli culture's perception of the Holocaust.

During the first few years, virtually nothing was done at the governmental level to commemorate the Holocaust. Some nongovernmental agencies undertook memorial projects, the best known of which was the Forest of the Martyrs planted by the Jewish National Fund. The only governmental agency to take action was the Ministry of Religion, which was far more representative of the religious camp than of the government itself. In a building under its care on Mount Zion the Ministry set aside a few rooms to store the torn fragments of Torah scrolls saved from the Nazis and prepared a Holocaust Basement to store jars holding the ashes of Jews burned in death camp crematoria.

The greater attentiveness of religious circles to the Holocaust is evident in the fact that it was the chief rabbinate that first fixed an official date to commemorate the Holocaust victims— the tenth of Tevet, a traditional Jewish fast day. This date gave the event a strong religious association, which was a factor in the government's choice of an alternative date when it finally passed a law on the topic.

Holocaust Day was established in 1952, but its form of observance was not fixed until 1959. Until that year, there were no visible signs of commemoration of the day on Israeli streets or in the homes. Places of entertainment operated as on any other day, and there were no special radio programs.[76]

The government's deemphasis of the Holocaust was evident from its long delay in establishing any national institution or shrine in memory of the victims. Proposals for such a shrine began to be offered almost as soon as the victims' fate became known. Plans for a project were approved at the 1945 Zionist conference, but only five years after the creation of the state did the government propose establishing a national institution to perpetuate the memory of the Holocaust victims and to research and document the Holocaust. Reading the debates in *Divrei Haknesset* (the Knesset protocol) surrounding the estab-

lishment of *Yad Vashem* (literally: a memorial and a name) one
gets a sense of how problematic the whole matter was to the
leaders of Israel. One individual in particular, a private citizen,
Mordechai Shenhabi, made the Yad Vashem proposal his life's
work and received much of the credit for its passage,[77] but the
government acted only after other pressures were exerted, not
the least of which, apparently, were the plans of Jews and
non-Jews to establish memorials abroad. Government leaders
saw these plans, some of which were eventually realized, as a
threat to Israel's status as the legitimate representative of the
Jewish people, authorized to speak on behalf of all Jewry,
including those who died in the Holocaust.[78]

Statism's response to the Holocaust was influenced to no
small extent by statist perceptions of the majority of the victims
as Jews who had surrendered to their fate rather than resist.
The behavior of the slaughtered was viewed as an extension of
traditional Jewish passivity. This critical stance toward the
Holocaust victims was carried over from labor Zionists of the
prestate period. They had experienced shame mixed with anger
at the image of their brethren who went "like sheep to the
slaughter."[79] An extreme expression of this attitude is found in
one kibbutz haggada: "Hitler alone is not responsible for the
death of six million—but all of us and above all the six million. If they had known that the Jew has power, they would not
have all been butchered . . . the lack of faith, the ghettoish-
exilic self-denigration . . . contributed its share to this great
butchery."[80]

But among the labor Zionists there was also a second interpretation of the Holocaust. During the war years and those
immediately following, analogies were drawn between the fate
of European Jewry, especially those who participated in resistance activity, and the fate of Masada's defenders.[81] The Warsaw ghetto was called "the Masada of European Jewry" and in
the yishuv the influence of the Masada myth grew following the
outbreak of World War II. The parallel of a persecuted minority, totally isolated and without effective force, surrounded by
a hostile world, without any hope, was obvious. Those who
drew the comparison intended to emphasize the heroism and
courage of those who, even under such circumstances, still
chose to fight rather than surrender.

The end of the war brought revelations of the full horror of
the Holocaust, direct confrontation with the survivors, perhaps

even guilt about how little the yishuv had done for the victims. There is even evidence of nostalgia and romanticization of East European Jewish life and the Jewish tradition among Zionist-socialists.[82] In addition, the Holocaust led Zionist-socialists to reassess their universalist principles and beliefs.[83] Their new mood led them to emphasize the bravery and resistance theme in an effort to come to terms with the Holocaust. They stressed, out of all proportion, the evidence of forcible resistance and rebellion by East European Jewry. It was a sign of their influence that the day memorializing the Holocaust victims was called "Memorial Day for the Holocaust and Ghetto Revolts." Yad Vashem's subtitle was "Memorial Authority for the Holocaust and Bravery." The date chosen for Holocaust Day was associated with the Warsaw ghetto uprising.

This strategy attracted some statists as well. The lead article in *Davar* (the paper most closely following government opinion) on the first Holocaust Day declared, "We return and will return . . . to the memory of the Holocaust and especially to the memory of the resistance fighters."[84] Minister of Education Dinur and others who discussed in the Knesset the establishment of Yad Vashem connected the heroic acts of physical resistance against the Nazis with the heroism of Israeli fighters in the War of Independence.[85] But this tactic was most characteristic of those who remained faithful to Zionist-socialism. They were the ones who emphasized the themes of physical courage and armed rebellion.

The characteristic approach of the statists, Dinur excepted, was consistent with their overall strategy of dissolution. The Jewish experience in the Diaspora, the persecution of Jews, was simply irrelevant. "German anti-Semitism, the Dreyfus trial . . . persecution of Jews in Rumania . . . they represent events from the past in foreign lands, sad memories of Jews of exile, but not emotional experiences and facts of life which educate and direct us."[86] As far as Ben Gurion was concerned, persecution was the natural consequence of living in a foreign land.

> The Jewish people erred when it blamed anti-Semitism for all the suffering and hardship it underwent in the Diaspora. . . . Must the whole world act like angels toward us? Does a people build its existence on the rule of righteousness—in the midst of other nations? Do Jews observe the rule of righteousness among themselves? Is there no jealousy and hatred among us? . . . Do we relate

to members of other groups and parties with sufficient understanding? . . . And we who are different from every people expect others to understand us . . . to accept us with love and fraternity, and if they don't we are angry and protest against their wickedness. . . . Is it too difficult for us to understand that every nation fashions its own way of life in accordance with its needs and its desires—and the context of its life and its relationships is the product of its historical condition. One cannot imagine that it will seek to adapt itself to the existence and mentality of the universal exception called Judaism. The cause of our troubles and the anti-Semitism of which we complain result from our peculiar status that does not accord with the established framework of the nations of the world. It is not the result of the wickedness or folly of the Gentiles which we call anti-Semitism.[87]

This incredible statement—that Jewish suffering stemmed from Jews' peculiar status as strangers among the nations—is all the more remarkable considering it was made in 1945. It suggests a complete misunderstanding of one of the greatest tragedies of Jewish history. In light of this it is little wonder that Ben Gurion had neither the capacity nor interest to integrate Holocaust symbols into his conception of statism.

The Holocaust symbolized exile, as both Zionist-socialism and statism perceived the condition of exile—deprivation, enslavement, defeat, humiliation, weakness, lack of alternatives. The statist and Zionist-socialist answer was to liquidate the Diaspora and transfer Jews and Jewish life to the Land of Israel. This answer also left its mark on the statist attitude toward the Holocaust during the first years of statehood.

But the problem the statists had with the Holocaust was like the one they had with Masada. Even if the events to which the symbol referred could be reformulated as heroic acts, the events themselves remained instances of overwhelming foreign enmity and defeat. Statism embraced symbols that by contrast pointed to victory and achievement, and to acceptance into the family of nations.

Statism, unlike the new civil religion discussed in the next chapter, did not seek to exploit the Holocaust to awaken guilt feelings among non-Jews or remind them of their moral obligations to Jews and Israel in the light of their behavior toward Jews during World War II. Statism sought to base Israel's relationships with other nations on terms of equality and mutual interest. The creation of Israel, after all, symbolized the break with the Jewish destiny of suffering and persecution. Statists avoided symbols that could be interpreted as placing Israel in a "sacrificial" role in its relation with other nations.

In addition, Israel sought to project the image of a strong confident state that ruled by virtue of its own power, yet interacted with other nations on the basis of friendship, trust, and mutual support. This image was inconsistent with the traditional Jewish self-image of a lamb among the wolves or a people that dwells alone—an image supported by the events of the Holocaust.

We must not forget that Israel was created with the support of a great majority of the world community of nations, and with military assistance from both major blocs. This strengthened statist perceptions that the renewal of Jewish sovereignty had created new conditions for relations with non-Jews. In their view the conflict with the Arabs was no exception. On the contrary, it was perceived as part of the normal course of relations between sovereign states—a conflict of interest but hardly a war of extermination between Jews and non-Jews.[88]

The same tendencies led the statists to deny any unique quality to the Holocaust. In the debate over German reparations, Pinhas Lavon, a member of the government and later minister of defense, responded to those who argued that accepting German reparations would blur the historically unprecedented monstrousness of the Holocaust. Jews were killed in the past, Lavon noted, and the only difference now was that more were killed in the Holocaust. There had been more Jews alive to begin with this time, and the Nazis had killed in a more efficient manner. Moreover, Lavon argued, the Nazi effort at genocide was not unique. The Turks had attempted it against the Armenians "and the blood of the Armenian people is no less precious to them than ours is to us."[89]

Mapai's Knesset delegation argued that opposition to reparations, to dealing with Germany, reflected an exilic approach inappropriate to a sovereign Jewish state. Diaspora Jewry had responded to persecutions by condemning their enemies, banning them (the rabbis issued a ban on Spain after Jews were exiled from that nation in 1492), or by fasting, prayer, and elegies. These, so it was said, provided a catharsis for the anger, sorrow, and frustration of a people unable to defend or revenge itself. But the new nation of Israel must now base its relationship with other nations upon *Realpolitik* and weigh its actions on the basis of its vital interests, not on emotional factors or the repayment of historical accounts. Foreign Minister Moshe Sharett said:

> He who objects to Reparations behaves as though there were no state. . . . What is the relationship between what has been said against reparations and the existence of the state? . . . Do the opponents have an argument that would not have substance if we did not have a State? Jewish morality, ostracism, no-contact, silence, refusal to forgive. . . . Would all this not be appropriate to the Jewish people . . . after every destruction? How have you changed? . . . What conclusions do you draw from the existence of the state? After all, there is no problem which can be approached except on the basis of the existence of the state. There can be no serious clarification of any crucial question that does not begin from this starting point.[90]

The statist response to the Holocaust, then, was not the cultivation of its memory but the dedication of effort to the development of the State of Israel. "The one suitable monument to the memory of European Jewry . . . is the State of Israel . . . where the hope of the Jewish people is expressed . . . and which serves as a free and faithful refuge to every Jew in the world who desires to live a free and independent life."[91]

If the Holocaust victims could express their opinion on German-Israeli relations, according to Ben Gurion, they would say, "what is good for the State of Israel is good for all Jewish people."[92]

In all fairness, even among Ben Gurion's faithful followers there were those who had reservations about his stance toward the Holocaust. We noted that Dinur supported efforts to memorialize the Holocaust victims. In fact, the debate over the establishment of Yad Vashem reflected the first signs of the decline of statism. Many of the speeches pointed toward an affirmation of at least some aspects of Diaspora life, as well as the religious tradition. This tendency found increased emphasis in the next few years in the Jewish Consciousness Program discussed in chapter six.

Ben Gurion himself agreed to the Jewish Consciousness Program, suggesting some moderation of his own position. He certainly reversed his attitude toward the Holocaust. In 1959 the law establishing the forms of public observance of Holocaust Day was passed. And in 1960 Eichmann was seized from his hiding place in Argentina and brought to Israel to stand trial, at the risk of Israel's friendly relations with other nations. The daring seizure was undertaken with Ben Gurion's full approval. This suggests that possibly Ben Gurion perceived the Holocaust as an extraordinary event that legitimized extraordinary action.

But the kidnapping and trial of Eichmann may also represent the statist tendency to demonstrate Israeli power—not necessarily an expression of a changing attitude toward the Holocaust and Diaspora Jewry. According to Harold Fisch, "The implication was that through the capture and trial of Eichmann Israel was somehow making good the failure of those who had died without resisting. The demonstration of state power that made the trial possible was a source of great and justifiable pride to the Israelis."[93]

The Eichmann trial is seen by many as a turning point in Israeli public consciousness of the Holocaust, resulting in a greater sense of identification by Israelis, young people in particular, with Diaspora Jewry. But the overtones of statist orientation remained visible. The lead article in *Davar* on Holocaust Day, 1960, repeated the Statist refrain: "The essence of the command 'to remember' that signals this day . . . must be to remember our own deeds . . . to what extent we were ready . . . to free ourselves from a life of dependence and bondage . . . The question is: What does the nation choose—a life of exile or the return to Zion?" The function of Holocaust Day, according to the same article, is to remind the Jewish people of its own sin in not unequivocally having chosen Zion.

SACRED SYMBOLS OF STATISM

The National Flag

The controversy over the choice of a national flag illuminates different conceptions about basic national values, which the flag presumably reflects.[94] Some felt that the flag, like other national symbols, should reflect the unique historical condition of the Jewish people, its traditions and culture. They favored a blue and white flag (the colors of the Jewish prayer shawl) with the Star of David at its center, in other words, identical to the flag of the WZO.[95]

Moshe Sharett argued on behalf of the government that the proposed flag for the new state must be distinct from the Zionist flag. He explained that otherwise it would embarrass Diaspora Jews who "fly the flag of the world Jewish people—the Zionist flag" but who, understandably enough, would not want to fly the flag of the State of Israel.[96] We do not find this explanation credible in the light of other statist positions. In our opinion, the statist demand to distinguish the national flag from the WZO flag is best understood as part of an overall effort to distinguish the state and the new period it had begun from the prestate period and from Jews living outside Israel. The statists there-fore proposed for the flag a symbol first suggested by Herzl himself—seven gold stars represening Herzl's vision of a seven-hour workday—a symbol that bore no relationship whatsoever to any element in the Jewish tradition. However, in order to placate the traditionalists, the government proposed that the seven gold stars be arranged in the form of a Star of David on the backdrop of a blue and white striped flag.[97]

In face of the criticism this proposal evoked, a new sixteen-member committee (including five ministers) was selected to choose the flag and they decided to adopt the WZO flag as the national flag.[98] The victory in this case went to the traditional-ists, who saw the state as anchored in the Zionist-Jewish tradi-tion, rather than to the statists.

The State Symbol

The Zionist movement had no official symbol of its own and discussions over the symbol of the state could not be resolved as readily as the decision over the flag. The proposal to adopt the *menorah* (plural *menorot*; a seven-branched candelabrum) was finally accepted after a debate that stretched from October 1948 to February 1949. The menorah was acceptable to all groups—religious and secular, traditionalists and statists—because it lent itself to multiple interpretations. The menorah, according to the Bible, was constructed in accordance with God's instruc-tions and placed in the Tabernacle in the desert. Gold menorot stood in the temple as well. Statists must have been particularly pleased by the second symbolic implication of the menorah. Titus's Arch in Rome displays the menorah as one of the items the Romans sacked from the second temple. Hence, the menorah signals the restoration of Jewish sovereignty—the return, as it were, of the menorah to its rightful heirs and the association of the new state with the earlier commonwealths. To pure secularists the menorah is also the symbol of light—a motif of great importance in civil religions of both the yishuv and the statist periods.[99]

The new symbols statism introduced were not only important representations in themselves. They were also of significance in that they replaced the older class symbols that had been used so widely in the yishuv period. The replacement of the red flag, the International, and *Teḥezakna* (the hymn of Zionist-socialism) was a gradual process. In the first years of statehood, class and statist symbols coexisted on an almost equal footing in labor Zionist circles.

Ben Gurion objected, not to class symbols *per se*, but to their usage in national ceremonials or on national buildings with which the entire population was expected to identify. In the bitter controversy over whether or not the red flag could be flown on school buildings he said, "The school will no longer belong . . . to part of the people but to all the people." Just as the national flag alone is raised above the Knesset, "because this place signifies all the nation" so "in schools, the home of the State, only the national flag will fly."[100]

STATIST CEREMONIALS

Like Zionist-socialism, statism utilized the concept mitzva whose origin in traditional Judaism refers to the commands of God, to signify one's obligation to obey the civil religion. Unlike Zionist-Socialism, statism could impose its commands by the law of the state. Yet statists preferred to influence through persuasion rather than use coercion.

This suggests the importance of civil religion to the political elite. No religion, traditional or civil, can exact adherence to, and promote internalization of, its system of sacred values without a process of socialization. The system of values and behavior is legitimated and internalized by symbols and ceremonies. We often associate ceremonials with the extraordinary, the very different. But ceremony may involve the routine and the everyday, investing what might otherwise appear to be a secular or habitual activity with sacred meaning. The state has the authority to impose many obligations upon the citizenry.

This, in turn, exposes it to the danger of alienating the public from a personal sense of obligation to fulfill its commands. National ceremonials, therefore, seek to evoke the sense of personal obligation and personal commitment to these commands.

An illustration is the proliferation of symbols and ceremonials associated with the Israeli army and the security needs of the state. Army service was compulsory; hence, it did not in and of itself signify identification with the state or the soldier's readiness to sacrifice himself on the state's behalf. But to fulfill its task efficiently the army required soldiers with strong national loyalties and security consciousness. Parades and military formations were one method of telling both the general public and the soldiers themselves that the army service was not only a legal obligation but also a national value. This helps account for the fact that such ceremonials were not deemed necessary during the period of the yishuv. Membership in an underground organization was in itself an expression of identification with the sacred values of the nation.

Archaeology

There are forms of activity not generally thought of as ceremonial which under certain conditions become symbolic, pointing to ultimate or transcendent values. For example, after 1948 archaeology became a national hobby and assumed cultic aspects. Ben Gurion encouraged this interest, which strengthened attachments to the Land of Israel.[101]

Amos Elon has noted that:

> Archeological finds have inspired nearly all Israeli national symbols, from the state seal to emblems, coins, medals, and postage stamps. For the disquieted Israeli, the moral comforts of archaeology are considerable. In the political culture of Israel, the symbolic role of archeology is immediately evident. Israeli archeologists, professionals and amateurs, are not merely digging for knowledge and *objects* but for the reassurance of roots, which they find in the ancient remains scattered throughout the country.[102]

He quotes the archaeologist (subsequently deputy prime minister) Yigal Yadin: "For young Israelis, a belief in history has come to be a substitute for religious faith. Through archaeology they discover their religious values. In archaeology they find their religion. They learn that their forefathers were in this country 3,000 years ago. This is a value. By this they fight and by this they live."[103]

The primary focuses of archaeological interest in the statist period were the Dead Sea scrolls. The scrolls were literary remnants of a second-temple Jewish sect, whose library in Qumran included both documents unique to it and biblical texts sacred to all Jews. The scrolls were discovered shortly before the creation of Israel and the scientific work involved in unwrapping and reading some of them took place in Jerusalem while the city was under siege. Great significance was ascribed to Israel's success in acquiring the scrolls (a fascinating story in itself). It was interpreted as an act of cultural redemption and the "return of a loss to its owners," an expression of the emphasis on the continuity between the State of Israel and earlier periods of Jewish sovereignty.

Yadin attributed symbolic importance to the date that his father, the archaeologist Eliezer Sukenik, acquired the first portions of the scrolls:

> I cannot avoid the feeling that there is something symbolic in the discovery of the Scrolls and their acquisition at the moment of the creation of the State of Israel. It is as if these manuscripts had been waiting in caves for two thousand years, ever since the destruction of Israel's independence, until the people of Israel had returned to their home and regained their freedom. This symbolism is heightened by the fact that the first three Scrolls were brought by my father for Israel on 29 November 1947, the very day on which the United Nations voted for the re-creation of the Jewish State in Israel after two thousand years.[104]

When Israel finally acquired all the scrolls, the prime minister called a special press conference to make the announcement.[105]

The religious-symbolic significance of the Dead Sea Scrolls is expressed by the structure which was specially built to display them. It is called the Shrine of the Book and stands opposite the Knesset. The scrolls themselves are inside a dome.

> Within the dome, the upward phallic thrust of an enormous, clublike structure is said to represent the national will to persist. This, the heart of the shrine, is reached through a dramatically unbalanced, off-center arched tunnel. . . . The rotunda evokes a chapel. In the middle, on an elevated pedestal shaped like a round

altar, the entire length of a Scroll of Isaiah is displayed in a great circular glass case. High above it is an opening to the sky, originally designed to jettison a thin spray of water from the dome. . . . No building in Israel is as clearly based upon the exploitation of anatomical shapes and erotic symbols. In the Shrine of the Book, archeology and nationalism are mated as in an ancient rejuvenation and fertility rite.[106]

The Shrine of the Book reflects the themes of return to the sources, rebirth and national renaissance; the same combination of ancient and modern expressed in the central myths of both the Dead Sea sect itself and statism.

Bible Study Circles

Statist leaders undertook a series of activities to inculcate an awareness of the Bible among the masses. Ben Gurion talked about the need for painters, sculptors, musicians, writers, dramatists, and educators to bring a consciousness of the Bible to the people because in the Bible Israelis will find themselves, their origins, their spirit, their purpose, and their future.[107]

Bible study circles were instituted throughout the country. The most popular effort to disseminate Bible consciousness was the annual Bible quiz which received a great deal of publicity in the mass media. These quizzes bore all the earmarks of national ceremonies, including the presence of the prime minister and other high government officials. The president was said to have composed some of the questions.

Other Gatherings

During the early years of statehood, there were a number of state-sponsored mass assemblies that had the character of ceremonials. Some were called for the ostensible purpose of discussing national issues, but the latent purpose was to create a climate of identification with the state through elaborate pomp and ceremony, including music, parades, and torchlight. These assemblies were criticized. The editor of Mapai's paper, *Hador*, was particularly critical of one gathering, which he termed "a profanation of both the sacred and the secular," an effort "to imitate the assembly at Mount Sinai."[108] Ben Gurion replied sharply to these criticisms. He answered the charge of excessive pomp and theatricality by commenting sarcastically that even at Mount Sinai, "there was no shortage of theatrical and musical effect . . . and, of course, there were torches."[109] He wondered whether those who were part of the exodus from Egypt appreciated the moral and historical importance of the assembly at Mount Sinai. Probably, Ben Gurion observed, many "were not too impressed with the ten commandments" which Moses gave them. Ben Gurion concluded that assemblies of great import are possible "in our days as well."[110]

Independence Day

Independence Day, the fifth of Iyar, commemorating Israel's declaration of statehood, was the chief holiday of statism. The major theme of the celebration was the inauguration of a new period in Jewish and world history, but, alongside the new and unique, Independence Day also symbolized continuity and succession. It was to be incorporated in the Jewish calendar along with Passover and Hanukkah—the two traditional holidays of freedom. The day the state was created was defined as "the day of days, the most honored and glorified day in the entire history of our exile . . . one of the three most marvelous days in the history of Jeshurun" (a biblical synonym for the Jews).[111]

Yet a suitable ceremonial for the holiday has troubled Israelis until the present. As *Davar* pointed out after the very first Independence Day, there was great joy, but people did not know how to express it, what to do.[112]

The official efforts in this respect suggest that the original notion was to recapture the experience of enthusiasm and wonder the declaration of statehood first evoked. Secondly, there was an effort to deepen the identification with the state and its institutions, to reaffirm the values and beliefs of statism. Not least important in this regard were army parades and demonstrations, which highlighted the early celebrations and attested not only to the renewal of Jewish sovereignty but also to the fact that this sovereignty had been achieved by the Jews themselves, by virtue of their own power and not as a gift from the nations of the world. Thirdly, the official celebrations were intended to demonstrate the strength and achievements of the state.[113]

In 1954 a new ceremony was introduced—the conferring of the Prize of Israel upon twelve outstanding writers and scholars. The number twelve was chosen as an association with the twelve tribes of ancient Israel. The ceremony's purpose was to demonstrate that "the holiday does not rely on military demonstrations alone" but honors men of science and Torah as well.[114] In distributing the prizes in 1956 Minister of Education and Culture Zalman Aranne said, "the culture of Israel brought us to the War of Independence; the Bible and Hebrew poetry were part of the arsenal which each of our warriors bore with him."[115]

Light and fire are popular symbols in both traditional and civil religions, particularly in nationalist-romantic movements. They evoke themes of renaissance and renewal. Light was a widely used symbol in modern Hebrew literature, which was known, not coincidentally, as the literature of the enlightenment. Light symbolizes good and beauty, wisdom and honesty, faith and hope for freedom. Fire is also a symbol of redemption—testimony to the victory of light over darkness. In addition, fire symbolizes qualities of courage, daring, energy, growth, and—above all else—eternal rebirth. Fire spreads light and warmth and can be seen from afar—hence it also symbolizes domesticity and fraternity.[116]

The huge watchfires lit at the opening of the Independence Day ceremonies were symbols of light and fire. The watchfires also had a particular Jewish meaning. Burning atop the hills of Jerusalem, they represented renewal of a custom recorded in sacred texts of lighting fires atop the mountains to notify Diaspora Jewry of the appearance of a new moon and the beginning of a new month. The watchfires were lit by twelve Israelis (the twelve tribe theme) originating from twelve different countries; each announced his place of origin—an obvious ceremonial symbolization of the ingathering of the exiles in the Land of Israel.

In our discussion of Zionist-socialism we pointed to the importance of dance in the civil religion of the yishuv. In addition to the happiness and joy expressed in dance, it was a particularly apt symbol of independence because it contained elements of freedom from both outward constraint and self-restraint. The original announcement of independence had been characterized by spontaneous mass dancing in the streets and it was this memory, more than any other, those who had been present in Israel at the time recalled. In the early Independence Day celebrations the dances were carefully orchestrated whether in the streets (youth movements, for example, were assigned set places in the streets) or in a dance festival called the parade of dances held in Haifa with hundreds of dancers and tens of thousands of spectators. Indeed, *Davar* referred to Independence Day as the new Holiday of Dances (an allusion to a day of that name celebrated during the first two commonwealth periods) and the new Holiday of Lights (an allusion to Hanukkah, also called the Festival of Lights).[117]

Another Independence Day custom, which showed the influence of Zionist-socialism, was ceremonial tree planting. Harold Fisch has noted the significance of the tree metaphor in early Zionist literature.

> The metaphor of organism which we noted as pervasive in Moses Hess also pervades the writings of many other Zionist thinkers down to the time of the creation of the Jewish state. It is, in fact, a fundamental metaphor. Israel is a tree to be replanted in its soil; this will assure its material rebirth. The spiritual and moral effects of that rebirth are the blossoms on the tree. The image suggests vitality and also liberation; the Jewish people, long artificially uprooted from its natural environment, will now resume the life granted to all natural, healthy organisms.[118]

Scholars, such as George Mosse and Robert Bocock, who have explored political ceremonials, have traced the symbols of tree, fire, and light in European political rituals.[119]

Unlike European rituals, statist ceremonials distinguished light and fire from trees. In addition, European tree ceremonials involved decorating the tree, whereas the Israeli ceremonial involved planting, as the symbol of the people returning to its land.

Independence Day was also marked by the dedication of new buildings, monuments, and parks. Many aspects of these and other ceremonies were directed in particular toward young people and new immigrants.[120] Special ceremonies took place in the immigrant camps and special efforts were made to transport new immigrants to the locations of the major ceremonials.

Special efforts were also made to involve local Arabs in Independence Day celebrations. Ceremonies took place in Arab villages, generally under auspices of the military, which was responsible in the early years for administering the heavily populated Arab areas. The ceremonies were aimed at the school age population in particular. Many of the restrictions normally placed on Arab residents in those days were lifted on Independence Day to permit Arabs to travel to sites of major celebrations.

Those who were concerned with the forms of celebration sought to introduce private, as well as public, rituals. Traditional Jewish holidays are marked by home and family ritual. More often than not the primary celebration takes place in the home. In 1952 the army commissioned one of Israel's leading writers, Aharon Megged, to prepare materials for use at Independence Day dinners at army bases. Megged wrote *Haggadat Haatzmaut*, structured in imitation of the traditional Passover haggada and built around recitations by the leader (the senior officer present at the meal), responses by all the soldiers, the raising of wine cups, and the like. The text was widely circulated and the entire population was encouraged to use it in their own homes.[121]

The tone of Megged's haggada is exemplified in the transformation of a traditional passage from the Passover haggada which begins, "He who defended our fathers . . . " and ends with the words "God will defend us." In Megged's text the passage ends, "and we defend ourselves." One of the best known passages in the traditional haggada observes that the Jews in Egypt were saved, "not by the hands of an angel, and not by the hands of a seraph . . . but by the hands of God himself." Megged's version: "not by the hands of an angel, and not by the hands of a seraph . . . but by the hands of the IDF."

Dinur offered a detailed proposal to celebrate Independence Day in the home.[122] He urged Israelis to sanctify Independence Day with a family meal at which the Declaration of Independence would be read. The home, he said, should be brightly lit and decorated with greenery and olive branches. Lights would represent "our going from slavery to freedom . . . from darkness to light . . . and the luster of our homes." The greenery would represent the return to the land. The olive branches would stand for Israel's desire for peace. Dinur offered additional suggestions to institutionalize the association between a festive family meal, Independence Day, and customs connected with other Jewish festivals.

The proposals to ritualize family celebrations of Independence Day were not adopted by any significant segment of the public. Even the public celebrations faded and changed over the years. Ritual celebrations in private settings, which demand so much more initiative than public celebrations, had little chance in an atmosphere of growing skepticism toward statist activity.

The transformation of public celebrations—growing emphasis on pure entertainment and a decline in importance of such events as army parades and other formal demonstrations—signaled the general decline of statism. Independence Day increasingly became a holiday for picnics. This gave it a familial focus but no national-statist component. We are not suggesting that Independence Day lost all its initial values. National flags, for example, continue to be flown from many homes. The decline of statism did not mean that the state lost its meaning for the citizenry, but it did mean people were less inclined to attribute absolute sanctity to the state or to represent it as the exclusive focus of loyalty and the source of one's highest obligations.

We ought not to be surprised at the decline of the civil religion of statism. It derived its authority from a natural source, not a supernatural one. It was thus far more exposed to changes in public confidence or commitment. The very ambiguity of the supernatural permits the interpretation of new events and changing conditions, or of the supernatural itself, in a manner that reduces inconsistencies. There are limits, of course. By the same token, the symbol system of civil religion contains some room for reinterpretation, but it has far less flexibility. In addition, the absence of a long tradition of observance gave an aspect of artificiality to the civil religious ceremonials.

Statist leaders might have responded to the declining importance of Independence Day by borrowing more traditional religious symbols and introducing more traditional themes in their public celebrations. They might have even coopted religious figures. But they chose not to do so. The religious element hardly found expression in the ceremonies, except for those celebrations aimed exclusively at the religious public which we will discuss in chapter seven. Apparently, statist circles, who repeated so often that Israel was governed by "law" not "halakha," and that state institutions were dominant over religious ones, were reluctant to legitimate statist values with religious symbols. Nevertheless, even in the statist period national leaders, the president in particular, customarily participated in the festive worship at a synagogue.

The World Bible Contest, as we noted, also culminated on Independence Day, but in the statist years, the quizzes emphasized not traditional religious elements but the continuity between the State of Israel and the biblical state. This conception was expressed in a cartoon published in *Davar*'s 1950 Independence Day issue showing an Israeli saying, "It's not easy, but I've undertaken to add a second volume to the Bible."[123]

Memorial Day for the IDF Fallen

The traditional religious dimension found more explicit expression in Memorial Day ceremonies, though even here the contrast between the statist and contemporary period is marked. In 1950 the government decided to dedicate the day preceeding Independence Day to the memory of those who fell in the War of Independence. This was done, partly as a response to demands from parents and widows of fallen soldiers, some of whom were then unhappy when the memorial holiday was set the day before Independence Day—particularly in the early years when the onset of the following holiday brought on celebration that bordered on revelry in some quarters. Statist leaders, however, favored the association between the memory of those who died to establish the state and Independence Day.

Memorial Day celebrations took place at various locations where special facilities or monuments had been erected to those who fell in the War of Independence. (These ceremonies in later years came to include the memory of those who fell in all wars on behalf of Israel, and in 1980 this change was institutionalized in an amendment to the law.) The most important celebration took place at army cemeteries. Army cemeteries are of special interest to our study.

In 1950 the government proposed a law establishing army cemeteries which denied the relatives of the dead any voice in where the fallen should be buried or how their graves would be marked. The proposal provoked vigorous opposition. A spokesman for the left-wing Zionist-socialist party, Mapam, chided the statists: "The only matter, in any event the first matter, you the Government propose to nationalize in our country is the IDF dead."[124]

Proponents of the law argued that the manner of burying and memorializing fallen soldiers must symbolize the cooperation and fraternity that had existed among them.[125]

Mosse has noted that in France, Germany, and England military cemeteries were cultic sites symbolizing, among other things, the cooperation and fraternal relations among those who fell,[126] but the Israeli proposal—granting the state exclusive authority—was more radical. Yielding to criticism in the Knesset, however, the final version that became law granted the relatives some voice.

The dead were also memorialized in monuments, forests, and parks, which sprang up all over the country in the first years of statehood. The monuments were of various types. Some were sculpted to symbolize war and courage, for example, the stone arrows extending out of the hills of Jerusalem or the statue of the wounded lion in Ramat Gan. Others were simply blocks of stone with a tablet bearing the names of those to whose memory the monument was dedicated.

The custom of memorializing the dead by monuments or planting trees is found in other countries as well.[127] These customs penetrated into European nationalism from Christian and pre-Christian sources and are unknown in traditional Judaism. In Jewish tradition one memorializes the dead through prayer and study of Torah—though the custom of visiting the graves of the dead is also firmly rooted in Jewish practice. The influence of traditional Judaism is found in the Israeli custom of establishing educational enterprises— libraries, rooms for study, even a corner of books—in memory of soldiers who died.

The various sites dedicated to the war dead provide locations for Memorial Day ceremonies, as do all army camps. Ceremonies include the lighting of torches, the lowering of the flag to half-mast, the firing of guns, the presentation of wreaths, and the recitation of the military *Yizkor* prayer (a version of the traditional Jewish prayer for the dead rewritten to suit the memory of fallen soldiers), often accompanied by a eulogy.

The original military Yizkor omitted such references as *kiddush hashem* (the traditional term for Jewish martyrology—an act which sanctified God's name) and the key section of the traditional Yizkor, the plea that the soul of the dead may ascend to heaven. The military Yizkor sanctified the heroism and courage of the fallen who gave their lives for the nation and state. There was no mention of God. Whereas the traditional version begins *Yizkor Elohim* (let God remember), the military version began *Yizkor am Israel* (let the nation of Israel remember). In accordance with the values of the new civil religion, discussed in the next chapter, a second version has been introduced which retains the traditional opening line. In military memorials today either version is used, depending on the location and the audience.

May Day

By coincidence, Independence Day and May Day fall close to each other. Since May Day is dictated by the Gregorian calendar and Independence Day by the Jewish one, the two holidays occasionally fall on the same day.

In the early years of statehood the May Day celebrations stressed national elements alongside traditional themes of halutziut and socialism. But May Day celebrations had lost none of their luster in those first years and, even among the moderate circles of the labor movement, May Day received almost as much emphasis as Independence Day. This is most evident in the equal coverage *Davar* gave to the two holidays and in the effort to link them as complementary—a national holiday and a labor holiday.

In fact, however, national symbols assumed priority over working class symbols even in the early years.[128] This tendency was strengthened by the course of the conflict between the left and right wings of the labor movement. The left stressed class symbols, and the right, which dominated in the conflict, stressed national ones.

In 1956 May Day fell during a period of national tension, a consequence of increased Arab *fedayeen* attacks and the announcement of a large arms sale by Czechoslovakia to Egypt. May Day was celebrated by busing masses of workers to frontier communities where they labored to construct and repair security installations, such as shelters and barbed wire fences. Afterward they returned to the cities to join parades conducted under the banner: "our faces are to peace and our hands to defense." The speeches at these celebrations stressed the association between class, national security, and worker solidarity.[129] *Davar* called the effort on behalf of the frontier communities "holy labor."

It is not surprising, therefore, that over the years May Day in Israel increasingly lost its special significance. It was emptied of its original meaning as an international, working-class holiday, and, as a national holiday, it could hardly compete with Independence Day. Each year *Davar* devoted less and less space to May Day, as the demonstrations and parades themselves became smaller and less glamorous affairs.

Traditional Jewish Holidays

The secularization of religious holidays that originated in the yishuv continued after the establishment of the state. For example, Passover celebrations stressed the theme of national freedom. That Passover ends only two weeks before Independence Day facilitated the association between the events the two holidays commemorate. This trend was prominently expressed in the kibbutz haggadot we have already noted which substituted the terms people of Israel, nation, or IDF for references to God. [130]

There were also efforts to add national elements to traditional celebrations. While a national leader such as Ben Gurion was reluctant to participate in synagogue services except on rare occasions, *Davar* noted that, following the conclusion of synagogue services on Simhat Torah (literally: the joy of Torah), many worshipers went to the prime minister's home to greet him. The story's headline read: "Simhat Torah and the joy of the state were combined." [131]

In addition to the introduction of statist elements and the transformation of traditional references into statist ones, religious holidays were secularized by the retention of Zionist-socialist components that had been introduced in the yishuv. But it gradually became clear that these secular components did not attract wide support among the people, particularly not among the new immigrants, despite the efforts to involve them in the transformed ceremonies. [132]

SUMMARY

As we noted in the first chapter, Ben Gurion and his followers sought to impose their version of civil religion more deliberately and explicitly than any other group of leaders in any other period. Concerned about the ideological cleavages of the past, anxious about the consequences of not integrating the masses of new immigrants, and confronted by acute economic and defense needs, Ben Gurion utilized those traditional symbols that could be interpreted as pointing to the centrality of the state and ignored those that could not. Ben Gurion affirmed his unbounded admiration for some aspects of the tradition. But he and other statists denied significance to that part of the traditional culture which originated in exile. They projected the modern settlement of the Land of Israel as the successor to the ancient period of Jewish national independence, discounting the intervening two thousand years.

The most important new symbol reflecting the dissolution strategy was Independence Day. We have defined dissolution as the affirmation of one strand in the tradition while ignoring others. How can such an approach incorporate new symbols? One can identify a strategy of dissolution when the new symbol is linked to a traditional one in such a way that one aspect of the tradition is deliberately emphasized at the expense of another.

As we noted, in the early years of statehood an association was drawn between Independence Day and Passover, an association facilitated by the occurrence of the former thirteen days after the conclusion of the latter. There were many references in the first years of statehood to Independence Day, the day of days, as a kind of culmination of the process which begins with the Passover celebration of the exodus from Egypt. Independence Day thus replaced Shavuot, the giving of the Torah which had been traditionally linked to Passover. The traditional paradigm was exodus (physical freedom) followed by the giving of the Torah (spiritual freedom). The new paradigm became exodus (freedom from foreign oppression by leaving Egypt) followed by Independence Day (achieving national autonomy by establishing the state). The new paradigm was strengthened by comparisons between Ben Gurion and Joshua.

It would be a mistake to think that Ben Gurion espoused statism or employed the dissolution strategy only as means to some greater end. Ben Gurion himself was a true believer. In this, however, he was part of a minority.

5 The New Civil Religion

We can only speculate about what factors led to the decline of statism. One factor was probably the vitality of Israel. As time passed the existence of the state no longer evoked such wonder, Arab threats no longer aroused such fear, as they had earlier. Second, as the great waves of immigration from 1949 to 1952 receded and immigration rates declined, statism, whose symbol system had pointed to the primary goals of defending the state and ingathering the exiles, necessarily lost resonance.

Under these conditions, problems that had been ignored in the enthusiasm of the first years of nation building captured public attention. The gap between the image of an ideal state cultivated by statism and social, political reality became more obvious and more troublesome. Ben Gurion himself was aware of this, but he attributed the new state's shortcomings to such factors as the multiparty system, and primarily to the galut mentality from which the experience of statehood would eventually free Israeli Jews.[1] Contrary to his expectations, problems, such as poverty and alleged ethnic discrimination, political favoritism, and corruption, intensified. This in turn raised questions of personal identity and meaning which had previously been subsumed in the struggle for statehood. It became increasingly clear in the 1950s that among many groups, young people in particular, statism was losing its attraction. Personal concerns were substituted for collective ones—national or working-class. (We will return to this problem in the final chapter.) No less serious, in the eyes of the political and cultural establishment, was the growing sympathy, especially among young people, for Canaanism.

Zionist-socialism and statism both represented efforts to imbue Jewish identity with secular national content. Canaanism, on the other hand, denied the necessity for such an identity. It sought to sever all ties with the religious-historical culture and rejected identification with Jews outside the Land of Israel. Sabras were far less likely than their parents to have a knowledge of the religious tradition. Their only contact with Diaspora Jewry was their association with the new immigrants. The negative stereotyping of Diaspora Jewry in Zionist literature and the school curriculum of the yishuv contributed to the young sabras' low regard for Jews outside Israel. It is not surprising that Canaanism attracted many of them, since it legitimated their ignorance of the tradition, their disdain for Diaspora Jewry, and their ambivalent feeling toward the new immigrants who were overwhelming the prestate settlers.

Many older veteran settlers retained nostalgic sentiments about the tradition and the Diaspora, despite their Zionist-socialist or statist ideology. The Holocaust, as we noted, strengthened these sentiments in Zionist-socialist circles. In the Knesset debate over memorializing the Holocaust, overtones of guilt emerged on the part of the older settlers, along with an implied fear that, by revolting against the Diaspora, they had produced a generation without roots, cut off from any attachment to Jewish heritage and cultural tradition.[2] Furthermore, the unwillingness of the sabra to welcome the new immigrants and integrate them socially and ideologically aroused fears among the political elite. One result was the 1957 Jewish Consciousness Program (discussed in the next chapter). The program was built on basic guidelines the government adopted in 1955. This is a convenient date to mark the beginning of the decline of statism.

Consciousness of the Holocaust also sharpened the perception of Jewish distinctiveness, which both Zionist-socialism and statism, each in its own way, had sought to blur. As we noted, the universalist principles of Zionist-socialism had not withstood the sense of isolation that overcame Jewry immediately after World War II. However, statist ideology and the support Israel received internationally prior to and immediately following the establishment of the state, reinforced universalist tendencies. The sense of Jewish isolation reemerged as symbols of the Holocaust gained ascendency in Israeli culture in the late

1950s. The penetration of Holocaust symbols, then, was both an effect and a cause of the decline of statism. These symbols could not penetrate statism as long as it was at its zenith. But once a weakened statism admitted the Holocaust memory, a memory its ideological system was unable to assimilate, that memory weakened statism even further.

When Zionist-socialism proved incapable of providing a satisfactory civil religion for the masses of new immigrants, statism arose at least partly in response to that failure. But statism also failed to provide an alternative collective symbol system for those Jews, particularly immigrants from Arab countries, who were committed to traditional Jewish culture. Statist efforts to reshape the immigrants' outlook and culture provoked the antagonism of the religious camp. Statists succeeded in undermining religious beliefs and traditional practices of many immigrants, but failed to replace the tradition with an alternative that could integrate them into Israeli culture and society. Consequently, the cultural and political elite began to realize that the negative attitude of statism toward the religious tradition had to be revised.

Even among those who acknowledged the need to create a symbol system that focused the citizens' loyalty and commitment on the state, many were reticent about granting it the degree of sanctity Ben Gurion's version of statism demanded. They shrank from the effort to represent the state as the primary source of values and the primary locus of identity and loyalty. Undoubtedly, in this regard Israel was affected by developments in Western political culture associated with the so-called decline of ideology, recoiling especially from ideology representing a totalistic world view of a quasi-religious nature. [3]

There are striking similarities between statism and what David Apter terms the *political religions* of new states. [4] Among them are: the representation of the state as a sacred value, the tendency of the state to provide direction in a variety of social and cultural realms, the demand for absolute loyalty from the citizenry to the state and its institutions, the mobilization of the citizens on behalf of state objectives, the identification of the state interests as superior to individual or subgroup interests, the demand for national unity, the emphasis on values of modernization (including industrialization and economic development), the tendency to charismatic leadership, and the effort to instill meaning and purpose into the lives of individuals by virtue of their identification with the state and its objectives. Another similarity is the tendency to represent the creation of the state as a sacred event and to stress both the association of the state with some golden era of past national glory, and to contrast the condition of freedom with the suffering that preceded the achievement of independence.

But there are important differences between statism and the political religions of new societies with their totalitarian overtones. Statism, unlike the political religions Apter describes, did not prohibit dissenting opinions, did not favor a one-party system, and did not affirm the unity and identity of state, party, and leader.[5] No Israeli statist supported, in theory or practice, the institutionalization of an antidemocratic regime.[6]

Apter notes the relationship between political religion and what he terms *mobilization systems* which he distinguishes from *reconciliation systems*. The latter are based on the principles of rule of law, democratic liberalism, limitation of governmental authority, tolerance, pluralism, compromise, negotiation, and gradual change. He explains that "many of the qualities that are found in the notion of totalitarian democracy are also to be found in systems that I shall call 'mobilization systems,' that is, those that are profoundly concerned with transforming the social and spiritual life of a people by rapid and organized methods."[7]

Statism, it is true, sought the social and political transformation of the nation, but it was neither prepared to use, nor capable of using, authoritarian measures to achieve its goals. In fact, statism combined elements of both mobilization and reconciliation systems. We think it fair to characterize statism as containing on one hand a strong tendency to totalism in the scope and nature of its goals, but on the other hand a tendency to democratic-liberalism in the means of achieving those goals. Indeed, this contradiction may be one reason statism failed.

Statism weakened the autonomy of Zionist-socialist institutions by transferring authority from the Histadrut and the labor parties to national institutions—the most important example being the elimination of the independent labor schools—but statism never substituted an alternative system of mobilization and support; and this too was a result of its unwillingness and inability to deviate from the canons of democracy and pluralism.

As Apter notes, the single party is a major source of organizational and propagandistic power to the political religions of new societies,[8] but whereas statism weakened the labor parties, it never created a statist party in their place. The elimination of the partisan educational systems and the creation of a unified system paradoxically led to the pluralization—even the neutralization—of the educational system at the value level. The state did not, could not, impose a uniform, rigid, carefully controlled system of values on the schools, nor could it establish ideological criteria for the employment of teachers.[9] The result was a value vacuum in some places, a plurality of values in others, depending on the teacher, the principal, the textbook, and so on.

We do not mean to imply that the decline of statism is attributable solely or even primarily to its democratic nature, or to the failure of nerve on the part of the statist leaders. After all, the use of authoritarian measures has not assured the success of political religions in other new nations, as contemporary developments in Asia and Africa attest.

There are other factors common to both Israel and other new nations that have led to the decline of political or civil religions in all these societies. The desire for economic efficiency and development creates a need to diffuse authority, thus weakening the attachment to transcendent values and symbols;[10] the achievement of a measure of economic growth whets the appetite for greater private satisfactions at the expense of public growth; the passage of time reduces the significance of the original revolutionary moment; and the institutionalization of the revolution has a special impact on youth, among whom there is a marked decline in the authority of revolutionary leaders. In Apter's words, "Prophetic statements lose the power of prophecy and 'young pioneers' are simply trying to get ahead like everyone else. . . . If revolt against church religion is iconoclastic, the revolt against political religion tends to be cynical."[11]

Finally, Apter notes the possibility that, as a result of the decline of political religion, modernization may come to be expressed in traditional terms. "Ritual and dogma," he says, may increase, as "political religion declines."[12] This comes very close to describing what happened in Israel, although it was not exactly like that. The decline of statism is partly the cause and partly the effect of a legitimacy crisis that Israeli society has not yet overcome, one the new civil religion is designed to confront. While the foregoing has gone over some of the factors that help account for the legitimacy crisis, the specific nature of that crisis merits separate discussion.

THE LEGITIMACY CRISIS AND THE GROWING IMPORTANCE OF TRADITIONAL JEWISH SYMBOLS

The legitimacy crisis and the inability of statism to provide a solution to it found strongest expression after the Six Day War. Israel's victory confronted it with a large Arab population that challenged its right to the land. Israel's claims to the conquered areas, and even its very right to exist, were disputed by voices that had hardly been heard before. Shlomo Avineri, an Israeli political scientist and former director general of the Foreign Ministry, observed in 1970: "Since the Six Day War there has existed in Israel a far greater sensitivity than ever existed previously to the objective injustice that has been the lot of the Arabs of Palestine. . . . There is today greater understanding of the position of the other side than in any period prior to 1967."[13]

The nature of the legitimacy crisis most troublesome to Israelis, however, is described in a 1975 interview with an army colonel:

> One gathers the impression that the future generation of commanders is immersed in a set of questions regarding our national existence which previous generations viewed as self-evident. The most prominent example is the question concerning our right to the Land of Israel and the Palestinian question. It appears that this does not stem from their loss of self-confidence, but from the fact that they are in general more skeptical and are unwilling to accept even the most basic topics in dogmatic fashion.[14]

The legtimacy crisis poses threats to Israel's capacity to defend itself. Special significance was attached, therefore, to the fact that the crisis did not pervade the camp of religious Jews. Israeli author Amos Oz notes that to religious Jews who believe in the promised land, Zionism is simple and self-evident. The Zionism of the secularist is more complicated, since he must answer the question, why here of all places? The secularist answer is that here was the focus of Jewish longings which "were originally linked with the belief in the promise and the promiser, the redeemer and the Messiah."[15] This led Oz to conclude that "the Zionism of a man without religious belief must necessarily have rifts in its structure of principles."[16] He noted that nonreligious man is condemned to an existence with built-in inconsistencies in various areas of life, including Zionism.

In other words, the absence of the religious belief left many Israelis, intellectuals in particular, without a firm basis for legitimizing the Jewish state. Statism, it turned out, was not self-legitimating, and Israelis were increasingly thrown back onto utilizing religious, or at least seemingly religious arguments.

The late Yaacov Herzog, a religious Jew, was ambassador to Canada and director general of the prime minister's office. He was a man of some influence on Israeli policy. His perception of the Israeli-Arab conflict is, therefore, of more than passing interest. It comes down, he argued, to a question of rights.

> It goes back to the problem raised by Rashi [a medieval Jewish commentator] in his commentary on the first chapter of Genesis. If the nations of the world say to the Jews: Ye are robbers; you have stolen this land, then the Jews can reply: "In the beginning God created the Heaven and the Earth": all the earth is the Lord's and He gave this land to Israel. Now this argument is very convincing for the Jews, but why should the rest of the world accept it? The answer is that the problem is intimately connected with one's outlook on history: whether it is an outlook of faith or a material-istic conception of history. If the latter, then the world will simply have to accept the fact that the concept of Providence and the place of man under Providence came from Israel, and that that concept has no validity without the Land of Israel. I believe this is the basic problem: whether the debate continues on the basis of "Ye are robbers!" or there is an understanding of the unique quality of the Jewish people and its separate path. If this becomes understood, there is a prospect that we will be accepted as part of the Middle East. In my view this is the key.[17]

Herzog's belief is apparently shared by many nonreligious Jews as well. In 1975 a special subcommittee of the Knesset's education committee was appointed to make recommendations to the Knesset on Israeli information abroad. The four-man committee included two members of the Labor party (successor party to Mapai) and two members of Likud. The draft summary of their conclusions noted: "The Bible must occupy a central place in Israeli information campaigns abroad which must stress the right of the Jewish people to the Land of Israel and the basic principles of the Zionist idea."[18]

The legitimacy crisis was sharpened by the fact that for a brief period Israel's security needs and the precariousness of its existence were no longer self-evident. Israelis are asked to make enormous sacrifices for their country. There is, perhaps, no other state that demands as much from its citizens in terms of taxes, military service, and other such contributions. Nor are these demands limited to a specific stratum. They are diffused throughout the Jewish population. It is inconceivable that the state could demand all that it does through coercion. Consequently, the legitimacy of the state, of its leadership, and of its goals is a vital matter for Israel. Before 1967 it was fairly easy to justify the demands of the state upon its citizenry in terms of Israel's very survival. From 1967 to 1973, when that survival seemed more secure, when Israel itself laid claim to newly acquired territory on the basis of its historical rights as well as its security, legitimacy required reinforcement. Traditional Judaism now appeared as an important foundation for Israel's legitimacy, especially since Israelis were being asked to make sacrifices for the sake of historical rights. Historical rights, in the case of Israel, necessarily evoke associations with the religious tradition of the Jewish people.

The trauma, loss of life, and suffering of the Yom Kippur War, and the burden of military service since then, has aroused further doubts among Israelis about the price they are being asked to pay for the state's existence. But it is significant that they increasingly feel that this is related to their Judaism. For those who do not feel an attachment to Judaism, alienation and emigration are the alternatives. For example, a soldier in the Yom Kippur War asked, "Can't one be a person? Not a person identified as a Jew, not a person identified as an Englishman, as a Frenchman, as a Turk—just a person? . . . Must I always be a person and a Jew? And if *Jew* says nothing to me, and *person* says something to me, can't I escape this killing . . . go someplace and only be a person?"[19]

Religious Zionism has an answer to the questions of Israel's legitimacy and to the necessity to continue bearing one's Jewish burden. It can also claim success in transmitting its values to its youth. Comments such as the following, which appeared in the army publication, *Skira Ḥodshit* (Monthly Review), are heard with growing frequency in Israeli society in general and the army in particular. A professor of psychology stated, "Every research study that I know from the present period finds basic differences between the religious youth and the secular youth. Religious youth are possessed of a far deeper and wider recognition of the significance of our presence here, greater identification with Israeli society as their society, and greater commitment to national objectives." A lieutenant colonel participating in the symposium added, "This is expressed in the Israel Defense Forces—officers want religious soldiers."[20]

Colonel (ret.) Zvi Bar, former commander of Israel's major officer training school, interviewed eleven field officers of the rank of colonel and above in 1974. He asked them how they felt about having religious officers under their command. His questionnaire provided them with three options: a willingness to accept religious officers; pleasure at being assigned religious officers; or doing everything within their power to have religious officers assigned to their command. All interviewees chose the last option. Four added that it is necessary to incorporate religious education in the public educational system since such education resulted in producing quality soldiers possessed of faith and a willingness to serve.[21] The decline of statism created the need for a new civil religion. The nature of the legitimacy crisis, together with the cultural traditions of the new immigrants, dictated the core values of what we call the new civil religion.

THE VALUES OR CREED OF THE NEW CIVIL RELIGION

The new civil religion seeks to integrate and mobilize Israeli Jewish society and legitimate the primary values of the political system by grounding them in a transcendent order of which the Jewish people and the Jewish tradition are basic components.

The term *Jewish people*, in the new civil religion, connotes a national group sharing a common history and fate, dispersed throughout the world but looking to the Land and the State of Israel, and destined to be reunited in Israel. Of particular importance in the Jewish people symbol is the notion of a people that dwells alone, an isolated people that can depend only upon its own resources. Of no less importance is the concept of the history of suffering culminating in the Holocaust which legitimized the Jewish people's rights to its own land.

The very notion *people* merits elaboration. The term in Hebrew is *am*, which also means *nation*. In fact, nation is the preferred translation. When Israelis use the term am with reference to the Jews they are as likely, if not more likely, to be thinking in terms of nation as they are of people. We translate am both ways in this volume depending on the context.

Am Yisrael refers to the entire Jewish people which is perceived as one nation. Indeed, the conception of the Jewish nation is probably the central Zionist myth and helps account for the different perceptions of Israeli and non-Israeli Jews regarding world Jewry's obligations to the State of Israel as the homeland of the Jewish people. A nation's homeland and a people's homeland are two quite different things involving quite different sets of responsibilities, loyalties, and obligations.

The term *Yisrael* (Israel) in the expression am Yisrael also lends itself to a particular confusion, because it suggests both the entire Jewish people and the people living in the State of Israel. Whereas no Israeli thinks of the term as including non-Jewish Israelis, it does blur distinctions between Israeli and non-Israeli Jews. One sometimes has the impression that the term is deliberately used because of its ambiguity. Similarly, reference is sometimes made to the culture of Israel where the referent (either Jewish culture encompassing the religious tradition or the culture of the state) is deliberately vague.

The new civil religion is unique in that it accords respect to Diaspora Jewry and it recognizes the past and present Diaspora as intimately connected to, and interrelated with, the Jewish state, yet possessed of a legitimate autonomy. An extreme, though not unique, formulation of this position is found in a review of a television program called "A People Alone," aired on Tisha Be'av night in 1980. According to the reviewer in one of Israel's most popular newspapers, the moral of the program was that

> Judaism succeeded in surviving in the Diaspora longer than in the Land of Israel—and this fact is imprinted upon Judaism. Hence, Judaism is different, perhaps even outside a national framework. It

is not purely national—but a way of life in accordance with a guide for life. Its nature and essence is observance of commandments. . . . Dr. Ben-Gal even compared the Jewish center in Babylonia, where the Talmud was created, to the Jewish center in New York today. The comparison raises thoughts. The fact is, in any event, that except for a relatively brief period of glory in the Land of Israel, Judaism reached its zenith in the Diaspora. Compare its achievements there in almost every area of life, and the wasteland of values and spirit in the new Israel.[22]

No statement better highlights the difference between the new civil religion and statism, which found no positive value in Diaspora culture.

The basic value around which consensus is generated within Israeli society is the commitment to Israel as a Jewish state. This commitment is reinforced by the fact that this is the aspect of Israel to which its enemies raise their greatest objection.[23] In chapter one we noted that 93 percent of the Jewish population affirmed that the State of Israel must be a Jewish state. We also noted that there are a variety of possible meanings to the term Jewish state, and that 83 percent of the sample believed that one meaning was a state in which a majority of the population was Jewish (only 10 percent said no) and that 62 percent believed that it means a state whose public image conformed to the Jewish tradition (only 18 percent said no). But the greatest consensus about the meaning of a Jewish state revolves around the ties between the State of Israel and world Jewry. Eighty-seven percent of the respondents believed that a Jewish state is one that senses a special responsibility for Diaspora Jewry (only 7 percent said no). The strength of this tie is expressed in the response to the question: "If there was a possibility for reaching a true and permanent peace settlement with the Arab states on condition that Israel undertake not to permit further aliya would you be willing or unwilling to agree to it?" Six percent agreed to such conditions and 3 percent said they were inclined to agree. Nine percent were inclined not to agree and 82 percent did not agree. In other words, 91 percent of the Jewish population of Israel is unwilling to exchange aliya for peace. Nothing better illustrates the Israelis' tie to world Jewry. This ought not to surprise us. To be an Israeli for the vast majority of Israelis is to be a Jew. This is the basic meaning of the Israeli identity, and hence peace with its Arab neighbors, for the vast majority of Israelis means not only Arab reconciliation with the people of Israel but also reconciliation with their Jewish identity.

This inevitably leads to an emphasis on traditional religious symbols, particularly in the wake of the decline of Zionist-socialism and statism, which both sought to secularize Judaism. If to be Israeli means to be a Jew, then it must mean, in some sense, to be religious. It ought not to surprise us, therefore, that the vast majority of the population (seventy-six percent) favors some tie between religion and state, and as much as forty-two percent felt that a Jewish state was a state which sought to conduct itself in accordance with Jewish law.

The Jewish Tradition

Eliezer Schweid noted that many secularists recognize the religious grounding of their own nationalist feeling and give expression to these sentiments in terms of traditional symbols, a process especially pronounced since 1967.[24] He contrasts the Israeli War of Independence in 1948 and the Six Day War, and observes that "the storytellers and poets of the War of Independence did not dare employ religious symbols or the language of the religious experience,"[25] whereas in the Six Day War "traditional symbols were . . . consciously perceived and fraught with meaning . . . there was no sense of recoil from using them."[26]

The growing association between Jewish nationalism and traditional Judaism is particularly troublesome to left-wing intellectuals, who in their continued battle to juxtapose religion and nationalism, themselves bear witness to the growing synthesis of the two.[27] A study by Simon Herman is also instructive in this regard. Herman compared the relative potency of Israeliness and Jewishness among a sample of eleventh-grade Israeli high school students. In 1965 and 1974, he asked students to mark their position on an Israeli-Jewish scale ranging from one to seven (the closer the student is to one, the more Israeli he feels himself; the closer to seven, the more Jewish). In 1965 the mean position of the entire sample was three and five-tenths—in other words, on the Israeli side. In 1974 it shifted to four and two-tenths, or just beyond the midpoint (4.0) and to the Jewish side. Among those students who defined themselves as religious the shift was from five and one-tenth to five and four-tenths; among those who defined

themselves as traditionalists, from three and six-tenths to four
and four-tenths; and among those who defined themselves as
nonreligious from two and six-tenths to three and one-tenth.[28]

The increased importance of the Jewish tradition is expressed in the increased use of religious symbols. Second,
whereas in previous periods traditional symbols underwent a
process of transformation and transvaluation, they now penetrate the culture in their traditional formulation. In other
words, in contrast to the recent past, Jewish symbols are
adapted in the context and meaning hallowed by the religious
tradition, without a conscious effort to change their form or
value (but, as we shall see, in an interpretation compatible with
national needs).

This does not mean that Israelis are becoming more religious.
On the contrary, the continued decline in the number of pupils
enrolled in religious elementary schools suggests that the number of Israelis who define themselves as religious is declining,[29]
despite frequent Israeli press reports of a turn to religion by
those raised in nonreligious homes. What we suggest is that the
Israeli is increasingly exposed to religious symbols which evoke
a positive resonance for him and serve as a basis of integration,
legitimation, and mobilization. In an earlier period, these
symbols, if not discarded, were radically transformed or
transvalued.

The importance of the Jewish tradition, however, is somewhat mitigated by the fact that the new civil religion, unlike
Zionist-socialism or even statism, lacks a coherent ideological
formulation. It lacks, as it were, a theory. This stems from a
number of factors. First, there is an inherent contradiction in
using the Jewish tradition as the basis for a civil religion that
serves a population in which the majority are neither believers
nor observers in the traditional sense. Elaborating an ideology
would only heighten the contradiction. Second, however important traditional Judaism may be in the new civil religion, the
two are not synonymous. The new civil religion affirms the
importance of traditional Judaism as a component of Jewish
identity and Jewish history, but it does not demand detailed
religious practice, nor does it limit its own concerns to those of
traditional Judaism. Hence, the articulation of the civil religious ideology would antagonize the religiously traditional segment of the population. Tension with this group is what
adherents of the new civil religion seek to avoid.

Something else merits notice. Western society in general has experienced a decline in nationalist sentiments and a concomitant decrease in the force of civil religions. The same is true in Israel as well. The new civil religion evokes less commitment that did either statism or Zionist-socialism or revisionism—a point to which we return in the final chapter.

The symbols of traditional Judaism have not only penetrated the new civil religion, but they have become an instrument for transmitting the values of the civil religion. It is important to understand what this means. It does not mean that Israelis are enjoined to observe the religious commandments, although some lip service is paid to traditional ceremonial. What it does mean is that respect and deference are accorded to the tradition itself and to those who observe it. The tradition is hallowed as representing the customs, ceremonies, and moral values of the people. Recently there has been the suggestion that those who strictly observe traditional religion are more faithful adherents of the civil religion. It is the stress on tradition which more than anything else distinguishes the new civil religion from earlier ones, and next is its emphasis on the Jewish people worldwide as one interrelated people.

God has reentered the civil religion, but only as a name, not as an active agent who confers legitimacy or to whom one can appeal for help. For example, the kibbutz haggadot from which God was previously excised now retain more, if not all, the traditional text. God has reappeared, but, more than renewed belief in God, this indicates instead renewed respect for the traditional text.

The absence of belief in God as an active agent distinguishes Israeli civil religion from the civil religions associated with other Western societies, and merits more attention than we will offer here. It probably stems from the fact that atheism was embedded into the civil religion of Zionist-socialism, and was left unchallenged by statism. In other words, in the culture in which today's political elite was reared atheism was taken for granted. By contrast, belief in God is assumed in American civil society, however inconsequential this assumption may be. The one notable controversy that developed in formulating the Israeli Declaration of Independence was the religious parties' insistence on, and leftist party opposition to, including the name of God. The compromise was to use a term, *rock of Israel*, which each side could interpret as it chose. In other words, in

Israel, unlike most Western societies, the use of the term God identifies one as "religious" which, in turn, associates one with a community, a particular weltanschaung, and a particular behavioral and attitudinal system. God is simply irrelevant in the new civil religion. There are nonorthodox religious Jews in Israel (Reform, who call themselves Progressive, and Conservative), but they have little public exposure. *Religious Jew* in Israel means an *Orthodox Jew*. Ben Gurion was prone to use the term God, but the public knew that his understanding of God was nontraditional. In general, belief in God is associated with religious orthodoxy and using the term labels one as an Orthodox Jew. This may change. Prime Minister Menachem Begin frequently invokes the name of God and the televised speeches of the former defense minister, Shimon Peres, point in the same direction. Peres, the most calculating of all Israeli politicians, is a weather vane, following the direction of public opinion. So far, however, the new civil religion emphasizes the Jewish people as the active, indeed the sole, agent responsible for the nation's achievements—an emphasis that recalls statism in particular.

Israel and the Nations of the World

The emphasis on Jewish peoplehood and the Jewish tradition has particular implications for the perceived relationship between Israel and other nations. The new civil religion has been most forceful in its assertion that Israel is an isolated nation confronting a hostile world. This idea is best understood when grasped in its mythic context.

MYTHS

The Holocaust

The growing importance of traditional Judaism and Jewishness is associated with the centrality of the Holocaust as the primary political myth of Israeli society, the symbol of Israel's present condition and the one which provides Israel with legitimacy and the right to its land, Israel. The Holocaust to a great extent fashions "our national consciousness and the way in which we understand ourselves and the world in which we live."[30] Its memory is omnipresent in Israeli society, cutting across differences in age, education, and even country of origin.[31]

The Holocaust is the most tragic event in modern Jewish history. However, it is not the Holocaust itself which concerns us here but rather its perception by Israelis. This relates, in turn, to traditional Jewish views of the non-Jew and the nature of Jewish-gentile relationships.

The traditional Jewish view of Jewish-gentile relations is symbolically expressed in the phrase, Esau hates Jacob. Esau is a symbol of the non-Jew, Jacob a symbol of the Jew. It is of interest to note the source from whence this statement entered the tradition. Genesis (33:4) describes the meeting between Jacob and his brother Esau: "And Esau ran towards him, and embraced him, and fell on his neck, *and kissed him*: and they wept." (Emphasis added.) Rashi, the medieval Jewish commentator, whose classic work is studied by traditionally religious Jews from early childhood, comments on the word "kissed."

> Dots are placed above the letters of this word and a difference of opinion is expressed as to what these dots are intended to suggest . . . some explain the dotting as meaning that he did not kiss him with his whole heart, whereas Rabbi Simeon the son of Johai said: Is it not well-known that Esau hates Jacob? But at the moment his pity was really aroused and he kissed him with his whole heart.

The sages felt it necessary to explain Esau's sign of affection. This is consistent with the main line of the Jewish tradition which found anti-Semitism to be the norm, the natural response of the non-Jew, whereas the absence of anti-Semitism required explanation. *Esau hates Jacob* symbolized the world the Jews experienced. It is deeply embedded in the Jewish folk tradition. Its resonance, however, rests on the fact that it not only reflects Jewish experience but, at the same time, it avoids a direct statement about non-Jews' feelings toward Jews. Such a statement, something like "all non-Jews hate Jews," would be not only offensive to non-Jews but clearly incorrect. Indeed, a little reflection suggests there is no category of people, non-Jew, that relates itself to Jews. Furthermore, not all non-Jews who do relate themselves to Jews hate them.

Jewish tradition itself recognizes the category of the virtuous non-Jew. But the allegory of Esau and Jacob evokes a sense of reality that functions to maintain a boundary around Jews and cement Jewish unity. It provides the traditionally religious Jew with a sense of his greater sophistication than the naive secular Jew, and at the same time strengthens his feeling that the secular Jew cannot escape his Jewish destiny. Finally, it provides some protection against the trauma of anti-Semitism since it prepares the traditionally religious Jew, at least psychologically, for this phenomenon. The religiously traditional Jew believes that the secularist lives in an illusionary world with regard to what he expects of the non-Jew. These tendencies are more pronounced in Israel than in the United States. In Israel they are experienced more intensely by the traditionally religious Jew, but are shared by a wider spectrum of the Jewish population.

The image of a naturally hostile non-Jewish world was rejected, as we have shown, by the leaders of the yishuv and the founders of the state. Zionism arose partly as a plan to resolve the problem of anti-Semitism. Non-Jews hated Jews, it was presumed, not because there was something innately wrong with non-Jews or Jews but because of the Jews' condition of homelessness. In the previous chapter we saw that Ben Gurion enunciated such a doctrine even in 1945 after the world learned the awful extent to which the Nazis had carried out their goal of genocide. Acquisition of a national homeland, Zionism promised, would restore the Jewish people to normalcy, and this would change the gentile's attitude toward the Jew. Furthermore, the rebellion against the Jewish tradition which characterized the early Zionists included rejection of values they perceived to distinguish Jews from non-Jews. Zionist-socialists, in particular, affirmed universalist-humanism. This ideology influenced Zionist activity and shaped the perception of reality which informed basic Zionist policy concerning relations with the mandatory power and, especially, with the Arabs. But a variety of factors, including perhaps the inability to create an adequate symbolic system to project this ideology, resulted in a reassertion of the older tradition.

Within the religious tradition one of the sharpest expressions of Jewish antagonism to non-Jews is found in the haggada. After the grace is recited, the Jew is enjoined to rise, hold up his ceremonial cup of wine and pronounce four verses that begin, "Pour out Thy wrath upon the nations who know Thee not." The text itself does not make clear whether God's wrath is beseeched upon all nations, or beseeched only upon particular nations, "who know Thee not." This is of little note to most traditional Jews. As far as they are concerned all nations in the words of the Psalmist (also included in the four verses), "devoured Jacob and laid waste his habitation."

When the kibbutzim introduced their own haggadot they had no problem deciding what to do with this passage. It was omitted. [32] Following World War II and discovery of the Holocaust, a number of kibbutzim reintroduced the verses, but after a few years they again disappeared. They have returned once more, albeit transformed and softened, since the Yom Kippur War.

From the point of view of the kibbutz, what we have here is a conscious manipulation of symbols; but symbols only reflect perceived reality. They reflect perceptions produced by filtering reality through prior symbols. A related fact is that symbols enforce codes, reinforce images, and socialize to a particular ideology. In the exchange below, with Ran Cohen, left-wing dove, Shmuel Tamir, former minister of justice, a hawkish nonreligious person ility of the political right, defends the need for a resolute military-diplomatic policy. (To understand Tamir's point it is helpful to know the verse in the Passover ceremonial: "For it was not one man only who stood up against us to destroy us, and the Holy One, blessed be He, saves us from their hand.") Tamir explained how he would justify Israeli national interest to his son.

> Shmuel Tamir: I would tell him . . . look, we Jews tried to convert and they would not absorb us. We tried to assimilate and they did not accept us . . . we concluded that we had no alternative but to become a nation like all the nations in the conservative, routine sense that solved the problems of all the nations. That we have to put a roof over our heads in the land from which we originated, where we grew into a nation, where we wrote the book of books. In that country we must be as numerous as possible, as strong as possible, as famous as possible in the whole region, and as decent as possible.

> Ran Cohen: I agree with you. But we can assume that the son of Mr. Tamir is an intelligent boy and will ask you: Daddy, must we rule over another nation that lives in our midst?

> Shmuel Tamir: I will answer you: I would reply to the boy, that they have murdered us in Munich because we are surrounded by a

hate and a desire to wipe us out. I will tell you what I tell him on the Seder night when we read the haggadah: "That in every generation they rise up against us to destroy us." Neither you nor I have found a solution to this source of evil but it is factually there.[33]

Symbols serve not only as heuristic devices to internalize values and ideology but also as prisms through which events are perceived and recorded. To what degree has the traditional religious symbol of the hostile gentile penetrated the public mind? Does it serve only to facilitate boundary maintenance, or has its specific content been internalized? We do not know. There is certainly evidence that it continues to resonate, particularly in periods of tense relations with Arabs. In August 1980, Israeli soldiers raided a terrorist base in Lebanon. Matters that do not concern us here raised questions among some Israelis about the wisdom and utility of the raid. Wide publicity was given to the raid, and the press was permitted to interview some participants. In a *Maariv* interview one commanding officer said:

> I believe in one thing; that Esau hates Jacob. That is a given form that did not change and still exists today. And if it is given, its implications are that we must indeed defend ourselves. To defend ourselves every day. And in order to do it properly, one has to enter within, and strike the terrorists. Everyone must see in this a holy service, a service to the Jewish people. For whoever enters the battle on its behalf is one of its servants.[34]

It is simplistic to believe that religious symbols by themselves account for Jewish attitudes toward non-Jews. Symbols forged by a powerless people in a hostile environment were deemed inappropriate by many in the early years of statehood and were ignored or replaced by symbols which pointed to a different conception of Jewish-gentile relations. The reality of the Holocaust, reinforced by the Six Day War and the Yom Kippur War, evoked an older, more traditional symbol system, which seemed to more adequately express the Israeli condition. But it is no less simplistic to deny that the traditional symbols themselves provide the Holocaust or later Israeli wars with particular meaning.

The Holocaust holds lessons for most Israelis beyond the pain, beyond the physical and psychological scars it left on those who were Nazi victims themselves and even many of those who vicariously experienced victimization. In this sense the Holocaust itself is a symbol. What meaning does it contain, as a symbol, for the Jewish people? The Holocaust can point to the possibility of evil or the reality of evil. It can suggest that we must guard against the aberration of Nazism, or that in a crisis the world will not rescue Jews in mortal peril. It can point to the world's indifference to the murder of Jews, or to the courage of a few, who stood up to Nazi terror on behalf of Jews. It can mean Nazi against Jew, or German against Jew, or Christian against Jew, or goy against Jew—or evil against good, strong against weak. It can suggest how monstrous a few can become, or how readily all of us can, by our silence or inaction, become complicit in monstrous crimes. It can point to the weakness of Eastern European Jews who allowed themselves to be murdered, or to the heroism and inner resources required to face death with dignity and faith, or to the courage of Jews who resisted and rebelled. Or the Holocaust can be understood as a demonstration of Jewish helplessness in the Disapora and the consequent importance of "Jewish power," which the State of Israel represents.

The facts do not necessarily lend equal support to each of these meanings, but a sufficient factual basis can be found to reinforce any one to which primary sentiments and world views might predispose a person. All these interpretations have found expression in the voluminous post-Holocaust literature, but not all have received equal emphasis in Israeli culture. Those institutions and occasions especially devoted to providing meaning to the Holocaust are particularly selective in their interpretations. Among those closer to the religious tradition there is greater propensity to view the Holocaust in terms of Israel against the Nations, than there is among nonreligious Jews, just as more Israelis than American Jews view the Holocaust this way.

The Holocaust image of a beleaguered Israel surrounded by an anti-Semitic world was reinforced by the perception of world reaction to Israel during the Yom Kippur War, but it also influenced this perception.[35] Many understood world reaction as an expression of anti-Semitism. This view was inadequate to account for American support to Israel, which was therefore explained as a result of American self-interest. Opinion polls indicating that many Europeans supported Israel in opposition to the official stance of their government were reported by the Israeli press but not perceived by most Israelis.

The fact that symbols shape our perception does not necessarily mean they deceive us. On the contrary, they may alert us to reality. Different symbols and perceptions accounted for the failure of world Jewry, and German Jewry in particular, to respond adequately to the Nazi threat. Nor does the fact that Israeli perceptions of a hostile world happen to suit the purposes of its political elite—to explain the failures of Israeli foreign policy, to legitimate the status quo vis-à-vis the Arabs, and to strengthen Jewish solidarity—make these perceptions any less valid. Widespread acceptance of the hostile world image is neither an elitist trick, nor the result of manipulation. It finds acceptance, however, partly because it is consistent with symbols deeply embedded into the culture of the people.

The symbol that relates the Holocaust to Israel's self-perception, and to the Jewish tradition's perception of Judaism's eternal condition, is the biblical phrase "a people that dwells alone" (Numbers 23:9). In the biblical story, the non-Jewish seer, Balaam, uses this phrase to describe the Israelites he sees encamped before him in the desert. There is a good deal of ambivalence attached to this meaning, consistent with the ambivalence of the entire episode and the curse-blessing which Balaam utters. Still, it is generally understood as the expression of a condition imposed upon Israel by the nations of the world, a condition willingly accepted by Israel because of its own superior virtues.

The concept of *a people that dwells alone* is embedded in the new civil religion. It serves appropriately as the title of a collection of Yaacov Herzog's speeches and writings. Herzog argues that Zionist leaders were wrong when they believed that once Israel attained independence the Jews would become accepted throughout the world. They were wrong, he says, because political Zionism mistakenly thought

> the idea of "a people that dwells alone" . . . an abnormal concept, when actually the concept of "a people that dwells alone" is the natural concept of the Jewish people . . . in the final analysis, one must come back to the idea that this is "a people that dwells alone." And not only in order to understand how it has managed to survive, but no less from the point of view of its right to exist, must one invoke this phrase.[36]

The symbol's impact is so deep that Israeli representatives utilize it without perhaps appreciating how it must sound to outsiders; how double-edged it is. Yosef Tekoah, former Israeli ambassador to the United Nations, for example, announced that Israel "should not be influenced by what *The New York Times* or any other paper writes." He related that when the Soviet delegate to the U.N. commented on how isolated Israel was, he replied, "You the ambassador of the Soviet Union have never read our history. We have always been a small and isolated nation, different and apart. It has not deterred us from our way of life and our destiny."[37]

The Holocaust is itself the symbol of Jewish history and the Jewish people, denoting the tragedy that may befall a people that dwells alone. It also denotes an Israel to whom the world owes a debt. The utilization of the Holocaust as a symbol of both Jewish history and contemporary Israel stands in sharp contrast to both the Zionist-socialist and statist perception of Judaism, Jewish history, and Israel. This is reflected in our respondents' answers to questions about Israel's right to exist and about the Holocaust.

In the analysis of the material that follows it is important to distinguish between respondents by their own perceptions of their religious identity. Respondents were asked to identify themselves as religious, traditional, or nonreligious. The terms are meaningful to Israelis and the distinctions are common ones in surveys of the Israeli Jewish population. As we noted, to be a religious Jew means to be what in America is known as an Orthodox Jew. The characteristics of a respondent who identifies himself as religious include strictly observing the Sabbath, covering the head at all times (with either a hat or a yarmulke), and drawing one's circle of friends primarily from among other religious Jews. Traditional Jews are the most difficult to define, since there is a great variation in their religious behavior. We suggest that their most important common attribute is the conscious observance of some but not all religious practices. This selectivity derives from a sense that one observes because of tradition, not because one believes that God commands observance. Traditional Jews respect the religious tradition but do not personally identify with the religious camp. However strict he may be in the observance of religious practices, the traditionalist is unlikely to wear a skull cap at all times. Nonreligious Jews include many who observe basic Jewish customs,[38] but they are less deferential to the tradition and more inclined to observe religious practices for family or aesthetic purposes, or simply from inertia. Finally, they are likely to be anticlerical. In our sample, 14 percent of the respondents identified themselves as religious, 44 percent as traditionalist, and 42 percent as nonreligious.[39]

Respondents were asked which of six reasons best justified Israel's right to exist.[40] Only 10 percent of those who identified themselves as nonreligious felt the best justification rested on the achievements of contemporary Zionism. Among those who defined themselves as traditional or religious the percentage fell to 5 percent and 1 percent, respectively. Seven to 8 percent of the members of all three groups justified Israel's right to exist in terms of the ancient settlement of the Land. These two responses would be characteristic answers of those attached to either Zionist-socialist or statist symbols.

Forty-eight percent of the religious, 16 percent of the traditional and as many as 7 percent of the nonreligious, anchored Israel's right to exist in strictly religious terms. Finally, 17 percent of the religious, 56 percent of the traditional, and 61 percent of the nonreligious felt that the most important justification for Israel's right to exist rested in Jewish history, Jewish suffering, and Jewish longing to return to the Land of Israel during the period of their dispersion. We can only stress again how much this is at variance with the Zionist-socialist and statist conceptions of what is important and relevant in Jewish history.

Respondents were also asked what, in their opinion, was the most important lesson to be learned from the Holocaust. Differences between religious, traditional, and nonreligious Jews were not statistically significant. Fifty-eight percent of the sample felt the major lesson was either that all the Jews in the Diaspora should come to Israel, or that there was a need for a strong and established, sovereign Jewish state. An additional 9 percent felt it meant there was no security in the Diaspora. Only 25 percent put the lesson of the Holocaust in general Jewish terms without mentioning Israel (the need for Jewish unity, self-defense, and self-reliance, or the need to be attentive to any evidence of anti-Semitism), and only 4 percent in universalist terms (the need to fight against antidemocratic practices and defend the rights of minorities everywhere).

In other words, to all groups, the lesson of the Holocaust is the insecurity of Jewish life in the Diaspora and the need for a Jewish state. But, contrary to the theories of classical Zionism

TABLE 1
BEST JUSTIFICATION FOR ISRAEL'S RIGHT TO EXIST BY RELIGIOUS SELF-IDENTITY (IN PERCENTAGES)

Justification	Religious	Traditional	Nonreligious	Total
Recognition of the nations of the world of the idea of a Jewish state	8.5	9.7	8.9	9.3
The suffering of the Jews in the Diaspora as a people without a homeland	16.5	31.7	32.3	29.9
The yearning of Jews throughout the generations to return to the Land	11.8	24.7	28.3	24.4
The settlement of the Land by the Jews in ancient times	7.4	7.8	8.4	8.0
The settlement of the Land in modern times and the War of Independence	1.1	4.6	10.2	6.4
God's promise to the fathers of the nation that the Land of Israel would be given to the people of Israel	48.5	16.0	6.7	16.5
Don't know or volunteered some other response	6.2	5.3	5.1	5.4
N	272	873	845	1990

TABLE 2
ATTITUDE OF THE NATIONS OF THE WORLD TO ISRAEL BY RELIGIOUS SELF-IDENTITY
(IN PERCENTAGES)

Attitude	Religious	Traditional	Nonreligious	Total
The nations of the world are always against us	27.6	12.4	10.9	13.8
The nations of the world are generally against us	26.5	26.6	24.5	25.7
It is impossible to generalize	37.1	52.8	56.2	52.1
The nations of the world generally support us	4.4	4.0	4.0	4.0
The nations of the world always support us	0.4	0.7	0.8	0.7
Don't know, no answer, or some other response	4.0	3.6	3.5	3.5
N	272	873	845	1990

embedded in the ideology of Zionist-socialism and statism, the creation of Israel did not reduce anti-Semitism. Rather, consistent with the new civil religion, the major themes of Jewish history emerge in the experience of Israel. It is directly associated with the suffering of Diaspora Jews and continues to reflect the eternal condition of the Jewish people—isolated and beleaguered. This perception, we noted, gains special emphasis after the Yom Kippur War. Respondents were asked what in their opinion was the attitude of the nations of the world to the State of Israel.

Forty percent of all respondents (35 percent of non-religious, 39 percent of the traditionalists, and 54 percent of the religious) felt that the nations of the world were always or generally against the State of Israel, whereas only 5 percent of the sample were willing to make the opposite generalization.

Masada

The renewed importance of the Masada myth is also associated with the decline of statism. The *Encyclopaedia Judaica* notes that "for Israeli youth it is a unique symbol of courage and, on its summit, the recruits of the Israel Armed Corps swear their oath of allegiance: 'Masada shall not fall again.' "[41]

Indeed, this ceremony in 1973 inaugurated Israel's twenty-fifth anniversary events.

But this is only part of the story. The main excavations at Masada began, as we noted, in 1963 under the direction of Yigael Yadin. The excavations added a new emphasis, experienced by every visitor to Masada who is led on a guided tour. Masada was the residence of a community of Jewish zealots whose zealotry extended to their religious practice no less than to their national commitments. The discovery of the ritual baths and a synagogue did much to focus attention on the specifically Jewish and traditionally religious aspects of the defenders' lives. It strengthened the asssociation of state—Jew—religion. Masada captured the imagination of Israelis and of Jews throughout the world, as the myth was related in stories, exhibits, and scholarly lectures. The State of Israel was the legacy of the defenders of Masada. Their courage and self-sacrifice legitimated the state and was an exemplary model for its citizens, but the defenders of Masada were also Jews in the fullest and most traditional sense of the term. All Jews could identify with them.

The Masada myth, however, also contains two other elements: isolation and defeat, which made it so problematic in the statist period, and the mass suicide. The first motif became less problematic with the decline of statism, particularly after the Six Day War, and especially after the Yom Kippur War. Both wars forced Israelis to confront the possibility of defeat and decimation, and they evoked, quite consciously and directly, associations with the Holocaust.[42] The sense of despair and isolation and the fear of defeat passed very quickly in the wake of the great victory of the Six Day War, but it remained long after the Yom Kippur War had ended, despite Israel's military achievement.

The most widely publicized association between Masada and the Israeli condition came in the exchange between Prime Minister Golda Meir and the American columnist, Stewart Alsop. The prime minister was reported to have turned to Alsop at a Washington press conference, and, referring to a recent column of his, said: "And you, Mr. Alsop, you say that we have a Masada complex. . . . It is true. We do have a Masada complex. We have a pogrom complex. We have a Hitler complex."[43]

Masada, then, represents the realization of the threat present throughout all Jewish history. It is a symbol of pogroms, of the Holocaust, and of what awaited Israel had it not won the Six Day and Yom Kippur Wars, and still awaits Israel if it does not remain stronger than its neighbors. In this respect, the Masada myth is a powerful symbol conveying a central tenet of Israel's new civil religion—reinforcing the notions of a people that dwells alone and Esau hates Jacob. This element of the myth, which statism was unable to digest, was most appropriate to the new civil religion. However, the final element, the suicide motif, remained problematical and, we believe, reduced the power of the myth.

We argue, in chapter two, that the suicide theme did not particularly trouble the yishuv. With the revival of the Masada myth, the Israeli elite also seemed untroubled by the suicide theme. Alsop reported that Golda Meir, at the luncheon mentioned above, delivered a "moving oration about the spirit of Israel, a spirit that would prefer death rather than surrender to

the dark terrors of the Jewish past."[44] Yigael Yadin was quoted
as saying, "Masada represents to all of us in Israel . . . a symbol
of courage, a monument to our great national figures, heroes
who chose death over a life of physical and moral serfdom."[45] In
other words, while suicide per se was not glorified, it was
subsumed by the theme of courage, as evidence of the defenders' love of freedom.

We suspect that for some Israelis the suicide motif represents a negation of Eastern European Jewish behavior. Whereas
both Masada and the Holocaust symbolized the eternal Jewish
condition of isolation, gentile hostility, and the threat of
annihilation, Masada symbolizes the activist, courageous,
Israeli response—suicide as the ultimate gesture of defiance
when all hope for freedom was gone—contrasted to the passive,
weaker Diaspora response of abject acceptance of fate. In this
view the Warsaw ghetto and other Diaspora resistance represent exceptions.

Such a contrast is challenged by historical scholarship about
Masada, on one hand, and by new interpretations of the response of the Holocaust victims on the other. We are not
concerned in tracing the assaults on the Masada myth which
question the reliability of Josephus's account (on which the
myth is based), or, assuming that Josephus's account is correct,
with disputing the moral and halakhic legitimacy of the zealots'
action.[46] The Jewish tradition did not glorify the zealots but
rather Rabbi Yoḥanan Ben Zakkai, who traded political dependency on Rome for the right to establish an academy at Yavneh.

To most Israelis, however, the aftermath of the Yom Kippur
War weakened Masada as a central political myth precisely
because it strengthened the identification of Israelis with the
Holocaust victims. The suicide motif was, as we noted, not
only a denial of basic Jewish values, a rejection of the Jewish
tradition, but most serious of all, an implied criticism of the
Holocaust victims. None of this was now tolerable. Yadin, as
early as May of 1973, was quoted as saying that young Israelis
tended to be disenchanted "with the grim example of self-
slaughter offered by Masada."[47] In 1980 he was reported to have
said that

> the true lesson we learn from Masada is not blind worship of the
> acts of courage of Ben Yair and his comrades. The lesson is in the
> words of Yizḥak Lamdan, "Masada will not fall again." We will not

judge them, for we did not face the same conditions, but we will strengthen ourselves so that we will not face the alternatives: to live as slaves or to die as free men.[48]

Yadin, who contributed so much to the popularity of the Masada myth, may thus have unintentionally written its epitaph. Yet new experiences may give the myth new force. The dramatic natural setting of Masada virtually cries out for mythic representation and it has recently become a popular site for the celebration of teenage rites of passage among many kibbutzim.

THE CELEBRATIONS OF THE CIVIL RELIGION

Holocaust Day

Since the Holocaust myth plays such a central role in Israeli civil religion, it is not surprising that its commemoration should be a central focus. We turn first to a discussion of that commemoration, following which we will discuss other rituals of the civil religion. Our emphasis throughout will be on how the symbols of traditional Judaism and Jewish peoplehood have penetrated the celebrations of the new civil religion.

The major Holocaust shrine is Yad Vashem, second only to the western wall in its sacredness as a shrine of the Israeli civil religion. It is the place to which foreign dignitaries are taken to celebrate and solemnize their relationship to Israel by sharing its identification with the victims of the Holocaust. Yad Vashem is the major memorial to the Jews and Jewish communities destroyed in the Holocaust. It is maintained as a religious location. Visitors are expected to cover their heads in accordance with religious custom. There are other monuments and museums devoted to informing the public about the Holocaust, or permitting the public to unite with the memory of the victims, but none other as important as Yad Vashem. Israeli schools devote much attention to the Holocaust, and classes visit Yad Vashem as well as other places dedicated to the memory of the civilization that the Nazis destroyed.

Two days mark off the Holocaust on the Israeli calendar. Major events commemorating the Holocaust occur on the Heroes and Martyrs Remembrance Day, a name which sounds almost as awkward in Hebrew as it does in English. On that day all places of amusement are closed. Schools and the army commemorate the Holocaust in a variety of ways. Regular T.V. programs are preempted and special programs devoted to the Holocaust are shown. Perhaps the most impressive moment of the day occurs when a siren sounds throughout the country for two minutes, during which time all activity ceases and every person stands in silent memory of the six million.

As we noted in the previous chapter, the setting of the Holocaust memorial a week before the two days devoted to Israel's independence is not coincidental. It was fixed on the twenty-seventh of Nisan, a date on which the Warsaw ghetto revolt was still in progress, and midway between Passover (when mourning rites are forbidden) and Memorial Day, which immediately precedes Independence Day. Religious circles had preferred the tenth of Tevet. Its original meaning had lost much of its significance and the rabbis had designated it as a day on which prayers in memory of deceased family members would be recited by those who did not know the dates of their relatives' deaths. There is no way of knowing the dates on which many of the Holocaust victims died, and the tenth of Tevet provided those who wanted to memorialize deceased family members in accordance with Jewish law an opportunity to do so. Obviously, the importance of the day would have been substantially increased if it had been named Holocaust Day; but, as we noted, statists preferred to stress the association of the Holocaust with the bravery of the ghetto fighters.

The name, Heroes and Martyrs Remembrance Day, coupling the Holocaust with bravery, was consistent with statist values and served as a response to Israeli youth who were especially troubled by the perception of the Holocaust victims offering little resistance to the Nazis. Hence, the stress on acts of forcible resistance by Jews—the best known being the Warsaw ghetto revolt. In recent years, Jewish resistance in other ghettos, even in the concentration camps, has been publicized. The public has also come to appreciate that resistance can consist in moral courage, as well as in armed force. Furthermore, for some Israelis, especially since the Yom Kippur War, it is Jewish suffering and the indifference of the world to that suffering which evokes an identification with the Holocaust, rather than the physical resistance or any other acts of courage by the Jews.

The Holocaust is so laden with religious symbolism and associations that it evokes and strengthens a sensitivity to the religious tradition and the Jewish people. Death naturally evokes religious associations and there is hardly any way to celebrate the memory of the dead without utilizing some religious symbols. More significantly, the Holocaust and its connection to the establishment of Israel associate Israel with Diaspora Jewry. This also evokes an association with religious Jewry. In other words, Diaspora Jewry, especially Eastern European Jewry which perished, is perceived as religious Jewry. We guess that the average Israeli, when asked to describe the Jew who died in the Holocaust, would think of a religious Jew, not a socialist ghetto fighter. The Holocaust, as we already suggested, is itself a symbol of the Diaspora. The difference between the statist period and today is that in the past, religion, Diaspora, and Holocaust, that is, defenseless Jews led as sheep to the slaughter, evoked negative associations, but now the association of the Diaspora with religion is more positive, the tragedy of the Holocaust evokes greater sympathy, and each symbol reinforces the other.

Independence and Memorial Days

The penetration of traditional Jewish symbols into the civil religion is also reflected in other civil or national holidays. It is probably least noticeable on Independence Day. Religious Jews sought to infuse Independence Day with religious ceremonial and we shall discuss this phenomenon in chapter seven. That ceremonial, however, is geared to religious Jews. It takes place in the synagogue or during regular prayer services. The political elite, in contrast, has not seen the need to infuse the national or civil ceremonies which commemorate the day with religious symbols. There are central synagogue services in the major cities on the eve of the holiday, which the president, mayors, and other civic leaders are likely to attend, but the public ceremonies themselves evoke historical associations related to the war of independence or other military victories. They neither begin with a prayer, involve the participation of a rabbi, nor evoke any religious association.

Independence Day, however, is not without traditional associations. Since 1963 one of the major events has been the Bible quiz, which involves high school competitors from throughout Israel and the Diaspora. The final competition on Independence Day is televised. Indeed, in 1976 the Bible quiz was labeled "the central event in the celebration of Independence Day."[49]

As we noted in chapter four, there has been continuing deemphasis of the holiday's public, political dimension, reflected most dramatically in the elimination of the military parade that was once the central event of the holiday.

The decline of statism and the difficulty or impossibility of infusing Independence Day with traditional religious symbols accounts for the failure of a clear pattern of celebration to emerge. In fact, two articles on Independence Day celebrations in *Ha'Aretz* were headed "Twenty-Eight Years of Search" and "The Symbol Has Not Yet Been Found."[50] And the results are reflected in public response to the day.

> Where has the joy of Independence Day disappeared? Why do the people of Israel express their real joy after the victory of Maccabi Tel Aviv [an Israeli sport team] or winning in the Eurovision [a European song contest that Israel won in 1978 and 1979], but require "organized joy" on Independence Day? . . . It is now a number of years that our Independence Day script has become one of monotonous boredom.[51]

By contrast Memorial Day, immediately preceeding Independence Day, now dedicated to the memory of those who died in all of Israel's wars, is rich in religious associations. Public ceremonies include the reciting of the traditional Jewish prayer for the dead. Indeed, in the national ceremony broadcast by radio, the prayer is chanted by a professional cantor.

Jerusalem Day

A civil holiday of special interest is Jerusalem Day. Unlike the holidays already mentioned, the Knesset has never established Jerusalem Day in public law, although workers are permitted to choose this as one of their optional vacation days.[52] The proposal to celebrate the establishment of Israel's control over East Jerusalem in 1967 was accepted by a government committee, but never adopted by the Knesset for fear of international repercussions. The city of Jerusalem plays the major

role in organizing the various celebrations which are attended
not only by local residents but also by tens of thousands of Jews
who come to Jerusalem from all parts of the country. Jerusalem
Day is celebrated on the twenty-eighth of Iyar, which generally
falls in late May. This was the date the old city fell to Israeli
troops during the Six Day War. The mayor of Jerusalem had
proposed that the holiday be fixed on the day the two parts of
the city, the old and new, were united administratively, thereby toning down the triumphalist elements of the celebration
and encouraging the Arab residents to participate. But popular
opinion, encouraged by the government, insisted on the
twenty-eighth of Iyar, and preferred to stress a uniquely Jewish
celebration on that day. A municipal committee established for
the purpose of recommending appropriate celebrations for
Jerusalem Day suggested evening ceremonies under five head-
ings. Three of the five suggestions involved prayer at various
locations in the city with participation by army officials, the
heads of the government members of the Knesset, and city
officials.

The Traditional Religious Holidays

Public commemoration of the traditional religious holidays
conforms more closely to the tradition than it has in the past.
These holidays are increasingly interpreted according to their
religious origin rather than in terms of sociological or historical
significance. But they are also invested with national meaning
in a manner consistent with a reinterpretation strategy, although with far less distortion of the religious tradition than
there used to be. For example, the army bulletin, *Informational
Guidelines to the Commander*, which appears just before Passover,
is devoted to the holiday. Its title in 1976 was: "Passover: The
Meaning of Freedom." The publication emphasized the holiday's celebration of national liberation. It downplayed one of
the central motifs of the religious tradition—that it was God
who took the Jews out of Egypt, that the holiday celebrates the
miracles God performed for the Jewish people. Yet the bulletin
also reminded the reader of the significance of the Seder ceremony, the festive ritual meal that inaugurates the holiday,
quoting the late Chief Rabbi Kook about the contemporary
significance of the redemption from Egypt.

The more popular army weekly, *Bamaḥaneh*, appears in magazine format and is intended for the average soldier and general reader. It also devotes material in each issue preceding a holiday, to that holiday. A recent issue preceding Passover contained eight articles, three of which related to the holiday.[53] One recounted the 1920 Arab riots that broke out on Passover. A second analyzed the character of Moses (lonely and isolated) and noted that "the most magnificent treatment of Moses, the most human and superhuman of all, and perhaps the most faithful to the truth, is that of the Torah." The third article treated the changes in the celebration of Passover in the kibbutz, stressing the return to tradition. Of the remaining five articles, one was an interview with the prime minister, one an article on the Israeli Armed Corps, one on the American marines, one on entertainment units in the army, and one entitled "The Jewish Life of Knesset Member Verdiger," dealing with an Agudat Israel Knesset member who also painted pictures of traditional Jewish life. The magazine's cover reproduced an 1849 drawing of Moses and the Egyptians at the Red Sea.

The penetration of traditional religious symbols into the culture of Israeli society and their incorporation into the civil religion is nowhere more pronounced than in the *kibbutzim*. One observer has said, "If secular Judaism has in Israel one outstanding civilian institution to witness to its character and the nature of its achievement, it is the collective agricultural settlement, the kibbutz."[54] A vast literature testifies to the groping of large numbers of kibbutz members for a more satisfying framework within which to raise and respond to questions of ultimate meaning than the framework provided by the established *weltanschaung* of the kibbutz.[55]

Our concern, however, is not with the personal dimension— the individual's search for meaning and his return to traditional Judaism—but rather the public dimension, the penetration of traditional religious symbols into the public life of the kibbutz. It was in the kibbutz, after all, that the most radical experiments in transvaluation and transformation occurred. But today there is a pronounced trend in the opposite direction.

The author of a book on kibbutz life offers an interesting illustration of this in an account of the celebration of Shavuot at one kibbutz. As we noted, despite its agricultural theme in the

Bible, the Jewish tradition has hallowed Shavuot as the day on which God gave the ten commandments to the Jewish people— symbolic, in turn, of the entire Torah. In rabbinic literature, Shavuot is called the holiday of the giving of the Torah. As late as 1964, however, this kibbutz celebrated Shavuot in the Zionist-socialist mode, as a harvest festival. A colorful parade of carts pulled by donkeys, trucks, and tractors circled a platform erected on the central lawn. Each cart displayed different products of the kibbutz. On the platform a prominent kibbutz functionary received the produce, evaluated it in monetary terms, and donated its value to the Jewish National Fund.

By 1966 the parade was eliminated and the produce was exhibited in cabins erected around the lawn. A picnic meal was served on the lawn. In 1969 and 1970 the exhibit was eliminated, but the picnic was retained and guest artists were invited to perform. Then, in 1971, "the harvest festival became again the traditional holiday of Shavuot. Toward evening the public was invited to listen to *drashot* [a rabbinical speech] on the subject of Shavuot as the holiday of the giving of the Torah."[56] We have already observed that kibbutz haggadot today, while not yet identical with the traditional text, are far closer to it than ever before.[57]

Virtually all kibbutzim publish their own bulletin. Two kibbutzim from each of the three major kibbutz movements were selected and the bulletins appearing prior to the holidays of Passover, Shavuot, and Sukkot were examined. All material dealing with the holidays was classified in accordance with whether it expressed a conception of the holiday as primarily agricultural, national, or religious in nature. Bulletins were selected for ten different years between 1948 and 1972. The percentage of religious material increased from zero in 1948 to around 40 percent in 1956, then remained fairly constant until the 1970s, when it jumped to 47 percent in 1971 and 53 percent in 1972.[58]

The phenomenon we have been describing here might portend a return to traditional Judaism. It is certainly related to the failure of either Zionist-socialism or statism to provide a meaningful symbol system.[59] But, first and foremost, it is an effort toward reintegration in the Jewish historical tradition through the utilization of symbols hallowed by the tradition. One kibbutz member observed:

We wanted to create in the Land of Israel a free Jewish nation, a nation whose culture is original, a worker's culture . . . and when we look back over forty years and we ask ourselves, has the kibbutz movement, and the State in general, succeeded in creating a different original culture that could stand against the religious culture based on the tradition and the faith—I think that with some isolated exceptions the answer is no. . . . I think in the present situation there is no alternative but a serious return to the tradition.[60]

Aryeh Ben Gurion, chairman of the interkibbutz committee on holidays, stated, "I am not a religious man, but I have a responsibility for the continuity of the people, and the people has a history."[61]

OTHER EXAMPLES OF THE PENETRATION OF RELIGIOUS SYMBOLS

Civil religion is expressed in myth and ceremony. These are associated in turn with sacred days, such as Tel Ḥai Day or Independence Day, and with sacred places. We have already had occasion to note the importance of Yad Vashem, Masada, and Tel Ḥai, but the most sacred of all places in the Israeli civil religion is the western wall. It is at the western wall that the most significant ceremonies associated with the civil religious calendar take place. It is to the western wall that Jews come to congregate and demonstrate when the most precious values and sentiments of the nation are to be evoked. The elitist army units, once sworn in at Masada, now take their oath of allegiance at the western wall. Demonstrations or fasts on behalf of Soviet Jewry or Syrian Jewry take place there. And it was the photograph of the paratrooper weeping at the western wall that captured the nation's imagination during the Six Day War—a symbol of the revolution that had transpired in the association of the Israeli with his past.

The western wall symbolizes everything that is Jewish-Israeli. It is the last remnant of the temple and hence evokes the national and religious glory of the past. It is also the symbol of the destruction of the temple, of Jewish defeat, and of the subsequent 2,000-year exile with all its humiliation, deprivation, and suffering. The western wall symbolized Zion to the Jews of the Diaspora, symbolized the place to which they

yearned to return and to which their prayers were directed.
The English term for the western wall is, quite appropriately,
the wailing wall. Cries and wails were the sounds the listener
heard from Jews praying at the wall prior to 1948.

Arabs, aware of the wall's significance to the Jews, "took
every opportunity to harass the hapless worshipers, scattering
broken glass through the alleys leading to the wall, dumping
their garbage and sewage against it, fouling it with urine and
feces."[62] Thus, the wall became also a special symbol of the
degradation of the Jew by his enemies. The wall is also associated with contemporary Zionist settlement. It was over
Jewish insistence upon their right to pray at the wall and sound
the shofar on the appropriate ceremonial occasions that Arab
riots against the Jews broke out in 1929. The wall was under
Jordanian control from 1948 to 1967. Under the terms of the
armistice agreement, Jews were to be permitted access to it.
Jordan violated that agreement. Thus, the wall today also
symbolizes the reunification of Jerusalem and the victory of the
Six Day War. The wall, in short, embraces symbolically almost
everything Jewish—historical, national, and religious—gran-
deur, degradation, suffering, yearning, and achievement.
Foreign dignitaries would no doubt be brought to the wall if not
for the fact that most countries, including the U.S., have never
recognized Israel's annexation of East Jerusalem, and hence
contest Israel's sovereignty over the western wall. The central
role of the wall recalls revisionism, but is in marked contrast to
the ambivalent attitude of Zionist-socialism, or the relative
neglect of statism.

Since the western wall is the central shrine in the Israeli civil
religion, it is interesting to note the extent to which it is associated in the minds of Israelis as a traditional religious symbol.
Rules pertaining to the proper conduct at the wall are religious
in character (men and women are separated as they approach
the wall, women are requested to cover their hair in accordance
with the strictest religious injunctions, and so on). The wall is
accepted as a traditional religious shrine, and the activity
deemed most proper at the wall is prayer.

One may argue that this is a result of the greater importance
religious Jews attach to the western wall, or that the rules are
the result of demands by the National Religious Party's representatives in the government, who insist on religious control
over the wall. But the whole population also views the wall as a

TABLE 3
IDENTIFICATION OF THE WESTERN WALL AS PRIMARILY RELIGIOUS OR NATIONAL BY RELIGIOUS SELF-IDENTITY
(IN PERCENTAGES)

Identification	Religious	Traditional	Nonreligious	Total
Primarily religious	66.9	39.7	28.9	38.8
Primarily national	7.4	29.7	49.1	34.7
Both religious and national	25.0	29.2	16.7	23.6
Neither or don't know	0.8	1.3	5.3	2.9
N	272	873	845	1990

traditionally religious shrine. Respondents were asked the following questions: "Is the western wall, in your eyes, primarily a religious site or primarily a national site?"

As might be expected, religious Jews were most likely, and nonreligious Jews least likely, to perceive the wall as a religious site, but the majority viewed it as a religious site. Even among the nonreligious, 29 percent perceived it as primarily religious and an additional 17 percent as both religious and national, together almost equal to the percentage who saw it as a primarily national site.

The Israeli Song Festival

The Israeli Song Festival was conducted annually from 1960 to 1974 in a special format. It constituted the closing event of Independence Day celebrations. New songs, whose selection virtually assured their subsequent popularity, were aired for the first time on radio and television before a live audience. The live audience then chose the three best among the twelve (originally ten) new songs.[63] In the first few years of the festival, the text of a number of songs derived from biblical verses, although there was nothing specifically religious about their content. In subsequent years, with few exceptions, the songs had no religious or even biblical associations. In 1972 and 1973 the text of five of the twelve songs carried religious associations and in 1974 six of the twelve entrees fell in this category.

ISRAELI ARABS

The Israeli civil religion has penetrated into the Arab sector. It has reached the most rural and backward Arab village, as well as the city. The most popular symbols of the religion are absorbed by Arab children in particular, as part of their identification with the society around them. Arabs learn about Jewish history and Jewish customs in their schools. They are surrounded by the symbols of the culture and they tend not to distinguish that which is Israeli and secular from that which is Jewish and religious. Hence, much is absorbed that is religious in nature—for example, eating matzot during Passover, despite the fact that leavened bread is readily available in the Arab village.[64]

Had the Jewish sector developed a totally secular civil religion or incorporated elements of traditional Judaism only at a superficial level, transforming and transvaluing them to serve statist purposes, it is conceivable, although unlikely, that a civil religion shared by Arabs and Jews might have developed. The ease with which Arab children absorbed at least superficial elements of traditional Judaism packaged as part of the national culture suggests the potency of the culture. But developments have gone in quite a different direction.

The Israeli civil religion today is permeated with the symbols of traditional Judaism and the association of Jewishness and Israeliness reminds the Israeli Arab of his minority status. Our study is concerned only with the civil religion and the political integration of the Jewish sector. We have avoided the Arab question because of its complexity, our own lack of familiarity with the details, and the absence of serious studies. This last betrays an avoidance stemming partly, we fear, from an unconscious effort to avoid the terrible dilemma posed by the Arab minority for the very basis of Israeli society. If Arabs are to be truly integrated, if they are to be truly equal, then how will Israel remain a Jewish state? But if Israel is not to be a Jewish state, then what have the Jews been fighting for, what has all their effort been about, what have they died for? And if the Arabs are not integrated, do they not pose a continuing threat to Israel's security?

There are precedents for the existence of minorities who maintain a distinctive national-cultural identity in the midst of a society dominated by some other culture, but, at least in Eastern Europe, North Africa, and the Middle East, which Jews and Arabs know best, the unfortunate precedents involve subjugated minorities, which paid a heavy price for their distinctiveness. Furthermore, the Israeli situation is special in that the minority is identified in national-religious terms with the dominant culture of neighboring countries who, Israelis believe, seek to destroy them and Israel. And it is this state of war or threat of war that reinforces the particularly Jewish elements of Israeli culture.

There are five theoretical options that Israel can adopt, none of which seems very attractive. Israel could: (1) seek to assimilate the Arabs into Jewish society and culture; (2) neutralize the Jewish elements in Israeli society and develop a syncretistic

culture; (3) encourage the development of one or more Arab
subcultures which would receive recognition, legitimacy, and a
measure of autonomy from the Jewish sector in a condition of
balanced pluralism; (4) institutionalize Jewish dominance of the
Arab population; or (5) expel the Arabs, an option no political
leader advocates.[65] Our study is concerned with political culture, not public policy, but the first three options touch our
immediate interest in civil religion and merit some discussion.

Assimilation

In some respects, the educational system in the Arab sector,
before changes were introduced in 1975, reflected the assimilationist position. The major language of instruction was Arabic,
but the stress was on Jewish history and literature, and students
were required to learn Hebrew. But even in education,
attempts at assimilation were halfhearted. Serious efforts to
assimilate the Arab population into Israeli society would have
meant far more attention to, and greater expenditure on, Arab
education, and the creation of integrated Arab and Jewish
schools. Furthermore, it would have required a willingness on
the part of the Jewish sector to absorb Arabs at all levels of the
economic system, to treat them equally for security purposes,
to provide opportunities for Arabs' social integration and to
encourage religious conversion of the Arab economic and educational elite. Few Israelis have ever taken this possibility seriously. Furthermore, since 1973 the emerging Arab national
identity makes such a policy impractical even if the anti-Arab
prejudice of the Jewish sector could be overcome.

Creating a Neutral Society and a Syncretistic Culture

The neutral society is essentially the Canaanite option. Some
radical Israeli secularists, while maintaining their belief in a
Jewish state, would, in fact, so dilute its Jewish content and
meaning that the requisite cultural obstacle to a neutral society
might be removed. The problem, as we have noted, is that this
would also undermine the Israeli identity of a large segment of
the Jewish population. Jewishness, as we have said, is what
Israel is all about to most Jews. Further, it is unlikely that a
truly secular state could survive in a region where all the neigh-

boring states are committed to Arabic, and in many cases to Islamic, national culture. In other words, a neutral or secular Israeli culture would require the Arab minority to sever its sense of identity with its neighbors and its history and would provide no cultural alternative, something even the assimilationist option (in theory) provides. Very few persons will give up something for nothing. A people certainly will not.

The Encouragement of National Minorities—Balanced Pluralism

It is theoretically possible that Israeli Arabs might have developed a number of minority subcultures on the basis of religion (Christian or Muslim), ethnic identity (the Druze considered themselves distinct from the Arabs, for example), or on some other basis or combination of bases. Such minority identities never flourished because Jewish society treated all Arabs the same. This was not official government policy. Such critical factors as the right to serve in the Israeli army distinguished Druze and Bedouin from other minority groups; but most Jews and Jewish culture in general lumped all minority groups together, assuring the emergence of a single Arab identity. Furthermore, Arab identity is increasingly shaped by the relationship between the State of Israel and the Palestinians of the West Bank who have succeeded, at least temporarily, in forging a national identity independent of their religious differences. It is significant that the bloody fighting between Muslims and Christians in Lebanon has not divided Israeli Arabs along religious lines.

The 1975 educational curriculum for the Arab sector, according to the ministry of education and culture, devoted greater attention to Arab history and culture, thereby encouraging the development of an Arab identity. This so-called encouragement simply gives ex post facto recognition to the reality of an Israeli-Arab identity. Since 1967, but especially after the Yom Kippur War, Israeli Arabs have identified themselves more and more as a national minority and have become increasingly vocal in asserting their demands for just treatment, better jobs, and so forth. Significantly, whereas these demands come from the younger, more radical, and presumably secular Arabs, whose barbs are often directed at the conservative Arab establishment, there has been a paradoxical upsurge in religious identification and practice among younger Muslim Arabs since 1973—an upsurge that is best accounted for by the association of Islam with Arab identity.

Israeli encouragement of an Arab national identity, including a measure of Arab autonomy, is fraught with the danger of turning the population into agents of enemy countries, of encouraging them to demand territorial separation from Israel and unification with a neighboring state. This option, therefore, harbors great risks and requires great patience and tolerance toward the inevitable outbreak of radical nationalism and anti-Israel sentiment that would result under even the best of circumstances. It necessitates a detailed understanding of the Arab sector in order to distinguish between security threats and the evolution of an independent Israeli-Arab identity. In the last analysis its success probably depends on factors beyond Israel's control. It hardly seems likely that Israel will consistently pursue such a policy.[66]

SUMMARY

Neither labor Zionism with its confrontational approach, nor statism with its dissolutional approach maintained its dominant position in Israeli political culture. The massive influx of traditionally oriented immigrants was an important factor in the decline of those civil religions whose ties to the religious tradition were relatively tenuous. The weaker the connection to traditional religion the greater the difficulty in sanctifying institutions and patterns of behavior. But the need remained for a symbolic system to legitimate the Jewish state and provide meaning to its Jewish identity. The very need which accounts for the decline of Zionist-socialism and statism also explains the rise of the new civil religion, characterized by the penetration of traditional religious symbols into Israeli culture. The symbols are reinterpreted, albeit less self-consciously than in Zionist-socialism. The reinterpretation strategy points the symbols away from God and toward the Jewish people, the Jewish state, and the particular needs of the state. In one sense, this form of reinterpretation is not especially dramatic. It is found in the older civil religions. Hanukkah and Passover, for example, had already been transvalued. In the case of Shavuot there was even a return to the traditional meaning of the holiday; and the Masada myth was invested with traditional religious associations.

Because the new civil religion was more closely linked to the tradition, it made greater use of its symbols for its own purposes. There was less irony, less playfulness, less explicit manipulation of the tradition. Instead, in the subtle process of reinterpretation, the authority of some contemporary religious leaders was invoked, as we shall see in chapter seven; and some of the newer symbols, such as the Holocaust, were interpreted to serve the immediate needs of the state, as we shall see in chapter six.

Finally, reinterpretation can work in two directions. It involves not only the transvaluation of traditional symbols but also the reformulation of the meaning of contemporary events in terms of traditional symbols. Thus, for example, the traditional concepts of Esau hates Jacob and a nation that dwells alone became explanations of reality and legitimations of Israeli policy.

6 Instruments of Socialization

The civil religion is in some sense a folk religion. It finds its wellsprings in the hearts and minds of a majority of Israelis, and the people expect those public institutions that transmit the culture to transmit the essential tenets of the civil religion. But not all Jews subscribe to the civil religion and not all who do feel very intensely about it. Great efforts are invested in socializing the population to the civil religion—in other words, in structuring the environment in such a way that the population will internalize the civil religion.

To a great extent, the symbols of which we spoke, the rituals, ceremonials, myths, and holy places associated with the civil religion, serve the function of socialization. In this chapter, however, we turn our attention to the neutral instruments of socialization which serve to transmit the civil religion without necessarily partaking of it.

THE MASS MEDIA

Dramatic changes have taken place in newspaper treatment of religion in the last few years. Newspapers in Israel are probably the single most important medium of cultural transmission. A few years ago, *Maariv*, a newspaper with one of the two largest circulations in the country, introduced a regular full-page feature devoted to world Jewry, in addition to its regular news coverage of Diaspora Jews.

Israeli newspapers today are more likely than ever to treat the traditional holidays as religious holidays in their traditional context. On the day before each holiday Israeli papers devote

167

articles to the holiday's significance. All articles appearing in the 1950–1974 Yom Kippur issues of *Maariv* and *Ha'Aretz*, dealing with the holiday, were analyzed.[1] The articles were classified as religious or nonreligious. Religious articles were defined as those which discussed positively Jewish values or Jewish ceremonials associated with Yom Kippur. Nonreligious articles were those which described in value-neutral terms the holiday's historical origins or its psychological basis. Between 1950 and 1958, 60 percent of the articles were religious; from 1959 to 1966, 73 percent were religious; and from 1967 to 1974 the figure was 80 percent.

Reference to traditional religious symbols has also increased sharply. Words bearing religious connotations were counted in articles about Israel or Judaism that appeared in *Davar* (the paper most closely following government opinion in these years) and *Maariv* during two-month periods in 1967 (preceding the war), 1968, 1972, and 1974.[2] Examples of words bearing religious connotations are holy, God, Messiah, shofar, land of the fathers, promised land, yeshiva, belief, Jewish destiny, eternity, Land of Israel, or religious experience. The number of such words increased in both papers from year to year. In 1967 the total was 61; in 1968, 100; in 1972, 131; and in 1974, 356.

The Yom Kipper War marked a sharp increase in the culture's penetration by traditional religious symbols. Newspaper coverage of the Yom Kippur War, in sharp contrast to coverage of the Six Day War, stressed religion and the role of the religious soldier. During the Six Day War the photograph that had captured the public's imagination was of a paratrooper in tears at the western wall. It symbolized the nonreligious Israeli confronting his own historical and religious tradition. The picture that captured the public's imagination in the Yom Kippur War was of a religious soldier reciting his prayers beside a tank. The manner in which the press trumpeted information about the participation of religious soldiers during the Yom Kippur War was unlike anything found in the press during Israel's previous conflicts. Interviewing newspaper editors concerning this phenomenon, one student found there had been no calculated effort to stress the role of religious soldiers—they had simply caught the imagination of both journalists and the public.[3] We suggest that the religious soldier caught the country's imagination not only because his courage made him an admirable

fighting man but also because his religious belief helped legitimate the justice of Israel's position—gave the war a holy purpose, so to speak. In other words, one outcome of the legitimacy
crisis was an increasing reliance on religion as a legitimating
factor. Religion filled the vacuum created by the decline of
other legitimating symbols.

Traditional Judaism and Diaspora Jewry also play a far more
prominent role than they once did on radio and television. A
certain number of program hours are devoted to religious programming and are geared primarily to a religious audience. In
the last few years these programs have become somewhat less
parochial. There is more effort to direct them toward a nonreligious audience. Of greater interest is the impression one has of
the growing presence of religious or specifically Jewish personalities and topics on programs of general interest geared to the
average Israeli.

Educational television programs directed to all school children today devote considerable time to religious motifs. Although there is a tendency to provide these motifs with a
nationalist interpretation, their traditionalist-religious basis is
not denied.

For example, a December 23, 1980, television program in a
series called "Basic Concepts of Judaism" was devoted to the
commandment incumbent on Jewish males to don *tallit* (a
prayer shawl) and *tephillin* (two black leather boxes containing
scriptural passages, which are bound on the left hand and head
during morning prayers except on the Sabbath and holidays).
The program opened with a Jew putting on a tallit and tephillin
while the announcer declared: "In the morning a Jew arises
from his sleep to reunite himself with his nation, reunite himself
with his creator." After the blessings recited while donning the
tallit and tephillin were heard, children in the audience were
asked about the significance of the tephillin. The youngsters,
students from nonreligious schools, gave nationalist, as well as
religious, responses. For example, "the tephillin reminds us
that we are Jews, that we are different from all other nations,"
or "that all the Jewish people must be united."

Israeli television has been under attack from right-wing and
religious circles who charge that it is dominated by left-wing
and antireligious elements out of step with popular sentiment.
We believe these charges at least until very recently are substan-

tially correct. In face of the dominance of these elements, the appearance of programs such as the one described above reinforces our sense of the strength and ubiquitousness of the new civil religion.

EDUCATION

In most societies, schools are the primary public institutions for socializing the population to the dominant values. There is widespread agreement in Israel that the schools have failed to instill in the youth either sufficient knowledge of, or necessary commitment to, the Jewish people, the Jewish tradition, and the State of Israel itself. If the schools have indeed failed, it is certainly not for any lack of declarations about the importance of the Jewish people and traditional Judaism as core values in the school program. Elad Peled, when he served as director general of the ministry of education and culture, reportedly said that Israeli schools do not provide the youth with the knowledge and consciousness to buttress their national-historical-religious identity. Peled, who served as a general in the Yom Kippur War, noted that he was impressed by the behavior of religious soldiers during the war and stated that it was necessary "to examine anew the spiritual equipment that the young people receive in the secular schools."[4] In 1974 his office prepared a new program to "increase education and study based on the Jewish tradition."[5] Two years later Aharon Yadlin, minister of education and culture, stated that Israeli education had two major goals—narrowing the educational gap and "transmitting to the young generation the ideals and spiritual tradition that were formulated in . . . the Diaspora and since the creation of the state."[6]

Such declarations are not as old as the state but they are as old as 1957, when the Jewish Consciousness Program was introduced into the school system. If the Jewish Consciousness Program has failed there is no reason to believe that more of the same, as advocated by Peled and Yadlin, will succeed. We argue that the Jewish Consciousness Program is the educational reflection of the new civil religion and that statements such as those of Peled and Yadlin thus suggest that the political elite continues to adhere to the new civil religion. We further maintain that the program's failure is not quite as complete as its critics suggest, but a large degree of failure is built into the program because of inherent contradictions within the civil religion itself.

As we indicated earlier, on August 8, 1953, the Knesset established a unified public education system. The law provided for public secular and public religious education according to the parents' choice. It abolished the older system in which labor, general, and religious schools had existed, each with almost total independence in matters of curriculum. The older system was both a reflection of, and an instrument for, the transmission of the earlier civil religions. The unified school system was expected to reflect and transmit the values of statism. In his statement defending the new law, the minister of education and culture, Ben-Zion Dinur, referred to the trend system as "ideological civil war organized by the state," and stressed that Israel must educate its citizens "to complete and full identification of every individual with the State, with her future, her survival." He observed that "the fundamental problem is the national capacity to become rooted in the Land . . . to implant the Land in the heart; to create in the heart of every single individual a sense of direct identification with the Land."[7]

The 1957 program was based on guidelines agreed to by members of the 1955 government coalition. The guidelines stressed the importance of "rooting youth in the nation's past and in its historical inheritance and increasing their moral attachment to world Jewry."[8] Schools were instructed to intensify studies of the Jewish tradition, Jewish history, and Diaspora Jewry. The intensified study of the Jewish tradition clearly had religious overtones (for example, prayer was studied as prayer rather than as literature; the portion of the Bible studied was the one to be read in the synagogue during the forthcoming week.

Parties of the left criticized this religious orientation, which they charged "comes to fill the vacuum that remains after abolishment of the labor schools." The leftist critics noted, for example, that a 1959 circular of the Ministry of Education and Culture no longer referred to the agricultural components of the Jewish holidays, but stressed only their religious aspects.[9]

Parties of the right generally defended the program. They had no objection to the stress on religious education and religious ideals, but they were disappointed by the absence of comparable stress on nationalist education and ideals.[10]

Zalmane Aranne, minister of education and culture, defended the program, arguing that knowledge of the Jewish tradition was essential "for the national education of the Hebrew nation,"[11] not for the purpose of religious education. According to Aranne, the surge of new immigration, the lack of experienced teachers, the prosaic image of the state, the sacrifices the youth might be called upon to make, and the gap between individual desires and social needs necessitated a "Jewish inoculation."[12]

Of particular significance was Aranne's statement on the goals of the program. He named ten goals.[13] Two referred to the state: "deepening one's civil responsibilities toward the state" and "preparing this generation for pioneering tasks." Two of the goals combined a statist and a Jewish-people orientation and might best be termed Zionistic; they were: "implanting a love for the national tradition" and "the command of integrating new immigrants." The other five goals made no reference to Israel, but oriented the student toward the Jewish people and the Jewish tradition. They included: "stressing the inner light that was the portion of the Jews of the Diaspora," "the cultural tradition," "the spirit of the people," "knowledge and respect for the world of religious Jewry," and "inculcating in the younger generation their supreme responsibility for the preservation of the Jewish people throughout the world." The final goal was "recognition of the mutual and ultimate interdependence of the State of Israel and the Jewish people of the Diaspora."

This last point is particularly important, since, in conjunction with the other goals, it indicates a virtual revolution in Zionist thinking. No longer was Diaspora Jewry perceived as destined for physical and spiritual annihilation, dependent on Israel for its existence and important only as a source of manpower and money. Now there was recognition of Diaspora Jewry as an independent entity with a proud existence toward whom Israelis had an obligation, from whom they could learn, and to whom they could look for various kinds of assistance.

The opposition, as we noted, was especially disturbed by the religious elements of the program. By the end of the debate, however, they were just as upset by the rationale for the program. They observed that the program's defenders seemed to assume that what integrated the nation was traditional religion.[14]

Since 1957, countless circulars and brochures containing suggestions and instructional guides have inundated Israeli schools on all aspects of the Jewish Consciousness Program. Teacher conferences and seminars have stressed its importance. Aranne, in his Knesset speech, emphasized that the program was intended to enrich the regular curriculum rather than change the number of hours devoted to each subject. For example, Bible classes once emphasized the theme of the Jewish people living in their own country in ancient times and teachers associated the biblical narrative with ancient Jewish history and contemporary archeological findings. The Jewish Consciousness Program emphasized the Bible in the perspective of the Jewish tradition, including rabbinical commentary.[15] Furthermore, the number of hours devoted to the most traditional of all Jewish subjects, the Talmud, was increased.[16] In addition to the regular curriculum, school assemblies, outside visits, and holiday celebrations reflect the emphases and goals of the Jewish Consciousness Program.

Yet the Jewish Consciousness Program receives far less attention in school than one might expect from the amount of attention the ministry of education and culture devotes to it. Somewhere between the ministry in Jerusalem and the student in the classroom a breakdown occurs. The ministry continues to stress the need for more and more Jewish programming, in part because they believe in it, and in part because it is a popular demand. But calling for more begs the question of whether or not there is some inherent defect or insolvable dilemma in the program as such. The program inherently, by its very nature, touches on the dilemma of the new civil religion itself, to which we return in the final chapter. However, before we undertake our own critique, we wish to examine—and take our distance from—some of the criticism the program has received from others.

There are those, of course, who find the Jewish and Judaic emphasis objectionable and favor nationalist or statist values.[17] But generally criticism of the Jewish Consciousness Program is directed less at the program itself than it is at Israeli schools. The criticism runs roughly as follows: Youth today lack Jewish-

Zionist values; they do not appreciate the importance of the State of Israel, of the Jewish people's right to the Land of Israel, or of Israel's continuity with the Jewish past; this is the fault of the schools. Since the Jewish Consciousness Program was supposed to impart such understanding, the program has obviously failed. This point of view has such currency among responsible Israelis that it deserves some attention.

First of all, it is not clear that Israeli youth lack Jewish-Zionist values. Our own survey results, those of Simon Herman,[18] Katz and Gurevitch,[19] and studies by the Israeli Institute of Applied Social Research[20] all indicate that the vast majority of Israeli youth accept the dominant values of the civil religion, that is, they believe that Israel should be a Jewish state, they do not doubt the right of the Jewish people to the Land of Israel, and they see the State of Israel as closely connected to Diaspora Jewry and all of Jewish history. The best proof of this is that, on those rare occasions when youth do assert anything suggesting political nonconformity, it throws Israeli society into near hysteria.[21] The legitimacy crisis to which we referred in chapter five exists in intellectual circles, but among the majority of the population it is a problem of the level of commitment, not one of manifest values. In the opinion of most observers we know, Israeli youth are more hawkish and more sympathetic to Begin and his policies than their parents are.

Even if one grants that large numbers of Israeli youth reject the civil religion, as the critics imply—and we do not believe this is the case—it would not follow that the Jewish Consciousness Program had failed. What rejection there is may stem from sources outside the school, and it may be that were it not for the Jewish Consciousness Program, rejection would be even more acute.

Finally, if the schools have failed to carry out the aims of the Jewish Consciousness Program, it may be because of the resistance of teachers to the program. A variety of teachers was interviewed concerning attitudes toward the program and the degree to which it had succeeded.[22] Whereas younger teachers were sympathetic to the program, older teachers, socialized to different values, were antagonistic. Their antagonism may have stemmed, not from a commitment to statism but from antipathy and antagonism toward religion or from a general decline of ideological fervor and a sense that the role of the school is to communicate knowledge rather than to transmit values.

The relative failure of the Jewish Consciousness Program, then, is not a reflection of the failure of the new civil religion, but is associated with the very legitimacy crisis that contributed to its rise in the first place and to the decline of Zionist-socialism and statism. The new civil religion helped to confront the crisis without demanding the same level of commitment and identification from the population insisted upon by its predecessors. The kind of intensive political socialization that characterized the older civil religions is inconsistent with the style of the new civil religion, which is much more open, flexible, tolerant, and pluralistic than its predecessors.

We have suggested that critics of the program have been either too harsh in judging it a failure or mistaken in condemning the program itself rather than those who resisted its implementation. However, these are caveats. Our central argument is that the program can never fully achieve the results its supporters hope for because of the contradictions inherent in the program. An antipathy to the Diaspora Jew who refuses to immigrate to Israel is built into the values of Israeli Zionism; moreover rejection of the religious tradition is a tenet of secular Zionism. Thus adherents of Zionism cannot transmit effective commitments to religion. The Jewish Consciousness Program has sought to solve this contradiction, and its failure is no surprise.

Zionism is the thread that has run through all the civil religions of the yishuv from the prestate period to the present. While there are many variants of Israeli Zionism, common to all is the notion that Israel is the center of Jewish life, that its goal is to ingather the exiles, and that all Jews are morally obligated to settle in Israel. No matter how sympathetic Israelis feel toward Jews outside Israel, no matter how deep their sense of interdependence with the Diaspora, there comes a certain point at which Jews who could immigrate yet refuse to do so call forth the Israelis' disdain. In fact, Zionist ideology is so deeply ingrained in the Israeli mentality that those who are especially sympathetic to Diaspora Jewry are inclined to blame themselves or the conditions of Israeli society for the absence of aliya. They pretend to themselves as much as to others that if Israeli society were more egalitarian, or more moral, or more religious, or less political, or more efficient, Diaspora Jewry would come. They refuse to accept the fact that even though the majority of the world's Jews love Israel, are willing to sacrifice on Israel's behalf, even to jeopardize their status in the Diaspora for Israel's sake, they not only do not want to live in Israel but they do not even feel any moral obligation to do so. To accept that would force those sympathetic to Diaspora Jewry to examine their own doubts about choosing Israel. They would rather attribute the absence of aliya to Israel's faults than to Diaspora Jewry. But the average Israeli knows the truth—perhaps because he feels that had he been born in the United States, Canada, France, or South Africa, he might not have made aliya. This feeling, not quite conscious, is often repressed, and the Zionist slogan of the obligation of aliya is consciously affirmed. This limits, however, the capacity of most Israeli Zionists to identify with Diaspora Jewry.

The second contradiction resides in the effort to develop an emotional attachment, respect, and even love for the religious tradition and religious symbols in a secular context. Religious values are not conceived to be observed and admired but to be experienced and cherished. How can youth possibly develop a reverence for the holidays, for religious texts, for symbols, for religious commands, when neither they nor their teachers nor their parents believe in the ultimate historical referents of the symbols or the substance of the texts or the obligation to obey the commands? The secular context denies the authenticity of the tradition by denying the authenticity of that which lies behind the tradition—whether the Divine origin of the Bible, the Divine will behind the religious command, or the Divine itself. The Jewish Consciousness Program is an effort to teach *about* religion. Such an approach is, so to speak, beside the point. It cannot develop a positive emotional response *to* religion. That schools are instructed to bring the youth into the synagogue; to teach prayer as prayer, not as literature; to teach the Bible as sacred text, not as ancient history moves in the direction needed to transmit religious attachments, but it only goes halfway. The very existence of separate religious schools, contrasting with the secular schools in which the young encounter the Jewish Consciousness Program, highlights the tradition as something outside their own lives. The life-style of the religious youth about which the secular youth studies in the program is not his life-style. The experience of the religious way of life to which the Jewish Consciousness Program exposes him necessarily confirms the *otherness* of the religious tradition to the secular youth. The religious school is not his school, the religious home is not his home, nor is the religious way of life his way of life. In the last analysis the secular youth only learns about how others pray, about how others view the Torah, about how others observe what they believe to be religious commandments. Perhaps in the grade school, prayer, ceremonials, and religious symbols can involve the child existentially, and he may not only learn about but even experience religion. By the time he reaches high school it is less likely. All this is true even when the teacher and family honestly attempt to implement the Jewish Consciousness Program.

The program may be less a failure than our analysis suggests because people do live with contradictions, but it is no wonder that the program has not been the success hoped for by some. We believe more of the same will have little effect on students.

THE ARMY

The Israeli army is a conscript army. Most of its soldiers in peacetime are eighteen- to twenty-one-year-old citizens undergoing compulsory military service. It is to them that the army's educational program is primarily directed. The program is heavily laden with efforts to socialize the recruits to the Israeli civil religion.

In the previous chapter we noted the importance that army officials ascribe to the Jewish religious tradition in preparing better soldiers. In discussions with army educational officers we were told that soldiers must develop better understanding of, and stronger commitment to, the Jewish tradition and the Jewish people—because this is, after all, what Israel is all about, and only with such understanding and commitment will a soldier do his best. We do not suggest that every officer is committed to these values, but this outlook informs the policies administered by top military leaders, educational officers, and field commanders. Significantly, this suggests that army leaders, who are necessarily concerned with motivation, do not believe statist values provide adequate motivation. It suggests that they have internalized the new civil religion.

The values of the civil religion are transmitted by various means: speeches by top officers, commanders' discussions with their men, lectures with outside speakers, special army chaplaincy campaigns, and training programs. Let us look at a few of these in greater detail.

All commanders receive the bulletin, *Informational Guidelines to the Commander*; all are urged to discuss bulletin topics with their men. The publication itself reflects the new civil religion. An example is the issue devoted to Holocaust Memorial Day,[23] which seeks to evoke a sense of Jewish peoplehood, respect for the religious tradition, and loyalty to the state in its treatment of this most somber day of the civil religious calendar.

The commander is told that in the course of his discussion with his men on the Holocaust it is appropriate to stress three points.

1. The Zionist solution establishing the State of Israel was intended to provide an answer to the problem of the existence of the Jewish people, in view of the fact that all other solutions had failed. The Holocaust proved, in all its horror, that in the twentieth century, the survival of Jews is not assured as long as they are not masters of their fate and as long as they do not have the power to defend their survival.

2. A strong State of Israel means a state possessed of military, diplomatic, social, and economic strength, and moral character which can respond properly to every threat from outside and provide assistance to every persecuted Jew wherever he is. The consciousness of the Holocaust is one of the central forces which stand behind our constant striving to reach this strength and behind the solidarity and deep tie with Diaspora Jewry.

3. The bravery of the Jewish people in the Holocaust cannot be examined only through the question: did they fight? The examination contains within it a prior question: what is bravery? This must be explored in light of the conditions under which Jews lived in World War II. Despite these conditions we are witness to Jewish rebellion and revolt when it was possible. Together with this, bravery was revealed in unfurling the banner of communal institutions, mutual help, education of the children, maintenance of the customs of Israel and its holidays, and in fostering the values of culture. By standing up under these conditions and refusing to surrender to despair the Jews made possible the continuation of the long chain of the Jewish people even in the inferno of the Holocaust and thereby helped the creation of the State of Israel.

The stance of the Jews in the Holocaust reflects moral and spiritual power which provides the basis for our stance in the continued conflict.

The commander is reminded that "the destruction of the traditional community of Eastern Europe reduced the proportion of religious Jews among the Jewish people. . . ."

Prior to each holiday, special lecturers are frequently invited to speak to the men on the importance and significance of the day. In addition, during the course of the year lecturers from the army educational unit will discuss such topics as Israel and Diaspora Jewry, Israel as a Jewish state, the Jewish tradition, and so on.

Special efforts are invested in the education of future officers. During the early 1970s, the officers' training course included lectures on the following topics:[24] What is Judaism? The uniqueness of the Jewish people. The people and the land in a Jewish perspective. War and the army in a Jewish perspective. The meaning of Jewish holidays in contemporary times. What is *Kiddush HaShem*? (Kiddush HaShem is a traditional term for public acts, including martyrdom, committed to sanctify the name of God. Israeli soldiers who die in battle are assumed to have died for Kiddush HaShem.) Is Judaism a religion, a way of life, or a constitution? The identity of the Jewish people.

All holidays were inaugurated with candle lighting as enjoined by religious law, with special meals as is customary throughout the army, and also with reading from the Bible and lectures appropriate to the holiday.

A bloc of time was devoted to strengthening the future officers' emotional commitment to Jerusalem, itself a traditional symbol for all the Land of Israel. Time spent in Jerusalem included meeting with students of Yeshivat Merkaz HaRav, an advanced talmudic academy led by the son of the late Chief Rabbi Abraham Kook. The cadets all visited Yad Vashem, and all were hosted for a Sabbath by families from Gush Etzion.[25]

The Jewish religion is incorporated into army life to a remarkable degree. The army has its own rabbinate, and its chief rabbi holds the rank of general. Religious equipment, such as a prayer book, a Bible, a shawl, and even tephillin,[26] are distributed free upon request.

In a formal sense, army life is conducted in accordance with the demands of religious law as interpreted by the army rabbinate. Admittedly, the laws are often violated in practice, and the rabbinate itself is compliant with the demands of a modern army, but at the same time serious efforts have been made, not only to conduct the army in accordance with Jewish law for the sake of religious soldiers but also to educate nonreligious soldiers, particularly officers, in the values of the religious tradition.

Among the most serious of these efforts has been the army chaplaincy's Awakening Campaign.[27] The forty-day period beginning a month prior to the Jewish New Year and extending to Yom Kippur is a period of repentance in the religious tradition. This is the period of the army's Awakening Campaign. (The term *awakening* in Jewish tradition implies new awareness of God and of the religious commandments.)

The campaign began almost by accident in 1950. In 1959 the chief of staff issued a standing order for all soldiers to participate. The order was issued despite vigorous protest by left-wing parties and a number of senior officers who charged religious coercion. Until the 1959 permanent order, annual permission to conduct the campaign had been required. The purpose of the campaign was described as explaining the principles of the Jewish New Year and Yom Kippur.

The standing order led to a gradual diminution of opposition within the army—an order is an order, after all—and an end to undisguised efforts by officers themselves, especially senior officers, to avoid participation in the campaign. Since the Six Day War there has been a growing conviction in the army that the Awakening Campaign has great value, not only because it increases the soldiers' knowledge of the tradition but also because it leads to a spiritual awareness. We must not exaggerate this phenomenon. Surely, many officers and men still find the campaign dull, distasteful, coercive, and a waste of time.

The campaign varies somewhat from unit to unit. It frequently includes soldiers gathering together, blowing the ram's horn, chanting liturgical songs, and listening to speeches delivered by army chaplains. Most army personnel consider these mass gatherings to be of little value. Of greater impact are meetings of small groups in each unit, in which the commander himself opens the discussion and the men hear visiting lecturers in a more intimate context.

Among units stationed on the West Bank the Awakening Campaign stresses the importance of the territories from a religio-historical point of view. Attention is given to the Jewish people's right to the Land of Israel from a religious point of view.

According to one nonreligious army officer, in difficult times the campaign provides important encouragement to soldiers and officers which both accept willingly. It is not enough, he says, for one to feel he is an Israeli soldier; he must feel he is a soldier of the Jewish people—and this means an awareness of the Jewish religion. The officer notes that the Jewish consciousness introduced and strengthened by the campaign will remain with the soldier all his life, thereby reducing social tensions and conflicts between religious and nonreligious Jews in civilian society.

STATEMENTS BY THE NATION'S LEADERS

The political elite in its public statements reflects the tenets of the civil religion. But statements by the elite also serve as important instruments for transmitting the civil religion. It is not within the purview of this study to consider the interesting question of whether the political elite articulates the civil religion and defers to its symbols because doing so increases its popularity or it does so because of a sense of religion's importance and a desire to inculcate its values. Without making a complete case, we suspect that both motives operate.

In his perceptive volume on Israeli society Amos Elon comments on the recent "revival among secular politicians, socialists, and liberals of a curious quasireligious piety. A kind of sentimental religiosity has seized the former rebels against orthodox religion and talmudic observance. They do not necessarily return to the orthodox fold. . . . Their newly found religiosity is of an atavistic, sentimental, almost mystical character."[28] But more is involved than simple deference or homage on the part of political leaders to traditional Judaism. There is a conscious effort to use the tradition and traditional symbols to buttress the social order; to associate the symbols and the emotional resonance evoked by the religious tradition, Jewish history, and the Jewish people with the state; and to utilize Israelis' most precious associations with the state to reinforce their commitments to the Jewish tradition and the Jewish people. It would be easy to identify such efforts with the political elite that emerged following the Likud triumph in 1977. Israeli President Yizḥak Navon, Prime Minister Menachem Begin, and Army Chief of Staff Raphael Eytan were all associated in personal and public life with the values and symbols of Israeli civil religion. But, as we shall see, similar statements were made by the predecessors of the Begin government—a phenomenon of greater significance, since nothing in the private lives or backgrounds of these figures would lead one to expect such commitment.

According to former President Ephraim Katzir, "The revelations of bravery and courage of Israeli soldiers in the Yom Kippur War stemmed from the spiritual inspiration of the religious tradition and the moral and eternal values of the Jewish Bible."[29] Former Prime Minister Yizḥak Rabin told a religious audience:

> I belong to those who were forced from an early age to engage more in matters of the sword than matters of the Book, but as the years passed I understand more and more the distinctive role in Jewish survival of study of the sources of the Talmud. . . . It is my impression that the Eternity of Israel has come from the spirit of two supreme values . . . study of Torah for its own sake . . . and the concept of *talmid hacham* [a master of sacred texts—a concept containing the notion of authority acquired by knowledge associated with ethical behavior].[30]

The former minister of defense, Shimon Peres, the present labor party candidate for prime minister, said in a television interview:

> Every time that Jews from America ask us: What are you doing about your image; why don't you explain yourselves better? and so forth; I ask myself: When did the Jewish people ever have the concept of image? Why, the Jewish image is very simple—every Jew is born in the image of God. What public relations firm can improve on this or deny this to us? . . . I believe that if all the Jews and the Jews living in Israel will not lose their firm belief that we can overcome primarily due to our own efforts, it will be a great thing for the Jewish people. The world—one cannot depend upon it. It is always possible to bring a wild man like Hitler or Idi Amin. . . . During twenty-seven years Israel has not ceased to be the center of the world stage, for better and for worse. I ask myself why. After all, we are a small country from a worldwide point of view. I believe that the reason for this is that we are in the midst of a reliving of Jewish history. This is the Jewish golden age of unique value. With all the pain, with all that happened to us, I think this chapter is the zenith of our history and I estimate it will continue for a long time.[31]

The former chief of staff, Mordechai Gur, said:

> Why is it so important to the Israeli army to extract fully and completely all the spiritual power inherent in the soul of the religious warrior? . . . The fact that for the religious warrior the Jewish people and the Land of Israel are supreme values in this world—this is what prevents any shadow of a doubt with respect to our right to live in this land in accordance with our tradition, in accordance with our moral values without excessive philosophizing and exaggerated and tasteless doubts. The obligation to belong to the Jewish people and this land strengthens the ties between the Israeli army and the Jewish people in the Land of Israel and between all the Jewish world. . . . For the religious soldier this is not only a way of religious command but a holy war. The readiness to fight is first and foremost an expression of the desire to live a full Jewish life. All this provides the religious soldier with much greater readiness to combine the sanctification of God in life with sanctification of God in death.[32]

These and similar statements by the nation's leaders are repeated at various times before various audiences. The civil holidays provide special opportunities for the nation's leaders to reiterate the association between the religious tradition, Jewish history, the Jewish people, and the state. The Holocaust Memorial Day is a particularly appropriate occasion. The major refrain is that Israel today, as before, is an isolated, beleaguered people standing alone against surrounding enemies. But two secondary refrains of no less interest are (1) that not only are Jewish lives at stake but the Jewish tradition is also at stake, and (2) Israel bears a special relationship to world Jewry and victims of the Holocaust. Here are the words of the Israeli president on Holocaust Memorial Day in 1976:

> Our decision is firm that the people ingathered again in its ancient homeland will preciously guard these eternal values for which a third of our people sacrificed their lives. . . . The Nazi devil sought not only to destroy the Jews but Judaism. . . . But the hatred that beat in the heart of that devil has not ceased to this very day and a great part of humanity has not learned the lesson of the Holocaust. Woe unto us if we remain complacent in the face of this reality.[33]

The term *sacrifice* is of special interest here. It implies that the Holocaust victims died purposefully—for the Jewish tradition, no less, according to the rest of the statement.

Closing ceremonies were held the following day at a number
of sites throughout the country. We base our discussion on the
reports of four speeches delivered at four different locations.[34]
The major ceremony was held at the Kibbutz Loḥamei Hage-
taot (the kibbutz of ghetto fighters) where 10,000 people heard
Yisrael Galili, a cabinet minister, say, "From those days we
learned not to dismiss an ideology that negates the existence of
the Jewish people. . . . Peace does not depend upon us, but it
does depend upon us to insure that Auschwitz will not recur,
that the strength of Israel will double, that we will be a continuation of the culture of Israel and be able to defend ourselves."

The chief of staff, in the ceremony at the monument to
Mordechai Anelewitz, leader of the Warsaw Ghetto revolt, said
to an estimated crowd of 7,000: "If you wish to know the source
from which the Israeli army draws its power and strength go to
the holy martyrs of the Holocaust and the heroes of the revolt. . . . The Holocaust . . . is the root and legitimation of our
enterprise."[35]

Zevulun Hammer, presently minister of education and culture, said at ceremonies in Haifa, "The Holocaust is not a
national insanity that happened once and passed, but an ideology that has not passed from the world and even today the
world may condone crimes against us."

Finally, Knesset member Hillel Zeidel said in Rehovot,
"Even the best friends of the Jewish people refrained from
offering significant saving help of any kind to European Jewry
and turned their back on the chimneys of the death camps . . .
therefore all the free world, especially in these days, is required
to show its repentance . . . by providing diplomatic-defensive-
economic aid to Israel."

While our impressions, as well as the evidence in this chapter, suggest that such statements reflect sentiments widely
shared by the Israeli public, these sentiments do not seem
sufficient to mobilize the public in actions that reflect devotion
and commitment to Israel or the Jewish people. One of the basic
problems of the new civil religion is its lack of authority—
political, intellectual, and emotional. Moreover, the new civil
religion has no influential leader who can inspire sacrifice and
dedication to the goals and values ostensibly shared by the
population. The new civil religion has not yet provided any
figure of national status, much less an individual perceived to
possess a radiant spiritual quality.

7 The Responses of Traditional Religious Jews to Israeli Civil Religion

We can distinguish four categories of response by traditional religion to modernization and secularization.[1] These categories are also appropriate in describing religious responses to civil religion.

The first response is rejection of and segregation from secular society and culture. This requires the creation of alternate structures and unique symbols of social distinction which serve to isolate the faithful from the influence of secular culture.

The second response is compartmentalization of religious life. Certain areas remain subject to the authority of traditional religion. Other areas are then defined as religiously irrelevant and, therefore, subject to the influence of secular and modern values and standards of conduct.

The third response is one of expansion and domination: the effort to impose traditional religion's values and practices on modern society, to reinterpret modern culture's values and symbols in the spirit of traditional religion, and to direct contemporary society in accordance with religious standards of conduct.

The final response is adaptation and reform: adjusting the values and practices of traditional religion to modern society by reinterpreting the values and transforming or transvaluing the practices to make them compatible with modern culture.

These responses are mental constructs; ideal types which help us distinguish between a variety of religious groups. They do not exist in pure form. For example, no religious group or thinker, regardless how adaptive or reformist, accepts all the values of secular society. Otherwise the religion would cease to be a religion. It is impossible for people to completely segregate themselves from contemporary society, nor can they reject all its values and practices. Some values and practices are certain to penetrate if only in the guise of technological innovation, which the rejectionists must employ to create their alternative system.

One problem in deciding what religious group falls into what category stems from the multiple dimensions of modernity and secularization. We want to distinguish between secularization as a process reflecting a decline of religious influence over the individual and society on one hand, and, on the other, secularization as a process in which surrogate religions come to fulfill the social functions once fulfilled by traditional religion. We are concerned with the latter type of secularization.

The community of religious Jews in Israel is subdivided structurally and organizationally into two camps, distinguishable from each other by the historical stance they each adopted toward the World Zionist movement. Those who favor affiliation are the Religious-Zionists. Among them, one finds a variety of responses to, and definitions of, Zionism. Among those who oppose affiliation with the world Zionist movement there is consensus as to the meaning of Zionism and unanimous rejection of Zionism as a civil religion. We will call this camp non-Zionist, but our reference, of course, is to religious Jews alone.

NON-ZIONISTS: REJECTION AND SEGREGATION

The majority of the non-Zionists, the Neo-Orthodox being an exception,[2] adopt an attitude of rejection and segregation toward modernity and contemporary society as well as toward Zionism. The non-Zionists are subdivided into many groups. The more moderate ones are identified with Agudat Israel,[3] the more extreme ones with the Edah Haredit.[4] There are differences, sometimes rather sharp ones, about the level of permissible cooperation with the State of Israel (the most extreme refuse to recognize its existence, much less its legitimacy) or about the level of acceptance of any value or aspect of modern society (until a few decades ago the most extreme opposed any formal education for girls, even religious education in their own autonomous schools). But all the non-Zionists reject the civil religion of Israel, not only because its content is objectionable but because its very existence represents an alternative to traditional religion.

Agudat Israel is a political party operating within the framework of the Israeli political system. Its delegates sit in the Knesset, it has played an influential role in some governing coalitions, and a representative once sat in the Cabinet. It has always engaged in the regular processes of political bargaining, whether in support of, or opposition to, government policies. Some of those who founded the organization in 1912 had been active before that in support of Jewish settlements in the Land of Israel. In fact, some had been members of the World Zionist Organization. They left that organization when it became clear to them that Zionism was not only a movement to secure international recognition for Jewish rights in the Land of Israel but an ideology or conception of Judaism in which the central components were territory, national identity, language, and secular culture, rather than traditional religion.

Rabbi Elhanan Bunim Wasserman (1875–1941), an important ideologue of the non-Zionists, for example, labeled Zionism as idolatry. Idolatry, he wrote, characterizes any belief that man's future can be affected, for better or worse, independently of God. Liberalism, democracy, socialism, communism, and all the other isms that "descended on our generation in such plentitude"[5] fall into the category of idolatry. Zionism is a particularly dangerous form of idolatry because it was devised by Jews who rebelled against God. The Zionists' answer to the question of "who will protect us in time of danger" is "we ourselves . . . the leaders, our 'national' youth, the heroes who have brought about a state of war between the Hebrew nation and the kingdom of God."[6]

Rabbi Shulem ben Schneersohn, the turn of the century leader of the Lubbavitcher *hasidim*, one of the largest and best known of all *hassidic* groups,[7] described Zionism as the effort to impress upon Jews

> that the whole purpose of the Torah and the commandments is merely to strengthen collective feeling. This theory can easily be adopted by the young people who regard themselves as instruments prepared for the fulfillment of the Zionist ideal. They naturally regard themselves as completely liberated from Torah and the commandments; for now, they think, nationalism has replaced religion, and is the best means for the preservation of society.[8]

Moshe Blau (1885 – 1946), political leader of Agudat Israel in the yishuv period, argued that in the Land of Israel, unlike the Diaspora, the distinction between religious and secular Jews and the necessity to wage war against the latter is not clear to everyone. This is a consequence of the Zionists' refusal to admit that their acts constitute a rebellion against Judaism.

> They desecrate the Sabbath . . . and still insist on their monopoly over Judaism . . . still declare themselves as perfectly proper Jews. Utilizing the idea of nationalism, a new concept in Judaism (heretofore defined by religion and Torah), they managed to capture Judaism for . . . their rule of rebellion against Torah and the commandments . . . [They] erased the differences between a Jew who observed Torah and a Jew who abandoned Torah, and . . . created conflict around the definition of the Jewish people.[9]

The categorization of Zionism as idolatry, an effort to replace traditional religion with *avoda zara* (the worship of strange gods), influences non-Zionist attitudes toward religious Zionism. The very term "national-religious" according to Elhanan Wasserman, proves that "the title religious is not sufficient . . . The name itself constitutes heresy against one of the principles of the faith. It is written: 'God's Torah is perfect' . . . We were warned, 'don't add, for whoever adds detracts.' If the nationalist idea is idolatry, the nationalist religious idea is partnership with idolatry."[10]

This is reminiscent of revisionist "monism," albeit a more radical version. According to the non-Zionists, even activity to which the Jewish tradition ascribes a positive value such as settling the Land of Israel and developing its resources is to be condemned when undertaken by secularists. In this conception, which stands diametrically opposed to that of the expansionists which we discuss below, the religious commandment is only fulfilled by conscious acceptance of its Divine origin. Activity has no merit if the person acting does not recognize the source that commands his behavior. Unlike the truly pious whose "love of God leads them to love of Zion" the agitation of Zionist leaders "in favor of Zion is not attributable to any religious feeling stirred in their souls."[11] The religious Zionists are really not much better since they distinguish between their religious commitment and their Zionism.

Anyone who limits the love and worship of God to one set of obligations and thinks that in addition he must "perform righteously . . . and love the Land of Israel and our language, Hebrew or Yiddish, and even adds an element of sanctity to love of the people, the land, and the language . . . " has turned even the most important religious injunction into idolatry.[12]

As we shall see, the non-Zionist charge was true of some but not all religious Zionists.

RELIGIOUS ZIONISM AND THE CIVIL RELIGION

Mizrachi, the religious Zionist organization, constituted itself as a separate party within the World Zionist Organization in 1902. From this one can assume that its followers, even those who rejected Zionism as a civil religion, were more moderate and less condemnatory than the non-Zionists. Furthermore the vast majority of religious Zionists do not reject modern culture and values as a matter of principle. This reduces the perceived social distance between them and Israeli secularists. In other words, most religious Zionists accept the value of secular education, notions of dress prevalent in contemporary society, basic cultural styles, and many other values not deemed in conflict with Jewish law. In addition, their cooperation with secularists is based on a positive evaluation of such relationships, an expression of the ideal of the unity of Israel and the fulfillment of Jewish obligations to the Jewish people or the Jewish nation. In contrast, even non-Zionists who are prepared to cooperate with secularists do so on the basis of considering the benefit for their own community (although the benefit may take the form of converting the nonreligious Jew, perceived as a benefit to the convert as well).

But even religious Zionists, who believe that traditional Judaism is fully compatible with Zionism, oppose total integration with the secularists. They maintain autonomous political, ideological, and social structures to insulate themselves from secularist influence. This segregation provides a basis upon which religious Zionists of all types are able to cooperate in the creation of independent institutions—political, trade union, athletic, educational, youth, cultural, and economic—as well as their own agricultural settlements. Religious Zionists have even created their own urban housing developments, although they are less rigidly segregated than those of the non-Zionists.

Segregation and Rejection Among Religious Zionists

Rabbi Moshe Avigdor Amiel (1882–1946) served as chief rabbi of Antwerp until his election as chief rabbi of Tel Aviv in 1936. His perception of Zionism was almost identical to that of the non-Zionists. He criticized the Mizrachi, to which he belonged, for underestimating the gulf that separates religious Zionists from secular Zionists. According to Amiel the violations of Jewish law which characterized Zionist enterprises in the Land of Israel were not simply a consequence of the fact that Zionist leaders were nonreligious. They stem, he said, from the basic conception of Zionism, which not only denies the fundamentals of traditional Judaism "but seeks to find substitutes in secular nationalism."[13] He accused Zionism of seeking to establish a new form of Judaism, of bringing an "idol into the holy shrine," of abandoning the core of Judaism and retaining only the shell. Our nationalism, he noted, has universalist implications. The Zionists "forget that the God of Israel is God of the whole world."[14] They retain only the Land of Israel and Hebrew, which they call Zionism, and abandon the rest of Judaism. Secular nationalism, he wrote, is worse than secularism without any nationalist ideology. Borrowing a phrase from the biblical story of the golden calf he likened secular nationalism to "a foreign God to whom they bow and say, 'this is our God O Israel'."[15] Amiel, in fact, rejected all nationalism as immoral since it chooses force instead of righteousness and stands, therefore, in total opposition to the spirit of Judaism.[16]

According to Amiel, religious Zionists who believe Zionism might result in the return of assimilated Jews to the religious tradition are wrong. Experience, he argued, demonstrates that those who adopt a national identity become less and less religious. This is not surprising, since they are embracing idolatry.

Like the non-Zionists, Amiel charged religious Zionism with the sin of according nationalism and its symbols absolute value, thereby admitting idolatry into a partnership with traditional Judaism.[17] Unlike the non-Zionists, he was prepared to cooperate with secular Zionists, within the framework of the World Zionist Organization, to further Jewish settlement and Jewish rights in the Land of Israel. At the same time, he also championed cooperation between Mizrachi and Agudat Israel and, at one point in the 1930s, favored reconsidering participation in the World Zionist Organization.[18]

It is difficult to classify Amiel within the typology we have proposed. As long as he favored remaining within the framework of the World Zionist Organization and cooperating with secular Zionists on a purely pragmatic basis his position was not very different from that of Rabbi Reines, whom we characterize below as a compartmentalizer. To the extent that he advocated withdrawal from the world Zionist movement, he is virtually indistinguishable from a small circle of non-Zionist rejectionists within Agudat Israel grouped around Isaac Breuer (1883–1946). Breuer's group favored aliya, Jewish settlements, and Jewish political rights in the Land of Israel. The one difference with Amiel was that Breuer opposed, not only participation in the World Zionist Organization but any form of cooperation with secular Zionists, a position that seems, in retrospect, utterly impractical.[19]

In 1935 Mizrachi formed a political alliance with the labor Zionist movement in the World Zionist Organization that extended to the institutions of the yishuv and continued after the establishment of the state. One result was weakened support for Amiel's position. Even those circles within religious Zionism which continued to favor cooperation with non-Zionists and opposed "unconditional partnership" with the Zionist organization[20] moderated their condemnation of Zionism. We don't believe this stemmed entirely or even primarily from pragmatic political recognition of the benefits derived from alliance with the labor movement. Amiel's position was really impossible for those who continued to define themselves as religious Zionists because, in the last analysis, the conception of Zionism as idolatry—the classic abomination, the worst of all biblical sins—is inconsistent with any form of cooperation with Zionism, let alone membership in the World Zionist Organization.

Compartmentalization among Religious Zionists:
The Pragmatic Approach

Rabbi Isaac Jacob Reines (1839–1915), a founder and leader of Mizrachi, opposed the very definition of Zionism as an alternative to traditional religion; that is, he disputed the assertion that territory, political sovereignty, language, and culture were the basic components of Judaism. He favored limiting the

Zionist struggle to political activity and practical efforts at
Jewish settlement of the Land of Israel. Therefore, he objected
to any cultural or educational activity of the World Zionist
Organization. Indeed, Mizrachi was established in 1902 to
oppose such efforts.

Unlike Amiel, however, Reines was far more friendly to the
idea of cooperation with secular Zionists—a difference that
stemmed from Reines's conception of Zionism as primarily a
pragmatic movement dedicated to achieving a secure refuge for
Jews. He did not believe cooperation toward this end did
anything to legitimate Zionism as a civil religion.

Reines was particularly sensitive to the charge that Zionism
sought to substitute the traditional Jewish conception of
redemption with national, secular redemption. The leaders of
Zionism, he said, "proclaim a simple solution that is not
directed toward a general redemption, is totally lacking in
spirituality, is entirely materialistic and political."[21] Zionism,
he emphasized, "is only an effort to improve the material well-
being of the people and add to its respect."[22] Those Zionists
who conceive of it as a Jewish national culture have distorted its
authentic meaning.[23] Religious Zionism, therefore, is a movement which affirms both religion and Zionism, not a merger or
combination or synthesis of Zionism and religion.

The contemporary representative of this compartmentalized
conception of Zionism is the Israeli scientist and philosopher,
Yeshayahu Leibowitz (1903–). (We will return to Leibowitz
below.)[24] Leibowitz's Zionism, he says, is summarized in his
being "fed up with being ruled by Gentiles."[25] It has no connection with religious faith. The concept of national redemption
and the return to the Land of Israel plays a marginal role in the
tradition according to Leibowitz. "The great heroic period of
the Jewish people was in the Diaspora."[26] Zionism is the desire
of Jews for political independence in their own land.[27] It has
nothing to do with the cultural, historical, or spiritual essence of
Judaism. Hence, the State of Israel cannot and ought not
concern itself with the problems of Judaism.

Leibowitz is aware that many religious and secular Jews
ascribe a sanctity to Zionist ideals and to the State of Israel. He
is adamantly opposed to any expression of civil religion. Only
God is holy and only His commands are absolute imperatives.
"Homeland, state, nation . . . are never sacred, that is, they

always must be tested and judged by something higher than themselves."[28]

The sacralization of nation or land or state is not only anti-religious but morally dangerous. Leibowitz accounts for instances of immoral behavior by Israelis toward Arabs as reflections of the pernicious doctrine that the "nation and its welfare, the homeland and its security are sacred."[29] He directs special criticism at religious Zionists who are partners in the civil religion of secular nationalism. "To the patriotic religious of our day the worship of God is not expressed in Torah and commandments but in service to the nation, the land, and the homeland—the religious Jew in this respect is no different from the secular patriot."[30] Unlike Reines, who perceived the cooperation between secularist and religious Jews as leading to a spiritual relationship and the return of the secularists to religion, Leibowitz does not believe there is a real basis for cooperation, since the civil religion, a distorted and counterfeit religion, will ultimately cause a split between truly religious Jews and the secularists.

The differences between Reines and Leibowitz partly reflect different stages of development of the Zionist movement. Reines's compartmentalized conception of Zionism and religion was already unrealistic by the 1920s as efforts to sacralize Zionism gained ascendency. It became increasingly difficult to represent Zionism as simply a political and materialistic movement. As the yishuv grew, it was impossible to overlook the secularist efforts to construct a civil religion, using conceptions of Judaism different from those of traditional religion.

Compartmentalization, even in Reines's terms and certainly in Leibowitz's, means that religion is simply irrelevant to the Zionist enterprise. Furthermore, given the central role played by Israel in Jewish life throughout the world, the implication of compartmentalization is to neutralize religion as a force in Jewish life. It is difficult for any religious believer to accept that his religion has no implications for the major social and political struggles that engage him. This is particularly true of the religious Jew, since Judaism seeks to encompass and direct one's entire way of life. Leibowitz believes that "God was not revealed in nature or history—he was revealed in the Torah." Hence "one must not attribute sanctity to a political-historical event such as the creation of the State of Israel."[31] His conception of Zionism, therefore, is consistent with his conception of Judaism. But we must add that his conception of Judaism is antithetical to the mainstream of traditional Jewish thought and utterly opposed to the tendencies of most believers to find religious meaning in historical events and natural phenomena. It is not surprising that Leibowitz is popular in secularist circles—he criticizes contemporary religious Jewry and its leadership, and he reduces religion to that which secularists perceive to be of trivial significance. Hardly anyone within the religious world, however, is influenced by his conception of the meaning and purpose of Judaism.

Compartmentalization then is unrealistic and unacceptable to most religious Zionists. Amiel's solution, the practical implications of which were isolation and segregation from the nonreligious and adoption of a rejectionist approach similar to that of Agudat Israel, had no more appeal. Not surprisingly most religious Zionists subscribe, at least in theory, to a synthetic approach that integrates Zionism and religion. This approach has been strengthened by the tendencies we have already noted to legitimate secular Zionism by selective use of traditional sources. But religious Jews who sought to integrate their religious and Zionist conceptions, who accepted Zionism as a movement of redemption and national rebirth containing a spiritual and religious dimension, had to answer the question: how can one ascribe a central role in redemption to a movement composed primarily of nonreligious—in many cases, antireligious—Jews?

The integrationist approach developed in two directions. One was expansion and domination, the other adaptation and reform.

Expansion and Domination: Rav Kook

Expansionism is the tendency to adapt the symbols and values of the civil religion to the categories of traditional Judaism. It is expanding the scope of traditional Jewish symbols to encompass activity and attitudes previously thought of as secular. It is, therefore, also a form of domination and, as we shall see, expansionists tend to think of their religious symbols in these terms. By and large, the expansionists sought to incorporate the general symbols of Zionism rather than the symbols particular to any variety of Zionist civil religion.

Rabbi Abraham Isaac Kook (1865 – 1935), first chief rabbi of Palestine, known as Rav Kook or simply Harav to his students and followers, is the most important figure associated with the expansionist response. His ideology, as we shall see, is directly related to important contemporary movements in the religious Zionist camp. His philosophy reflects an effort to resolve the theological problems raised by secularism in general and Jewish and Zionist secularism in particular.[32]

Whereas most religious thinkers accepted secularism as a fact of life, however unpleasant, Rav Kook defined secularism as a superficial manifestation lacking inner content, meaning, or a firm foundation in existence. But, like every aspect of reality, it contains sparks of holiness which stem from a Divine source and are hidden throughout all creation. Everyone is obliged to attempt to uncover the sparks of light and holiness concealed behind the manifestations of secularism and expand the influence of holiness to all areas of life.

All human beings are partners in this effort but the primary responsibility rests upon the Jewish nation since the expressions of holiness and good stem from and are influenced by the unique qualities of *knesset yisrael*, the hypostasis of Jewish spirituality which is particularly attached to and associated with the Divinity. In accordance with Rav Kook's philosophy of "all encompassing unity" everything that is good and positive from a moral or aesthetic point of view stems from Judaism and Torah even when no association is apparent.

As a consequence, religious Jews dare not segregate themselves from modernity and contemporary society; nor are any manifestations religiously neutral, as the compartmentalizers believe. On the contrary, it is important to identify the positive aspects of modernity and secularism by revealing the associations between these elements and their sacred sources. In Zionism, in particular, according to Rav Kook, there is a large measure of holiness.

Unlike Rabbi Reines who denied the existence of messianic and civil religious aspects in Zionism, Rav Kook represented Zionism as a movement of redemption whose spiritual base is evidence of its foundation in the religious tradition. The expansionists denied the autonomous legitimacy of national symbols, such as state or territory, but they refused to perceive any deep chasm separating them from the advocates of civil religion. On the contrary, the participation of secularists in the Zionist

movement is a sign of coming redemption—the revelation of
the good within the evil, the holiness within the secular. The
secularists take part in this God-inspired, holy enterprise even
if they themselves fail to acknowledge its divine origin.[33]

Rav Kook accorded particular sanctity to those elements of
the tradition which had a more nationalist basis, such as settlement of the Land of Israel. He interpreted, in an especially
radical fashion, aspects of the tradition which supported nationalist claims. For example, he and his followers held that the
Jewish nation (people) possessed absolute sanctity uncondi-
tioned by their behavior—a result of their natural and unchang-
ing qualities.[34]

Jewish national revival, according to Rav Kook, is not only
reflected in their return to the Land but in their experiencing
the full gamut of life and creativity which was neglected during
exile—a return to nature, creativity, the cultivation of values of
heroism and beauty, and the renewal of public and private
vitality. In this respect, Rav Kook's conceptions are very close
to those of Zionist-socialism. He shared, in fact, an attitude
which can only be characterized as "negation of the Diaspora."
The 2000-year Jewish exile, according to Rav Kook, was not
only a period of dispersion and travail but an unfortunate social
and spiritual experience characterized by closedness, divisive-
ness, spiritual weakness, and detachment from nature and
accomplishment.[35]

Unlike the Zionist-socialists or statists, however, negation of
the Diaspora did not extend to a condemnation of Diaspora
Jews. The condition of exile imposed the necessity for Jewish
segregation and exclusive devotion to spiritual matters. But this
is an unnatural state. National revival, therefore, necessarily
entails a revolt against the exile. This revolt, however, has its
negative side. In reaction to the excessive spirituality of the
Diaspora, the rebellious (that is, the secular Zionists) show
signs of exaggerated concern with the territorial or physical
aspects and neglect the spiritual dimension of national existence. The self-segregation which characterized Diaspora life
stemmed from the necessity to preserve and strengthen the
dimension of holiness in the life of the people. Hence, it is not
surprising that the revolt against this isolation and segregation is
characterized by an apparent weakening of the holy dimension
and a strengthening of secularization.[36]

Therefore, one can understand manifestations of heresy in the Zionist enterprise, but they are, nevertheless, harmful. Zionists must appreciate that the merit of their efforts stems from the eternal bond between the Jewish nation and Land of Israel on the one hand, and God and his Torah on the other. Religious Jews must cooperate with secularists in the effort at national redemption. This will help the latter understand the true nature of their motivation and their goals. They will then return to the God of Israel and the Torah. In turn, the secularists will impart certain of their qualities to religious Jews, who now lack these qualities.[37]

Rav Kook saw manifestations of holiness in sports, which strengthen the body, in physical labor, in education, in science and languages, and in the fields of culture, art, aesthetics, and manners.[38] But he attached greatest significance to the nation. The individual is perfected only by his total incorporation into the life of the nation. On the other hand, complete national life is not possible unless the nation possesses its own territory and establishes a system of social and political institutions which will provide full expression to the national spirit.[39]

The renewal of independent statehood, he believed, would permit the sanctification of all aspects of life by directing them in accordance with the Torah. According to Rav Kook, many of the commandments of the Torah are intended to sanctify life within an independent statist framework and their fulfillment is only possible within that context; hence the value and sanctity of a Jewish state which will represent the spirit of Judaism. Speaking of the state he would not live to see established, Rav Kook said:

> That the State is not the greatest happiness for man can be said about a normal state whose merit does not exceed that of a society of mutual responsibility. . . . But this is not true of a state upon whose existence the noblest ideals are inscribed. . . . Such a state is truly the greatest happiness and such a state is our state of Israel . . . whose only wish is that God shall be one and His name one which is truly the greatest happiness.[40]

Expansion and Domination: Rav Zvi Yehuda Kook

After the establishment of Israel many of Rav Kook's followers applied his conceptions to the state and its institutions, the

Israeli army, in particular. The establishment of the state became in their eyes a vivid expression of the beginning of redemption. The leading circle of followers were grouped around the *yeshiva* (academy for advanced Talmudic study; plural, *yeshivot*) Rav Kook had founded, Merkaz Harav. The spiritual leader of this circle was the head of the yeshiva, Rav Kook's only son, Rav Zvi Yehuda Kook (1891–1982).

In a speech delivered before his students in honor of Independence Day (1967), about a month before the outbreak of the Six Day War, Rav Zvi Yehuda termed the establishment and survival of Jewish national sovereignty a religious command and a sign of redemption. His answer to the problem of how sanctity can be attributed to a state and its institutions which appear to be of a secular nature is that holiness is an unconditional attribute of certain objects; such objects can never be deprived of their sanctity.[41]

Israel, according to Rav Zvi Yehuda, is the state the prophets foresaw.

> Our prophets and their successors, our rabbis, said the following about the State: the seed of Abraham, Isaac, and Jacob will return and establish settlements and exercise independent political control. We were not told whether they would be righteous or not righteous. The prophet says: "When I will gather the House of Israel . . . they will dwell in their own land . . . they will dwell there in safety and build homes and plant vineyards" [Ezekiel 28: 25–26]. It speaks of building of homes and planting of vineyards, not the establishment of yeshivot.[42]

Rav Kook, the father, spoke of the effort required to expose and activate the elements of sanctity within the nation and to impose sanctity upon the Zionist enterprise. He believed that as the process of redemption unfolded, more and more Jews would become religiously observant and the light of divine holiness in the Jewish nation would be revealed to all. To the son, on the other hand, the existence of the State and its achievements in the fields of statehood, security, and the economy are manifestations of the revelation of holiness. "The real Israel is the Israel that has been redeemed: the State of Israel and the army of Israel, a nation which is complete; not the exiled Diaspora."[43]

The contrast between Zvi Yehuda Kook's message and his father's reminds us of the differences between statism and the civil religions of the yishuv. In prestate formulations the messianic element was an ideal vision. Like Ben Gurion, Zvi Yehuda Kook's formulation presents the creation of Israel, the War of Independence, and the ingathering of the exiles as the realization of the vision.

Rav Zvi Yehuda gave special emphasis to the religious commandment to conquer all of the Land of Israel in accordance with God's promise to the Jewish forefathers as recorded in the Bible. Prior to the establishment of Israel he objected to compromising any portion of the Land.[44] He refused to sign a manifesto after the Six Day War which included a statement to the effect that all the Land had now been liberated.[45] Therefore, it is no surprise that the IDF assumes special importance for Rav Zvi Yehuda and "everything connected to it, the various types of arms, whether manufactured by us or the Gentiles . . . all is holy."[46]

Israel's victory in the Six Day War and the liberation of Judea and Samaria is another clear sign of redemption. Any withdrawal from these territories would interrupt the process of redemption and would violate religious commandments. Resistance to world pressure to withdraw is a holy obligation and an expression of national pride, a contrast to the condition of humiliation in which Jews lived while in exile. This is another expression of redemption.[47]

While the significance of this element of national pride is shared by the civil religions there is an important difference between their view and Zvi Yehuda Kook's view. They saw national redemption as a process in which the Jewish nation would overcome its isolation and become integrated into the community of nations. Religious Zionism instead tended to emphasize the distinctive status of the Jewish nation which would be retained, albeit in pride and glory, after redemption. According to Rav Kook, the Jewish nation had a mission to assist in the redemption of all humanity, but his universalist thrust is neglected by Rav Zvi Yehuda. The son lays greater emphasis on the great gulf separating Jews and gentiles. The Holocaust demonstrates the iniquity of the gentiles and their enmity to the Jews. One cannot trust the gentiles nor is there any need to consider their opinions. The Jewish nation must act in accordance with its own interests, relying only on its own powers and its trust in God.[48]

The Holocaust uprooted the Jews and Judaism in the most radical and cruel manner from foreign soil and, therefore, it too paved the way to redemption. "This total collapse, the total uprootedness . . . of knesset yisrael from its presence among the Gentiles and in their land. . . . This is the expression of the light of light and rebirth of a holy people."[49]

The Expansionist Response and Gush Emunim

Until the Six Day War, Zvi Yehuda Kook's position was barely known, much less widely influential in religious Zionist circles. A coterie of young disciples did form around him in the early 1960s. Many of these disciples later became politically active. But all the broader public knew about his philosophy or his father's was that it extended religious legitimation to Zionism and the state, affirming as matter of religious principle the importance of cooperation between religious and secular Jews. Both Rav Kook and his son were popular figures in religious Zionist circles, partly because their behavior was considered especially saintly and partly because they told religious Zionists what they wanted to hear.

The influence of Rav Zvi Yehuda's special message and his role as visionary and spiritual leader became most pronounced after the Six Day War when he was embraced by political circles who opposed any Israeli withdrawal from the territories captured in the Six Day War. Rav Zvi Yehuda's influence reached its zenith with the establishment of Gush Emunim, in the wake of the Yom Kippur War.[50] This movement has had an important impact on cultural and political developments within Israel. It is led by some of Rav Zvi Yehuda's most ardent followers and has exposed large segments of the public to his point of view. Even within Gush Emunim, many have not been directly exposed to his teaching—his style is very difficult to follow, particularly for those unaccustomed to a sermonic-kabbalistic mode of expression—but one need not study an ideologue's writings in order to be influenced by his basic ideas. The dominant themes in the literature of Gush Emunim and circles sympathetic to it are those first expressed by Rav Zvi Yehuda. If Gush Emunim is innovative, it is in the effort to realize in practice the notions presented by Zvi Yehuda Kook.

The national awakening within the religious camp, for which Gush Emunim is in a sense the standard bearer, is to a large extent an outcome of the Six Day War and the Yom Kippur War. The wars strengthened strains of messianic expectation, commitment to the notion of Jewish sovereignty over all the Land of Israel, the sense that contemporary events reflect in a very special way the hand of God and the revelation of His intentions, and the belief that the IDF is in a special sense the instrument of God.

The achievements of the Six Day War—victory over the Arab armies, the liberation of Jerusalem and the holy places, the extension of Israeli control over all the West Bank—evoked intense enthusiasm among religious Jews who saw in these events some special revelation of God's intentions, evidence of the fulfillment of messianic promises. Hence, any willingness to withdraw from the territories conquered in the Six Day War was a challenge to the perception of messianic fulfillment and a threat to the continuity of the redemptive process. Chief Rabbi Goren promised that "the hand of the clock will not move backwards again. The process of redemption will continue and will progress. No power on earth can exile us again and steal from us the Land, promised to our fathers."[51] But other factors were also important in changing the self-image, ideology, and conceptions of religious Zionists.

The Six Day War was preceded by a waiting period in which Jews all over the world lived in trepidation for the fate of Israel. This experience evoked a sense of Jewish solidarity on one hand and distinctiveness from the gentile nations on the other. It strengthened deeply rooted tendencies in the Jewish tradition to stress the uniqueness and isolation of the Jewish people. These strains, central to Zvi Yehuda Kook's thought, were especially pronounced in religious circles and reinforced the support of many religious Jews for a militant foreign policy. The Yom Kippur War enhanced these tendencies even further, lending even greater weight to expansionist formulations.

Rabbi Yehuda Amital, founder of one of the major religious Zionist yeshivot, spoke of Israel's war as a biblical phenomenon. "All two thousand years of our exile we didn't know war . . . we knew many terrible troubles . . . in exile there is no war."[52] The Yom Kippur War had a messianic dimension because it was a consequence of the "establishment of the Kingdom of Israel." The war was not only between the State of Israel and the Arab states but a confrontation between the Jewish nation and the nations of the world—in which the anger of the gentiles at the establishment of Jewish sovereignty brought them to "fight for their very existence as gentiles." The war will result in the "search for the meaning of Jewish suffering, an examination of the meaning of these wars and our purpose. And from this will emerge an identification with the Jewish people in the search for Jewish uniqueness and a recognition of the difference between Israel and the nations—this is the first condition to every spiritual ascent."[53]

The wars also strengthened the sense that national solidarity was a sacred value and that religious Jews were obliged to cooperate and participate with secularists in areas of general social and political concern. Here also, the expansionist position seemed vindicated.

But other developments in Israeli society, in addition to the wars, strengthened the influence of expansionism. For example, while most religious Zionists accepted the principle of cooperation with secularists, pragmatic considerations limited such cooperation. Religious Zionists were a numerical minority in Israeli society and self-conscious about their minimal contribution to the leadership and development of Zionism, and to the establishment and maintenance of the state. They felt obliged, therefore, to adopt defensive, segregationist policies to protect themselves from secularism.

The civil religions of the yishuv and early statehood were especially important in this regard. The defensiveness of religious Zionists reflected their response to dominant civil religions which posed as substitutes for traditional religion, supported by large communities of believers committed to their values and symbols and prepared to struggle on their behalf.

The expansionist response as formulated by Rav Kook and his son reflected a readiness to battle secular civil religion by assimilating it into traditional religion. Yet fear of secular influence and civil religion were present even among those who favored expansionism. Rav Kook, despite his radical conceptions, was very cautious in his own relationships with secularists. He never joined the World Zionist Organization or integrated the institutions of the chief rabbinate he headed into the general organizational framework of the yishuv.

In this respect, as in others, Gush Emunim and religious circles close to it demonstrate a readiness to implement the principles of Rav Kook more consistently than he himself was prepared to do. We suggest that this results partly from the declining status of the civil religion and its reduced capacity to command the devotion and commitment from its followers that it once did. At the same time, the rise of the new civil religion and its penetration by religious symbols reduced secularist antagonism toward religious Jews and the religious tradition, a phenomenon particularly marked in the wake of the Six Day War.

These developments strengthened the self-confidence of religious Zionists and their willingness to relax their previous posture of segregation and defensiveness. This relaxation has, in turn, contributed to their readiness, indeed their anxiety, to cooperate with secularist circles and engage their own energies in general social and political issues. These currents were reinforced by the Six Day War which turned the conception of Jewish sovereignty over all the Land into an operational concept. The commitment of so many religious Zionists to this ideology, contrasting with the hesitation and misgiving in most secularist circles, ended their status as political satellites. For the first time in the history of political Zionism, religious Zionists asserted leadership in political and social fields—in their own settlement of the newly captured territories and in their political defense of Israel's foreign policy.

The fact that their stance was presented from a religious perspective permitted the expansionists to assert a claim for leadership within the religious Zionist camp based on their uncompromising struggle for religious principle. This also permitted the Mafdal, the political party of religious Zionism, especially the circles of younger people attracted to expansionism, to free itself from a position of inferiority vis-à-vis Agudat Israel.[54]

Agudat Israel had always represented itself as more principled in religious matters—they characterized the Mafdal as compromisers always accommodating to secularism and conceding on religious matters. This negative image affected even many Mafdal supporters. However, the issue of retaining and settling the West Bank, once it was put forward as a religious issue, permitted its advocates to turn the tables on the religious non-Zionists, most of whom had tended to adopt a rather pragmatic foreign policy stance.

Finally, the self-confidence and ideological solidarity of the expansionists was strengthened by the development of a network of religious Zionist high school yeshivot at which many of the most influential teachers had studied at Merkaz Harav or been otherwise influenced by Rav Zvi Yehuda Kook. Many teenagers from religious Zionist families were exposed to notions of expansionism and messianic conceptions of Zionism even before the Six Day War. The war provided an opportunity to concretize these notions at the same time it reinforced the belief that they were rooted in reality.

Expansionism and the Symbols of Civil Religion

One of the interesting aspects of expansionist incorporation and sacralization of the civil religion is that it returned vitality to some of the symbols and values that had been declining. This was particularly true of Zionist-socialist symbols. Some concepts revitalized by religious Zionism, such as the tie between the Jewish nation and the soil, paradoxically had been first presented by Zionist-socialists in opposition to the values and behavior of traditional religious Jewry.[55]

Gush Emunim spokesmen, for example, utilize the language of Zionist-socialism borrowing such terms as *halutziut*, "sacrifice," or "redemption of the Land." They also evoke myths of defense and settlement such as Tel Hai. Indeed, they emphasize the common denominator between themselves and the *halutzim* of the labor movement. A leader of Gush Emunim compared himself to the militantly antireligious writer Brenner in his deep attachment to the Land of Israel. He coupled such molders of the rabbinic tradition as Rabbi Akiva and the Ramban together with the founders of modern Jewish settlements. "This is all one thing for me. A very very simple feeling!"[56] Another Gush Emunim spokesman noted that in many respects the new settlements were a continuation of the efforts of the second and third aliyot, even though these earlier settlers were not conscious of faith and sanctity.[57]

Gush Emunim and Zionist-socialist adherents share more than common terminology, myths, and values. They share devout dedication and loyalty to their symbols and values. But there are also pronounced differences besides the radical difference in attitude toward traditional religion. Gush Emunim does not accept either the class identity or the universalist thrust of Zionist-socialism (or the attendant incorporation of foreign ideologies into the Zionist symbol system). Furthermore, unlike the Zionist-socialists, Gush Emunim includes in its concept

of settlement urban development; and ḥalutziut, to Gush
Emunim, does not necessarily mean an equal division of property. Indeed, the conceptions it shares with Zionist-socialism
tend to be conceptions that are common to Zionism as a civil
religion in all its manifestation but that found more pronounced
emphasis in Zionist-socialism. As one Gush Emunim partisan
phrased it:

> For much of the Zionist movement socialism was very impor-
> tant—even more important than settling the land. We have
> changed that order. For us, the most important thing is *hitnaḥalut*
> [settlement] and the social form of our settlement is quite second-
> ary. . . . The emphasis of social form over hitnaḥalut is a foreign
> influence and therefore dooms labor Zionism to failure.[58]

At a ceremonial level, one civil religious holiday which the
expansionists have fully incorporated and sacralized in their
own terms is Independence Day. Zvi Yehuda Kook and his
followers attribute great religious significance to Independence
Day. But, significantly, they omitted from Independence Day
a thanksgiving prayer included in the services of other, traditional holidays because the chief rabbinate did not attribute
equal status to Independence Day. Only after Chief Rabbi
Goren, an expansionist himself, sanctioned the prayer in the
wake of the Yom Kippur War did Rav Zvi Yehuda and his
students follow suit. This is consistent with expansionist defense of the autonomy and authority of religious institutions:
"we come from Torah and God to the state and the government, not from the government . . . to Torah."[59] The state and
its institutions are, in the last analysis, perceived as subject to
halakha. Most expansionists today insist on a rigid interpretation of Jewish law in virtually all matters that do not involve the
general security of the state. Even the interests of the national
economy have to give way when they conflict with Jewish
law.[60]

The expansionists' innovation has been not in the introduction of changes in traditional customs and symbols but in
expanding the meaning and relevance of these customs and
symbols. But even this expansion has extended only to circumscribed areas. The expansionists never incorporated realms of
activity or values and concepts that were foreign to the accepted
spirit of traditional Judaism, despite Rav Kook's theoretical
formulations in this regard. The sanctity of the nation of Israel

and the Land of Israel, the commandment to settle the Land, the desire for a return to Zion and national redemption are, after all, legitimate and important symbols in traditional Judaism which lend themselves to an interpretation that includes the values and activities of secular Zionism. Hence, the expansionist response was able to extend religious legitimation to the Zionist enterprise, indeed to represent it as an expression of messianic redemption, while continuing to affirm the comprehensive and absolute validity of the religious tradition.

The Adaptationist or Reformist Response

The final response is characterized by a theoretical readiness, however tentative and cautious in practice, to radically reinterpret traditional symbols and practices in order to adapt them to the values and symbols of Zionist civil religion. Rav Kook legitimated symbols and values expressing nationalist motifs, but these were extensions of symbols and values rooted in the religious tradition. The adaptationist response, associated primarily with the religious kibbutz movement and the broader Torah V'avoda (Movement for Torah and Labor), the religious labor Zionist movement,[61] extended religious legitimacy to the symbols and values of Zionist-socialism, despite the fact that many basic conceptions of Zionist-socialism were foreign and even contrary to those of traditional Judaism. Both the expansionists and the adaptationists favored cooperation with the secularists. Both respected the devotion, idealism, and contributions of secularists, although the adaptationists were more effusive in this regard. Both remained critical of the secularists' refusal to embrace traditional Judaism and their violations of Jewish law. But a major theoretical difference consisted in adaptationist acceptance of secular Zionism as an autonomous ideology. Unlike the expansionists, adaptationists viewed the civil religion as having great merit, as capable of moving its adherents to acts of enormous good. And they did not necessarily attribute these positive qualities to the secularists' inner or unconscious spiritual attachment to traditional Judaism.[62]

The extension of religious symbols to new realms of activity and new conceptions of reality involved the adaptationists in some departure from the religious tradition. The very readiness to legitimate totally new values reflected a weakening of commitment to religious authority. This has been reflected in the tendency, in practice though not in theory, of Torah V'avoda to minimize the importance of rigorous observance of the minutiae of Jewish law.

A good illustration of the subtle but significant differences between the expansionist and adaptationist responses is found in their divergent conceptions of exile and the Diaspora. The expansionists negated the Diaspora because the condition of exile limited the influence of Judaism and reduced the possibilities of directing all areas of life in accordance with Torah. Torah V'avoda presents the culture and behavior of Diaspora Jewry as morally defective. Reflecting the influence of Zionist-socialism, Torah V'avoda sees the Diaspora as having been characterized by class differences, economic exploitation, and nonproductive labor. National renewal becomes moral renewal—a return to the life of labor and creativity based on principles of equality, righteousness, and social cooperation. Torah V'avoda claims these values were associated with the Bible and Jewish life in the first and second commonwealth periods. An article in a Torah V'avoda journal referred, for example, to "the simplicity and innocence of the original Hebrews and the pure Judaism without the exilic taint and filth."[63]

There is even ambivalence toward the rabbinic tradition in the call for "a return to the original biblical life, built upon righteousness and justice" which, the author notes, the Jews themselves have partly abandoned.[64]

The literature of Torah V'avoda reflects Zionist-socialist influence in its call for the creation of "a new Hebrew man"[65] and the accusation that Mizrachi was exilic in its orientation because it was insufficiently concerned with conquest of the Land.[66]

The Adaptationists' Style

The adaptationists, more than the expansionists, utilized many of the terms of Zionist-socialism extending sanctity to such conceptions as settlement, *halutziut*, and labor. As we noted in chapter two, avoda means labor in contemporary Hebrew and service to God in traditional religious terminology. Hence, the double allusion in the following statement. "The life of avoda . . . is Torah itself, the realization of the spirit of Torah in practice. Avoda is holy avoda, the avoda of Torah."[67]

The blurring of secular and religious terminology is deliberate. It reflects the tendency to merge the values of the two realms. Another example is the decision to permit secular study in the study room of a religious kibbutz where, traditionally, only study of sacred text was deemed appropriate. A more striking example is the transformation of the rabbinic statement, "the world stands on three foundations: Torah, avoda, and acts of mercy," to "Judaism stands on three foundations: religion, nationalism, and social justice."[68] But despite the apparent similarity between adaptationists and Zionist-socialists, for the adaptationists, as for the expansionists, terms such as Torah, messianic redemption, or holiness, applied to physical labor, settling the land, establishing kibbutzim, or defending the state, bore direct transcendent referents.[69]

Symbols and Ceremonials among the Adaptationists

The adaptationists incorporated the symbols and ceremonials of Zionist-socialism as an addition to, rather than as a substitute for, traditional symbols and ceremonies. Despite the term holy rebellion with which Torah V'avoda characterizes its efforts, the adaptations and reforms were almost never in overt conflict with religious law, however permissive they may have been with the spirit of the tradition. Even here, most of the adaptations originated and remained confined in the religious kibbutzim. The religious kibbutzim attracted a more radical element and, by their very nature, produced a more radical response. As a self-contained community based on an innovative way of life, the kibbutz had to create symbols and ceremonials to express, reinforce, and religiously legitimate its singular perception of reality.

Like Zionist-socialist kibbutzim, the religious kibbutzim sought ceremonials that would associate traditional holidays with agriculture and nature. They adapted many of the rituals described in chapter two, confining themselves to those which did not violate religious law. In the words of one kibbutz member,

> Despite our tie to the tradition, we don't find the same emotional satisfaction in the holidays that we might have found abroad. Hence, there is room for innovation and one might say that the innovation is also traditional because we only seek the ancient

sources and try to return them to our lives in order to create once again the strong tie between the nation and nature, between nature and the celebrations of the nation.[70]

In addition, tree planting rituals and dancing were adapted from Zionist-socialism and invested with religious meaning.[71] Virtually alone among the religious Zionist groups, religious kibbutzim also celebrated May Day. Red flags flew, work ceased, and kibbutz members joined in May Day parades of the labor movement. But, traditional religious terminology was not applied to these events.

Beginning in 1950 the religious kibbutz movement devised a more elaborate Independence Day religious service than that proposed by the chief rabbinate.[72] Of special importance was the self-consciousness of the innovators that they were responding to their own perception of religious legitimacy or to the insistence of the religious public rather than to the decisions of rabbis.[73]

Innovation by public rather than rabbinic decision was extended to other matters by religious kibbutzim. This was particularly true of topics in which traditional practices were perceived as contrary to national or social-ethical principles. For example, Jews are prohibited from milking cows on the Sabbath by religious law. Rav Kook suggested that the labor be performed by non-Jews. The religious kibbutzim rejected this proposal as contrary to the principle of national pride and self-labor.[74] But they were unwilling to violate religious law by simply milking the cows themselves in the customary manner. Instead they tried alternative methods of milking. However, these measures won approval from very few rabbis. The introduction of milking machines ultimately resolved the problem to the satisfaction of a more substantial number of rabbis.[75]

Whereas, in practice, there was a reluctance to deviate from accepted halakhic principles, the religious kibbutzim sought to reform the religious tradition to meet their needs and to adapt the tradition by incorporating civil religious symbols. In the process they found that they could not always anchor what they would like to have done in rabbinical authority. They had to seek new sources of religious legitimation, but their own ties to the tradition precluded them from taking the final step that would have led to a break with orthodoxy—declaring that legitimation for religious change, or the power to interpret the tradition authoritatively, resided in the religious public rather than with the rabbis, presumed masters of religious law. Had the religious kibbutzim believed that a large segment of the religious public would have followed their leadership, they might have been encouraged to issue such a declaration. In the last analysis, when faced with the choice, even the radical religious elements within Torah V'avoda chose to maintain their ties to the religious camp rather than break them and enter the ranks of Zionist-socialism or opt for independent religious status.

Yeshayahu Leibowitz is an exception. We categorized him as a compartmentalizer, a radical critic of the civil religion. But in the early years of the state, Leibowitz left the ranks of Torah V'avoda to establish a group, Haoved Hadati (The Religious Worker) within the ranks of the labor movement. He proposed restructuring the halakha in order to apply it to the reality of a sovereign Jewish state.

Leibowitz maintained that the halakha developed in the Diaspora was not suited to the conditions of an independent state. In its present formulation, he argued, the law is directed to the concerns of the individual or of a religious subcommunity for whom state services are performed by foreign rulers. Therefore, he maintained, changes must be introduced so that the state could be directed in accordance with the principles of traditional Judaism. Furthermore, he did not assign this task to the rabbis, but to the religious public "acting in accordance with its understanding of Torah and with the honest intent to preserve it. In other words, the changes are made from the need and necessity to maintain the Torah and not for the convenience of people or the gratification of their personal desires."[76]

Leibowitz suggested, for example, the need to reform the laws of Sabbath observance to permit work by those engaged in providing state services. In fact, such work would be the fulfillment of a religious obligation.[77] He criticized the expansionists who claimed they wanted to extend religious law to include the entire public and the operation of the state without acknowledging that this required the introduction of changes in the law itself.

Leibowitz's call to the religious public went largely unheeded. His party remained a marginal group exercising little influence on the labor movement or the religious public.

Adaptationism as a religious response remained confined to the religious kibbutzim and small circles close to it. Following the establishment of Israel, adaptationist influence diminished even there, reflecting the decline of Zionist-socialism and the subsequent rise in influence of the expansionist response. Expansionist influence is keenly felt today among younger elements within the religious kibbutzim and in the religious Zionist youth movement, B'nei Akiva, which has always been associated with the religious kibbutz movement.[78]

THE RELIGIOUS ZIONIST MASSES
AND CIVIL RELIGION

We have identified four theoretical responses of religious Zionism to Zionist civil religion as expressed in the work of various religious leaders and in the behavior of institutions guided by these responses. We have not discussed the responses of the masses of religious Israelis who identify themselves as religious Zionist, vote for the Mafdal and send their children to religious Zionist schools. While the vast majority of them would reject adaptationist efforts to legitimate halakhic deviation, in practice many of them are adaptationists. They sometimes deviate from both halakha and traditional custom in their effort to accommodate themselves to modernity and to what the modern state and modern society deem appropriate. At the same time, they don't try to justify their actions ideologically or seek to express them symbolically.

This is not surprising. Masses generally are neither behaviorally consistent nor ideologically self-conscious. Hence they don't readily fall into any of our categories of responses. Elements of segregationism may also be found among the masses of religious Zionists, even among those who are in other respects adaptationists. For example, regardless of their acceptance of modernization, of secular education, or of nationalist symbols and values, most religious Zionists object to educating their children with children from nonreligious homes—even if the curriculum is under religious control. Many neither feel at ease with, nor even think it proper to mix socially with, nonreligious Jews. In fact, it is the very inconsistency in the behavior of the masses that leads us to suggest their response is most aptly labeled compartmentalization—though not in the sense we presented it above.

The religious Zionist public has absorbed values and symbols of the civil religion alongside traditional religious values and symbols without really integrating them. Two striking exceptions are Independence Day and Jerusalem Day. Almost all religious Zionists invest their celebration with an aura of sanctity and religious legitimation. In addition to the special synagogue services and prayers, the religious public participates together with the secularists in the civil ceremonies associated with these days. Religious circles also participate in civil-religious ceremonies such as tree planting on the fifteenth of Shevat (Tu B'shvat), which in addition to its religious origins carries Zionist motifs of national regeneration and a return to the Land.

The interpretation of traditional holidays such as Passover and Hanukkah show the influence of Zionist civil religion. For example, themes of national freedom, glorification of physical resistance, and attention to the theme of self-liberation were added to the holidays' traditional themes, despite the fact that these additions conflict with the traditional spirit.[79]

Generally, religious Zionists accept the civil religion and its symbols as long as they don't perceive them to be overtly antireligious. When, as they did in the past, they involve attacks on the religious tradition or violations of religious law, religious Zionists leaders are outspokenly critical, confident of support among the religious Zionist public.

When the agricultural settlement Nahalal celebrated its fiftieth anniversary, *Davar* observed that avoda (labor) for its founders was like avoda (worship) of God. An article in the religious Zionist press replied: "without faith in the God of our Fathers, and the Torah . . . avoda . . . inevitably becomes the cult of the barn and the chicken coop, the tractor and the combine."[80]

During the statist period, the cult of the leader associated with Ben Gurion aroused strong criticism in religious circles, particularly the perceived effort to dress the Prime Minister in the mantle of the messiah.[81] Statism was further accused of seeking to create a nation without ties to the historical people of Israel or to Jewish history,[82] of "converting the Jew of Judaism into the new Israeli of the State of Israel,"[83] and of "placing the state and its army at the center and the Torah in a corner."[84]

The decline of statism and the rise of the new civil religion brought a more positive reception from religious Zionists; some thought it signaled a return to religion. Even more careful observers greeted these changes with satisfaction. This has increased the self-confidence of religious Zionists, something we noted as an important factor in the rising influence of the expansionists. It is also reflected in the support religious leaders offer in the mobilization of the public on behalf of national-social goals. We have noted the foreign policy stance of religious leaders. The most outspoken oppose any Israeli withdrawal from the territories captured in the Six Day War. But this stance is rooted in religious sources and frequently goes beyond that which the political elite would like to hear. It constitutes a form of pressure by the expansionists, in particular, on the political establishment. What we are referring to here are statements by rabbis, for example, urging Israelis in general and synagogue worshipers in particular to fulfill their civic responsibilities in volunteering for the Civil Guard,[85] giving birth to more children (even though birth control pills are religiously permissible),[86] saving money rather than spending it,[87] or simply not becoming depressed by Israel's economic and security problems.[88] These calls are in turn based on religious sources and provide religious legitimation to civic values.

Similar statements were made before 1967 but they are far more common in recent years. They suggest the sense of mutual purpose that the political elite shares with a rather wide spectrum of religious leaders. Both a cause of and effect of this association between Judaism and Israeliness is the fact, noted in chapter five, that high school students who identify themselves as religious score higher on scales measuring the strength of Israeli identity than do nonreligious students.[89]

However, the religious camp, including the expansionists, stands outside the civil religion. The religious Zionists are pleased with contemporary developments, and they have played an important role in shaping the civil religion, especially since the 1977 Likud victory. Certainly one can point to their own nationalist-Zionist reinterpretation of the tradition. But despite political cooperation, adherence to a common set of symbols, and compatible policy orientations, traditionally religious Zionists are divided fundamentally from civil religion's adherents by conflicting sources of authority, ultimate obligations, and appropriate ritual behavior.

8 Summary and Conclusions

We have discussed the varieties of civil religion in Israel in some detail. We begin this final chapter by returning to a question raised in the first chapter. Does every nation-state have a civil religion? If not, where can we expect one to develop? The answer depends on the extent to which the nation-state views itself as a moral community.

Only a few years ago liberal Western thinkers assumed that the nation-state was the natural context for societal life. Today the concept nation-state has come under increasing challenge from several directions. At the heart of these challenges is an assumption that the nation-state no longer constitutes a moral community. By moral community we mean a group of people drawn together by shared conceptions of right and wrong, of good and evil or propriety and impropriety, of the function and goals of their community—that is, by shared conceptions of reality or, in other words, a common religion. Some have challenged the possibility of identifying a moral community, or of determining the public interest (a byproduct of the existence of a moral community). They have argued that the nation-state is undermined by conflicting interest groups based on occupation, class, race, religion, ethnic origin, or ideology who do not share a common vision or sense of participation in a single moral community. Each group, they claim, has a special concern only for its own welfare. No group is willing to sacrifice its own good to assure the good of the other groups. Others have argued that it is not group interest that undermines the nation-state as a moral community but individual interest—the affirmation of self, the concern with self, the belief that it is only in one's private, emotional life that one finds ultimate meaning. The

214

preoccupation with self has become the ascendent theme in Western society. Hence public life has lost its purpose and no longer engages the efforts of serious people.

Some allege this empirically, others affirm it normatively. The latter argue that allegiance or loyalty to a nation-state is evil because moral communities are dangerous. The conception of a moral community leads to authoritarian and totalitarian ideologies. Indeed all totalitarian states view themselves as moral communities entitled to suppress individual freedoms in the name of collective purposes. Others argue that the nation-state is either too broad—it destroys meaningful relations of simpler subcommunities based on family ties, propinquity, common origin, belief—or too narrow—it separates mankind, creating artificial barriers to the emergence of international or supranational structures, which would accommodate a more authentic sense of shared humanity.

Except for a few bolder visionaries, these critics do not propose to abolish the nation-state. But the notion of nation as a moral community has suffered from their attacks. The alternative to the moral state is the welfare or service state—a state that views its primary role as satisfying the demands of its citizens or mediating between the competing demands of citizens or groups of citizens. The concept of a service or welfare state has its roots in ideas of Hobbes, Locke, Hume, and Adam Smith, in the notion that "a good society can result from the actions of citizens motivated by self-interest alone when those actions are organized through the proper mechanisms."[1] It stands in contrast to the moral state whose function is to fulfill some goal or realize some vision beyond the political demands and immediate self-interest of its citizens, and to educate its citizenry to the significance of that goal or vision.

The concepts of welfare state and moral state are obviously ideal types at opposite ends of a continuum. In reality a state can survive neither by completely disregarding the welfare of its citizenry nor by functioning without any sense of purpose. Without both common purpose and attention to individual needs, a state could not mediate conflicts, allocate resources, or determine what welfare or service to provide. But it seems clear that states can be distinguished from one another by how closely they approach one or the other end of the continuum.

Israel's founders conceived it as a moral state. No leader was more explicit or insistent than Ben Gurion in arguing that Israel was created with a purpose beyond the satisfaction of its citizens' needs; but every Israeli political leader shared this conception. Setting aside the question of the authenticity of the leadership's commitment in this regard, it can be cogently argued that Israel could not survive if it were not a moral community.

From its inception, the majority of the yishuv rejected that school of thought which defined the sum total of the Zionist goal as the normalization of Jewish existence. The majority of the yishuv sought to establish a moral Jewish community in the Land of Israel. It was this ideal that attracted Jews from all over the world into Zionist activity.

Since its establishment, Israel's problems of survival, economic and especially military, have remained so acute, and required such sacrifices by its citizens that no simple, utilitarian calculus could have mobilized the energy and commitment necessary. If all that Israel's citizens sought were their personal satisfaction, then they could achieve it better elsewhere. If all that the different occupational or ethnic subgroups sought were their own self-interest, the state would collapse, since divisions at home would render it incapable of withstanding pressures from without. Hence, whether Israel's leaders have a real vision and sense of purpose or not, they must not only act as though they do but they must also involve the populace in that vision and purpose.

Emile Durkheim introduced the conception of moral community and it was he who pointed out that beliefs and rites are what unite the members of the community and give expression to their conceptions; in our terminology, beliefs and rites are the building blocks of the civil religion which integrates the society, legitimates the social order, and mobilizes the population on behalf of social goals. In other words, Israel needs a civil religion. Unlike either economically advanced, wealthy, militarily and politically secure Western societies or insulated, parochial, traditional, resource-poor, nonachievement-oriented societies, Israel cannot be indifferent about its citizens' commitment to the nation's moral purposes.

We have argued that there are two ideal types of societies; one is the moral or visionary state, the other a welfare or service state. The former requires a civil religion, the latter does not. But since neither ideal type exists in reality (all states are ranged along a continuum between the two models), it follows that the closer a state falls to the visionary end the more highly developed its civil religion will be. Likewise, the closer the state falls to the welfare end of the continuum the less highly developed its civil religion will be, or it will have no civil religion. Israel stands closer than most Western nations to the visionary or moral end of the continuum, which is why we expect to find a more elaborated and explicit civil religion there. The question becomes, what is the content of the civil religion? What is the source of its symbols, how does it use these symbols, and to what do they refer?

The various civil religions of both the yishuv and the state attest to the centrality of Judaism and Jewishness. Jewishness is both cause and effect of Israel's civil religion. On the one hand, it provides symbols and referents for the civil religion. On the other hand, Israelis feel the need for a civil religion because they assume that their society is Jewish; in other words, that Israel is a moral community whose essence is defined by a shared Jewishness. Therefore, they require a civil religion to express that sense and to provide symbolic meaning to Jewish history and Jewish continuity as reflected in a Jewish state. The significance of the Jewish component of Israeli civil religion is evident in the comparison of the core values and beliefs of Zionist-socialism and the two civil religions of statehood in table 4.

This chart also reflects the increased importance of Judaism and Jewishness in the new civil religion. The new civil religion affirms the indivisibility of Israeliness, Jewishness, and the religious tradition. This is consistent with the increased penetration and reinterpretation of Jewish symbols. These symbols are no longer transformed or consciously selected but reinterpreted; they now play a much more important role in policy formation, a point to which we will return.

Our discussion of civil religion indicates there are two interrelated but analytically distinguishable features of civil religion: core values on one hand and symbols on the other. We think more needs to be made of this distinction in the general literature on civil religion. We will return to this below.

How does one account for the changes in Israeli civil religion, the decline of one variety and the rise of another? One can point to two basic causes, which in turn relate to the two basic features of civil religion.

TABLE 4
CENTRAL VALUES AND BELIEFS OF ISRAELI CIVIL RELIGIONS

New civil religion (1956–)	Statism (1948–1956)	Zionist-socialism (1919–1945)
1. The survival of Israel is a necessary condition to the continued existence of the Jewish people.	1. Same	1. Same
2. Jewish history has meaning and the creation of Israel, as a peak event in the development of that history, therefore has critical meaning.	2. Same	2. Same
	2a. The State of Israel should serve as an exemplary state and *a light unto the nations*.	2a. The ultimate purpose of Zionism is the creation of a just society for Jews which will serve as an example to the world.
3. The state of Israel is intimately associated with, if not identical to, traditional Jewish conceptions of Zion.	3. No. But it is intimately associated with biblical conceptions of the Jewish people living in their land.	3. The same as statism.
4. Israel must be a Jewish state and there is a relationship between religion and Judaism. Some measure of religious observance, of knowledge about and respect for the Jewish tradition are important attributes of the good Israeli. The state itself should incorporate traditional Jewish symbols.	4. There is no inherent relationship between religion and Judaism. Moral behavior and loyalty to Israel are the essential attributes of the good Israeli.	4. There is no inherent relationship between religion and Judaism. Moral behavior and loyalty to the principles of Zionist-socialism are the essential attributes of the good citizen.

	Column A	Column B	Column C
4a.		Israel is the spiritual heir of the first two commonwealths. The Bible embodies the basic cultural values of Judaism and Israel should conduct itself in accordance with those values.	
5.	Israel's immediate tasks include both the protection of world Jewry and affording conditions for the ingathering of world Jewry. But Israel must also help preserve Jewish identity in the Diaspora.	Tasks include protection and ingathering. Preserving Jewish identity in the Diaspora has less importance.	Similar to statism.
6.	Anti-Semitism is a constant in world history. It finds contemporary expression in hostility toward Israel.	No. Anti-Semitism is the outcome of exile. The state is a solution to the problem of anti-Semitism.	Same as statism except it is Zionism which is the solution to anti-Semitism.
7.	The world respects power and Israel's only real safeguard is its own power. Secondarily, it depends upon world Jewry for help.	Statism emphasized the importance of power even more than the present civil religion but felt less threatened.	Less emphasis on the importance of power than in either of the other two civil religions.
7a.		That which Israel or Israelis do will in the last analysis determine whether Israel succeeds or fails.	Same as statism.
7b.			Class ties and solidarity between Jewish workers in the yishuv and the workers of the world must be developed.
8.	A Jew who takes Judaism seriously must strive for aliya.	Aliya is the necessary condition for survival of the individual Jew.	Same as statism.

TABLE 4 (Continued)
CENTRAL VALUES AND BELIEFS OF ISRAELI CIVIL RELIGIONS

New civil religion (1956–)	Statism (1948–1956)	Zionist-socialism (1919–1945)
9. It is important to develop a consensus of the Jewish people and avoid situations of conflict with the Diaspora.	9. Israel and the Diaspora must unite around the symbol of Israel rather than develop a consensus.	9. Israel and the Diaspora are in a state of tension. Unity can be achieved around the symbols and values of the Jewish working class.
	9a. Negation of the Diaspora, an important value of statism, not only points to the necessity of ingathering but negates Diaspora culture.	9a. Same as statism.
10. Israel wants peace. The core of the Arab-Jewish conflict stems from Arabs unwillingness to accept the Jews' right to their own state in the Land of Israel.	10. Same.	10. Differences of opinion.
11. All Israeli Jews must share the same basic values and symbols and emphasize that which is common to them. However, within such a framework, pluralism of ethnic Jewish cultures is tolerable.	11. Israel's survival requires cultural integration and the centralization of functions by the state. The state and its institutions (especially the IDF) are the proper focus of devotion and loyalty. They symbolize the collective Jewish people. Cultural uniformity is therefore necessary.	11. The Jewish workers must unite in a distinct community which will preserve its particular institution until the entire yishuv will share its values and symbols.

First of all, Israel has undergone radical changes in its demographic composition during its brief history. The immigrants who came both before and after the establishment of the state brought their own particular conceptions of what Israeli society should be like. In some cases the conceptions were clearly articulated in ideological terms but more often they were vague notions more suitable to symbolic than ideological formulation. The contrast between the values and symbols of Zionist-socialism on the one hand and the new civil religion on the other reflect, among other things, the differences between the labor movement which led the yishuv and the immigrants who comprised the dominant population group after the establishment of the state. Most of these later immigrants were Oriental Jews from more traditional Jewish communities in Muslim countries. Of the three dominant civil religions we discussed, statism is least reflective of the values and symbolic conceptions of any large population group. The point must not be overstated. There is no question but that the masses of immigrants were attracted by symbols of statehood, intoxicated by the idea of an independent Jewish state after 2,000 years of exile and a decade of intolerable suffering. This aspect of statism remains a legacy of the new civil religion as well. But on the whole, while Zionist-socialism and the new civil religion represent popular conceptions, statism is the creation of a political elite. Even this must be qualified. Zionist-socialism was an elitist ideology which self-consciously sought a symbol system corresponding to its ideology and values. However, unlike statism, it was developed for a subcommunity which saw itself as pioneering for the Jewish people. Hence in the new civil religion, and even in Zionist-socialism, one can speak of the political elite's role in articulating, refining, and providing frameworks and channels of communication for a civil religion generated by the adherents themselves. Statism, by contrast, was an ideology and symbol system generated by a political elite.

We can restate these distinctions with the help of four models of public (civil) religion, which, according to John Wilson, can be ranged along a continuum of religious representations. The opposite extremes of the continuum are at one end the *social* model, in which the collectivity itself is the sacred object, and at the other end the *theological* model, in which public (civil) religion is identified as a separate realm with a belief or meaning system "independent of the society, its culture and its poli-

tics."[2] Religious Zionism, in a manner of speaking, is a theological model. As far as religious Zionists are concerned, traditional Judaism is the appropriate civil religion for Israel. Their
conception was never dominant and need not detain us. Wilson's social model is close to our understanding of Zionist
socialism. The collectivity, in this case the subcommunity of
labor Zionism, was the sacred object. The Zionist-socialist goal
was to extend its boundaries to include the entire yishuv but the
concern was the needs of the collectivity; culture and institution
were secondary. The kibbutz, as it understood itself, is the best
illustration of the social model of civil religion within the
context of Zionist-socialism. Wilson's two intermediate models
fit the new civil religion on one hand and statism on the other.
Wilson calls one a *cultural* model. Here, the symbolic unity of
society is identified by the rituals or symbols which constitute
"evidence for the generally held values or orientations to the
society."[3] It is not the group itself which is necessarily sacred
but "the object of religion is the culture which may have cosmic
significance attached to it."[4] This characterizes the new civil
religion and explains why we were able to identify its sources in
popular celebrations of holidays and belief in myths.

  Wilson's second intermediate model, the "political" model,
conceives of public religion in terms of a particular political
order "requiring fundamental commitment and deserving final
loyalty."[5] Statism is closest to this model and this explains why,
perforce, our search for expressions of statism led primarily to
statements by the political elite and the analysis of public
ceremonies and myths the elite sought to impose, rather than to
anything generated by the civil society. Following Wilson's
analysis, theoretical purity would have required us to analyze
what cultural or social models of civil religion, if any, coexisted
with statism. This question takes us beyond the boundaries of a
concluding chapter. No political or social model of public
religion coexists with the new civil religion.

  We stressed that one cause for the changes in the civil
religion, the move from Zionist-socialism to the new civil
religion in particular, was the changed composition of the
population. Statism, however, was not rooted in the social
culture but developed as an effort of the political elite to overcome the legacy of conflict among the subcommunities of the
yishuv and to socialize the new immigrants to its perceptions of

Zionism and the needs of a modern state. Statism was an elitist response to changes in the composition of the population. It sought a solution to problems likely to arise from the incompatibility of Zionist-socialism with the new immigrants' conceptions. As we indicated, statism sought to unify Israeli-Jewish society around the state and was intolerant of symbolic diversity. It generated the thinnest of all symbolic systems, perhaps because it was so single-minded in its purpose, or, put another way, because the interplay between values and symbols was so one-sided in statism. In no other civil religion were symbols less important in shaping policy.

The development of Israeli civil religion as we understand it challenges the theory that civil religion is a response to pluralism, which creates problems of integration requiring the elevation of a universalistic legal system to the sacred realm to solve them.[6] Even if we ignore Zionist-socialism because it was only the dominant, not the exclusive, civil religion of the yishuv, the new civil religion is certainly not a response to pluralism. It is a response to the failure of statism to provide a meaningful symbol system. But it is not quite accurate to characterize statism as a response to pluralism either. In some respects statism might be most appropriately characterized as an intermediate civil religion developed during the hiatus between a new population's arrival and its translation of numerical dominance into political and cultural dominance. The civil religions of the yishuv did not suit the new immigrants, even those who came from eastern Europe. But in the 1950s the immigrants, Oriental Jews in particular, lacked significant political influence. The elite determined, on its own, what had to be done with the immigrants in the best interests of the state. Hence, in a manner of speaking, statism simply filled the gap until the new immigrants were in a social, economic, and political position to make their own voices heard.

But the changes in the civil religions are more than a response to different population groups with different values and symbolic associations. They also reflect new political pressures and new sources of support and hostility in the international arena, to which Israel's security problems make it so sensitive. Symbols serve as prisms through which reality is interpreted. There is no question but that symbols shape perceptions. The metaphors of a nation that dwells alone or Esau hates Jacob influence the way in which Israelis see the world. But these symbols are also understood or selected from a reservoir of available symbols because they correspond to political reality. There are limits to the capacity of symbols to be reinterpreted. If they are infinitely elastic then they point to nothing tangible and meaningful. Hence, symbols must be radically transformed or replaced when completely new political conditions suggest new values and new symbolic forms for their transmission.

Israel is faced with hostile neighbors, and their hostility involves more than competition for the same resources and territory. These nations reject Israel's very right to exist. This was not clear in 1948. A more subtle but equally dramatic change is Israel's position in the international arena—and Israel's awareness of this change. In 1948 its leaders believed Israel was a nation like all other nations. True, it had its own cultural tradition, but, after all, every nation has its own cultural tradition. The universalism that characterized statist values and symbols was not syncretism but an assertion that Israel is different in the same way that every other state is different, which also means that in most ways it is the same. Israel was different, statist leaders believed, but not exceptional in most respects. It has become increasingly clear to most Israelis that this view of Israel is mistaken. Israel is judged by different criteria than those by which other nations are judged; even Israel's friends relate differently to Israel than they do to their other friends. And this is true not only of governments but of public opinion as well. (This isn't always evident. Some Israelis believe this is only an Israeli perception, not an objective assessment. Others argue that the unique criteria by which Israel is judged sometimes acts to its advantage. But Israel is disadvantaged often enough, and not just according to its own perceptions, so that even many self-critics admit that statist assumptions of Israeli normalcy are inadequate to explain Israel's situation or guide its policies.) By contrast, the symbols and beliefs of the new civil religion do offer many Israelis an explanation of Israel's predicament.

We have observed that Israeli civil religions rose and declined in response to the changing composition of the population and changes in both the internal and external environments. But there may also be a more general reason for the changes. A recent article on civil religion, which docsn't even mention

Israel, noted that "many civil religious experiments appear to have short life spans, with periods of weakness and ultimate failure, although not necessarily total disappearance. Although we do not wish to rule out as impossible the staying power of civil religions in the modern world, such experiments . . . seem more often sprinters than marathon racers."[7]

Quite apart from the causes particular to each state and its civil religion, there is a problem in sustaining long-term commitments and evoking passion and dedication through the use of symbols that are not rooted in a sacred tradition or in a tradition perceived as sacred. We are alert to the danger in the discussion that follows. We will argue that the reason civil religions decline is their failure to generate passionate long-term commitment and that the reason for this failure is the inadequacy of civil religion as such. But this is more than the obvious tautology it appears to be. Civil religion, we assert, must be analyzed in terms of values and symbols. These are interrelated, but values and experience do exist independently of symbols. Values are not simply explications of symbolic referents. It is values that are primary. Values link the civil religion to the political environment. The symbols only tend to express or reflect the values. The symbols socialize the population to the values. The endemic problem of civil religion is that ideally it begins with a value system that in turn generates an appropriate symbol system. The values and beliefs sacralize the symbols. Thus the symbols retain a sacred character only so long as the values continue to evoke commitment and passion. The decline of civil religion stems from its failure to generate symbols sufficiently sacred to transcend the values themselves. In other words, unlike traditional religious symbols, symbols of civil religion are not reinterpreted to accommodate changing political environments and changing values but simply rejected once they no longer fit the situation. (This isn't always the case, as our discussion in chapter seven shows, but examples of the reinterpretation of civil religious symbols to suit new values are unusual.) By and large, civil religion fails to evoke deep and lasting commitment because its symbols are too closely associated with values and beliefs; they lack independent validity; they are not perceived to be rooted in the very nature of reality, the way religious symbols are. A declining traditional religion may perpetuate symbols empty of meaning. But this hints at the independent power of traditional religious symbols; they can persist as empty shells. The symbols of a declining civil religion are simply discarded.

The search for more lasting symbols, symbols with independent validity, leads consciously or unconsciously to symbols of traditional culture—traditional religion in particular. Such symbols are already sacralized. The tendency to seek traditional symbols is found in Muslim, Buddhist, and Christian countries as well as in Israel. This tendency is either absent or less noticeable in welfare or service type states, which either depend less on civil religion or have none at all. The welfare or service type states are those most heavily influenced by Protestant religion and Western European traditions. Hence they are the last places one ought to look for an understanding of civil religion.

The reliance on traditional religious symbols should not be mistaken, however, for a generalized return to traditional religion. To say that a civil religion has adopted traditional symbols on a wide scale is not the same as saying that the traditional religion is the civil religion of a particular society. In this respect, we register emphatic disagreement with those who argue that this is true of Israel or indeed of any other contemporary society.[8] In chapter one we indicated the reasons why traditional Judaism is not suitable as the civil religion of Israel. Most of the reasons listed there can be generalized to other societies. The basic reason that civil religion must be distinguished from traditional religion—even if there are no secularists who reject the traditional religion, even if there are no dissenting minorities with loyalties to other traditions (or one chooses to ignore such minorities), even if the religion is not transnational and even if traditional religious values and those of the nation-state are compatible—is that without exception in the modern world, political authority can be distinguished from traditionally religious authority.[9] Regardless of how deeply traditional symbols penetrate the political culture, no matter how basic they are to integrating and mobilizing the population and legitimating the social order, traditional religion and civil religion remain distinct unless either civil religious leaders abrogate the right to exclusive interpretation of the meaning of the symbols or there is no distinct, traditionally religious authority.

Even reliance on traditional symbols raises problems for civil religion. They are invested with sacredness, they do legitimate, they do invoke commitment—but not for everyone. Moreover, as indicated in chapter one, traditional religious symbols point to values inconsistent with the needs of a modern state.

A respectable body of Jewish scholarship believes that traditional Judaism, in its period of critical formulation, deemphasized national and political goals, stressing instead a religious message directed to the individual Jew, a message that proved especially appropriate to the needs of a homeless, powerless people.[10] The original Judaic self-conception was one of a nation rooted in its own territory, but conditional upon the people's behavior. And even then memories of origins and experiences outside their own land influenced the Jewish people. Moreover, traditional Judaism never elevated political sovereignty or national unity to the level of a supreme value. The prophetic tradition is characterized by a critical posture toward government. This is most keenly expressed in the notion of the Kingdom of God.[11]

In the postbiblical period Judaism underwent a change. It became the world view of a people without a territory, without power, without the instruments of a nation-state. Judaism always retained memories of past national glory and messianic expectations for its restoration but this too was appropriate to the symbolic-ideological baggage of a people outside its own land.

It might be argued that if, under conditions of exile, the tradition had evolved in one direction, it could, under conditions of a Jewish state, evolve in another direction.[12] Indeed, our discussion of religious Zionism in the last chapter pointed to such a possibility. But this requires reformulation of the religious symbols. We suggested three approaches or strategies in the reformulation of traditional symbols: confrontation, dissolution, and reinterpretation, all of which are found in Israeli civil religion. The problem is that traditional religious leaders are particularly sensitive to any reformulation initiated by others. However, as we observed they are most comfortable with the reformulation characteristic of the new civil religion.

The most conspicuous difference between the new civil religion and its predecessors is the difference in attitude toward secularism (defined as the rejection of traditional religious belief and observance) and traditional religion. To Zionist-socialism and statism, secularism was a positive value and traditional religion was something they tolerated. The new civil religion tolerates secularism (accepts it as a fact) whereas it affirms traditional religion as a positive value (even though this affirmation stops short of recognizing a personal obligation to observe the commandments).

One consequence of the different attitudes toward secularism and tradition is that symbols incompatible with the values or experiences of the society at any particular point in time were rejected or radically transformed by Zionist-socialism and statism. Those traditional symbols adopted were uprooted from their religious context and integrated into a secular culture system. In contrast, the new civil religion adopts the symbols of the tradition because of their centrality within the tradition. Of course, the new civil religion is also attracted to particular symbols because of their association with the value of national survival. Furthermore, the new civil religion is indifferent to the divine origin claimed for the symbols by traditional religion. But on the whole there is an inherent sanctity in the symbols of the new civil religion lacking in those of its predecessors.

THE NEW CIVIL RELIGION:
PROBLEMS AND PROSPECTS

The particular relationship between the new civil religion and the religious tradition has implications for the former's survival. As we noted, the new civil religion relies on symbols already sacralized by the tradition. Their sacralization is reinforced by the fact that they are adopted with a minimum of reformulation. They are adopted more because they are traditional symbols, than because they serve the interests of the civil religion. True, they are reinterpreted, but even the reinterpretation is general and unself-conscious, not the rigorous application of an ideology that finds specific national meaning in every traditional symbol penetrating the national culture. Whereas Zionist-socialism and statism desacralized symbols in the very process of transforming them, the new civil religion legitimates the concept of tradition by implying that the symbols of Israel are the symbols of the tradition. Unlike its predecessors, the strategy of reinterpretation does not legitimate change. It cannot, therefore, be used to undermine the new civil religion as the strategies of confrontation and dissolution undermined the previous civil religions, which utilized them. This augurs well for the prospects of the new civil religion.

At the same time, the new civil religion does not insist upon the observance of the commandments, nor does it affirm the tradition in all its detail. It affirms the notion of public rather than private observance, in two respects—public in the sense that the injunction falls on the state rather than the individual and public in the sense that the state ignores what the individual does in private. Furthermore, the universalist element of traditional religion is absent. There is no concern with man *qua* man and his relationship with God. Whereas Judaism places man's obligations to God at the center of its value system, inferring his obligations to the community from his relationship to God, the new civil religion places the individual's obligations to the nation at its center. The tradition is affirmed as the primary expression of the national culture, not as an independent value-symbol system of transcendent origin. This permits the new civil religion to adopt the symbols without having to rigorously reinterpret them. But it reflects the relatively theoretical weakness of the new civil religion which results in an imprecision, a kind of flabbiness that leaves unresolved questions of the civil religion's ultimate authority. The new civil religion does not evoke the same intensity of commitment that Zionist-socialism or statism did, or that traditional religion does, because it is ambiguous about its source of authority. Indeed it does not even resolve the question of whether primary loyalty belongs to the Jewish people or to the nation-state. The problem may be endemic to the cultural model—as opposed to the social, political or theological models—of civil religion proposed by Wilson, but it remains a problem nonetheless. If the new civil religion's ability to sacralize its symbols suggests greater survival potential on one hand, its lack of success in evoking loyalty and dedication suggests a relative instability on the other.

The second problem of the new civil religion is not peculiar to it but stems from the challenge to the entity on which all civil religions are based in one way or another—the nation and the collectivity of which it forms a part. We began this chapter with a discussion of the way this value has been challenged with growing frequency. National loyalty, national commitments, old-fashioned patriotism all seem to be on the decline in Western society. Nationalism is under attack by those who would replace it—or by those who feel it is being replaced—with either transnational loyalty, emphasis on the self, or subcommunal loyalty.

The substitution of a supranational or international commitment for a national one is relatively unknown in Israel. No one urges this, it attracts no significant group, constitutes no menace to Israeli nationalism. The substitution of obligation to self for obligation to society is another matter. The condition of modern consciousness may have reduced the power of any broad collective ideology to evoke the kind of commitment or transmit the sense of identity it once did.[13] Israelis may adhere to the values of their civil religion, to the idea of the concentration of world Jewry within the borders of Israel, to the maintenance of Jewish attachments and orientations. They may affirm the continuity of Jewish history and tradition expressed in the state of Israel through the observance of public ceremonials and proclamations. But at the same time these values may be internalized at a rather superficial level by many Israelis. Indeed this may account for the apparent inconsistency between opinion polls showing almost unanimous assent to the principles of the civil religion and the lack of commitment to these values sensed by virtually all Israelis. Civil religion may be threatened by a turning inward, by private religion's becoming an alternative meaning system.[14] The phenomenon of a return or conversion of young Jews from secular homes to traditional Judaism is a matter of frequent comment in both religious and secular circles. What is less frequently noted is that the overwhelming majority of such converts embrace non-Zionist rejectionism rather than some version of religious Zionism. In other words, what the secular Jew seeks is a meaning system that has a collective dimension but speaks to his condition as a person and a Jew rather than to his condition as an Israeli. Within the religious Zionist camp religious extremism is on the increase. It takes the form of increased punctiliousness in personal observance coupled with growing indifference to matters of national-collective concern.[15] A flurry of interest in Eastern-oriented religion has also captured some attention in the past few years. While the immediate cause is probably imitation of Western cultural trends, the phenomenon reflects the failure of civil religion to provide an adequate response to questions of ultimate meaning. Finally, there are efforts by some to recapture, in small communes or intimate groups, the original meaning of Zionist-socialism, of communion with nature, of the experience of humanity.[16]

Privatization also means the search for symbols of ultimate meaning in spheres not ordinarily regarded as religious. For example, some observers have noted the increased importance of soccer, the intense personal identification of many Israelis, Oriental Jews in particular, with teams and individual players. One can, it has been said, trace a process among age groups in which the eldest continue to find greatest involvement with traditional religious symbols, the middle-aged with national ones, and the youngest with private ones, sports in general and soccer in particular.

Privatization then is found in Israel. It doesn't compete with nationalism so much as it undermines the nation's claim to primacy of identification and loyalty. Yet this must not be exaggerated. Nationalism in Israel is not an "endangered loyalty." The essence of Israeli civil religion consists in its Jewish component, which in turn reinforces cultural, political, and perceptual differences between Israel and the rest of the world, between Israel and its Arab neighbors, and between Israeli Jews and the Israeli Arab minority. These differences in turn reinforce the Israeli's sense of isolation and his need for collective reassurance. If a Jew chooses to remain in Israel, he perforce chooses to remain part of the nation. One cannot live as a Jew in Israel and substitute private, personal concerns for national ones.

A third development troubling many states has been the undermining of national loyalties by ethnic allegiances. Israel has experienced a growing emphasis on ethnicity and ethnic celebrations. In marked contrast to everything statism stood for, this development legitimates and celebrates the distinctive customs and traditions of a variety of Oriental ethnic groups, generally the most underprivileged groups in Israeli society.[17] The 1981 elections were characterized by ethnic appeals and slurs and the success of an ethnic slate in capturing three seats in the Knesset. There is a pervasive residue of ethnic hostility.[18]

There is no doubt that Oriental Jews are increasingly outspoken in their hostility toward the dominant Ashkenazi establishment (Ashkenazi Jews are those from Europe). Oriental Jews sense that they have been objects of discrimination and humiliation and one even hears the demand for reverse discrimination. But this may also explain why ethnic solidarity has not undermined the Orientals' sense of national identity. The surge of ethnic identification is not an affirmation of primordial ties and the desire to affirm a subcommunal identity but a search for a weapon to strike back at an establishment that is perceived as having closed its doors to Jews of oriental origin. Ethnic loyalties, therefore, do not clash with national ones. On the contrary, opinion surveys indicate that Oriental Jews are more hostile to Arabs, more hawkish in foreign policy, and more sympathetic to Begin and the Likud than are non-Oriental Israeli Jews. The Oriental Jews are particularly hostile to the universalist legacy of Zionist-socialism and statism. Oriental Jews constitute the largest group among the traditionalists (as distinct from strictly religious or secular Jews), and the new civil religion resonates loudly for them. In addition, their relative lack of education may make them more susceptible to symbolic manipulation.

In summary, two of the three tendencies that undermine national loyalties and commitments in the West are also present in Israel but do not constitute quite the same menace. We turn now to an analysis of the problems and criticisms that have been raised with particular regard to Israeli civil religion.

The most cogent criticism of Israeli civil religion from a traditionalist perspective is that made by Baruch Kurzweil, although his own position is by no means typical of religious Jewry. Kurzweil, less concerned with contemporary Israeli culture than with its intellectual antecedents, argues that faith and belief in God and Torah constitute the core of Judaism. Paradoxically, at the historical moment that this faith declined, Jews turned toward their past. Unable to live in accordance with traditional conceptions, with its true essence, the nation searched its past in order to reinterpret the tradition to make its contemporary life meaningful and assure its survival.[19] Kurzweil directed his sharpest criticism at Aḥad Haam (1856–1927), who is really the unacknowledged father of Israeli civil religion. Aḥad Haam, according to Kurzweil, refused to confront the real dichotomy between the contemporary Jewish self-image and the Jewish belief in God and religion which lies at the core of Judaism. Anticipating the civil religion, Aḥad Haam transformed references to God into references to the Jewish people. He used such terms as *sanctification, holy spirit,* and *prophecy*, but he used them to refer to this world. "The God of Aḥad Haam was created by the nation. His prophets are messengers without a sender."[20]

Kurzweil notes that Karl Kraus (1874–1936), the renowned Viennese satirist, stylist, poet, and critic, sensed the imminent danger facing Zionism from its infancy. The danger was that it would avail itself of the spiritual-religious foundations of ancient Judaism as a "decoration for its national-secular purposes."[21]

Zionist-socialism and statism were at least self-conscious about their transformation and transvaluation of traditional symbols. They rejected Diaspora Jewry and a large chunk of Jewish history and culture. Hence, even when they argued that they were reviving the original meaning of Jewish symbols, it was clear they were rejecting its traditional referent. In contrast, the new civil religion protests its affirmation of the entire tradition. As we have seen, however, it too chooses selectively, it too transforms and transvalues. Nowhere is this more evident than in the avoidance of any conception of an active, intervening, judgmental God—in the substitution of self-reliance for reliance on God. The new civil religion, like its predecessors, continues to substitute the people of Israel for God, but it is far less explicit or honest about it. Thus, the Ḥanukkah or Passover myths continue to be recited as paradigms of Jewish bravery, courage, and desire for freedom—not in their traditional formulation.

This criticism, despite its ring of truth, invites as an answer the question: "Who cares?" Almost no one, as Kurzweil sensed in the last years of his tragic life, least of all the religious Zionists who have contributed so much to, and become heroes of sorts in, the new civil religion.

A second criticism pertains to the interrelationship of the civil religion and policy formation. Symbols shape perceptions of reality. Ideally, however, the symbol is rich in layers of meaning and vague enough in its reference to lend itself to various interpretations. This versatility facilitates a productive interchange between symbol and audience or between symbol and policymaker. Symbols ought to point in a general direction while they remain free to shift within the range of that broader compass.[22] It seems to us that many symbols of the new civil religion have been transformed into slogans, not prisms

through which reality is perceived but prisons which constrict
the interpretation of reality within such narrow boundaries that
the interchange between symbol and respondent is entirely
one-sided. In other words, the symbol becomes so unambigu-
ous that one must either adopt it with its specific policy implications or abandon it.

This process is not new. To cite two examples from the past
whose legacies remain, Zionist-socialism's interpretation of Tel
Ḥai included the lesson that one never abandons a settlement;
and Ben Gurion reduced the meaning of Zionism to the imperative of aliya. While neither of these symbols have been absolute
constraints on policymakers, as the Israeli withdrawal from
Sinai and the ongoing relations between Israeli leaders and
Diaspora Zionists demonstrate, they have posed impediments
to rational policymaking.

The deleterious effect of the symbol *cum* slogan on policymaking tends to be indirect. It operates primarily on the mass
public and, as a result of the democratic process, constrains the
policymaker. The negative impact of the mass media can be
seen in its need to reduce reality to simplistic categories readily
comprehended by, and of interest to, the masses. This has led
them to emphasize extremist positions of all types and to facilitate the transformation of symbols into slogans. It seems to us
that this process is especially noticeable in recent years. It also
seems to us that since the Likud came to power, government
leaders have been subjected to the symbols and slogans of the
new civil religion in a direct way. In other words, the intervention of the masses is no longer necessary. Menachem Begin and
many of his chief advisors seem to be prisoners of a one-dimen-
sional interpretation of the symbols of the new civil religion.
They are more personally committed to these symbols than
were their predecessors. If the leader of the Labor party,
Shimon Peres, is guilty of hypocrisy, as some believe, paying
lip service to ideas he doesn't hold, Menachem Begin is charged
with sincerity. He really believes in the slogans he utters. This
helps explain the success of the Likud in the last two elections,
since it is a far more authentic representative of the new civil
religion than is the Labor Party. It also explains the present
weakness of the Mafdal, the party representing religious Zionism. Many of Mafdal's supporters, particularly those who were
traditionalists rather than rigorously observant, abandoned it in
the last elections to vote for the Likud. At the same time,

precisely because the new civil religion in its present format provides so narrow an interpretation, it runs the risk of wearing itself out. The public may tire of what it comes to perceive as the preaching of political leaders. Not only that, but many Israelis see the large-scale concessions to the program of religious parties made during recent years as a result of religious coercion and as a betrayal of classical Zionism. The possibility of a backlash cannot be dismissed, however little evidence there is for it today.

The transformation of symbol into slogan may be a problem endemic to any modern civil religion. Our particular fear for Israel stems from its vulnerability and the relatively greater role civil religion plays in its public life.

This leads us to a third and final criticism of the new civil religion. Not only have its symbols been transformed into slogans but into slogans unsuited to the tasks facing Israel internationally and at home—particularly the task of dealing with its own Arab minority. The new civil religion may nurture chauvinist tendencies and encourage isolationism and intolerance toward non-Jews in general and Arabs in particular. It is true that the most extreme pronouncements come from within the ranks of religious Zionism, the expansionists in particular, and rely on motifs they find rooted within the religious tradition.[23] But there is a difference between expressions of rejection and hostility toward non-Jews which originate under conditions of oppression and persecution, and expressions made under conditions of Jewish sovereignty and dominance.[24] Religious non-Zionists, no less than expansionists, are acutely suspicious of non-Jews. They suspect them of an obsessive desire to destroy Jews and Judaism. But these attitudes are mitigated in practice by a tradition of extreme caution against provoking non-Jewish antagonism and by a strong dosage of political realism. The expansionists combine traditional Jewish conceptions of the hostile non-Jew with a faith in God's active intervention. Many believe this combination leads to an unrealistic politics and to a worldly sense of self-confidence alien to traditional Judaism. These propensities have grown in influence since the rise of the Likud to office.

The Holocaust is of special importance in this regard. We argued in chapter five that the Holocaust symbol could lend itself to many interpretations. We demonstrated in chapter six how the new civil religion gave this symbol a particular meaning. Of all the policy consequences of the symbol, none is more deeply entrenched than the notion that Jews can only rely on their own strength and never on assistance from others. Obviously there will be some merit or truth in a maxim that cautions anyone against excessive reliance upon another. It is clear that even without the Holocaust such a maxim would serve as a guide to policymakers. But we believe that Israel's sense of isolation and distrust of its allies is profoundly influenced by the Holocaust symbol, resulting in behavior that could antagonize allies and become, in the end, a self-fulfilling prophecy.

Those critical of the new civil religion have suggested alternative symbols and myths from within the tradition. Israeli civil religions have relied on myths and symbols that stressed motifs of courage, heroism, and continuing struggle for national honor and freedom. According to a previous generation of secularists the heroes of these myths—the Maccabees, the zealots, the defenders of Masada and Bar Kokhba were heroes neglected by the religious tradition. Paradoxically, some secularists today would evoke alternate myths and heroes identified with moderation and political realism—the very qualities once scorned as exilic and unbecoming a new Jewish people emerging in its own land. The retired general, Yehoshafat Harkabi, a foreign policy dove, has argued for the demythologization of Bar Kokhba and his futile, self-destructive revolt against the Romans.[25] He has proposed two alternate heroes whose political message is the opposite of what the civil religions have preached—Jeremiah, the prophet of peace who advocated surrender to the Babylonians prior to the destruction of the first temple, and Rabban Yohanan ben Zakkai, who opposed the revolt against Rome which led to the destruction of the second temple. Ben Zakkai surrendered to the Romans and reached an agreement that allowed him to establish a center for the study of Torah in Yavne, rather than Jerusalem which was then under Roman siege.

Can one transform the new civil religion with traditional symbols such as the spirit of Yavne? Perhaps it is possible. But there is not much support for such an approach among the secularists who are most critical of the new civil religion. Most of these secularists are somewhat antagonistic to the Jewish tradition in general; they favor a return to the antireligious motifs of the former civil religions rather than a reinterpretation of traditional Judaism in line with their political propensities. Yet, as we have shown, we do not see the potential for an effective symbol system that draws upon nontraditional sources. We are not happy with the new civil religion. It offends our understanding of traditional Judaism, our moral sensibilities, and our sense of the requirements for rational policy formulation. But we are committed to the notion that Israel must have a civil religion and we have no alternative to propose. We fear that any serious decline threatens Israel's survival. We believe superficial adherence of many to the present civil religion helps account for increased emigration, increased crime, a declining work ethic, and other social pathologies. We also believe that the civil religion must rely primarily on traditional religious symbols. This stems from our commitment to Israel as a Jewish state; we believe Judaism is the only source of symbols which can fulfill the functions of a civil religion.

These last lines are written in early August of 1982. Israeli troops have encircled West Beirut. While it appears, as of this moment, that they will not enter that part of the city, the issue has not been resolved. Most Israelis, members of the government in particular, know that the entry of Israeli troops would cost the lives of a good many soldiers and of many more Lebanese civilians. It is abundantly clear that in the process, the communications media, foreign governments—the United States in particular—and public opinion throughout the world would condemn Israel. United States leaders have regularly warned Israel not to enter West Beirut. Nevertheless, many Israelis anticipate an entry.

All we have written about the new civil religion, the centrality of the Holocaust myth, and the core values of Jewish history and Jewish peoplehood is relevant to understanding why Israel is apparently prepared to behave in a manner that not only many of its friends but even some of its own citizens consider irrational. As we noted in this last chapter, the present government of Israel, more than any of its predecessors, acts in accordance with the symbols and representations of Israel's civil religion. These symbols are filters through which even the country's leaders perceive events and evaluate policy. A recent front page quotes Begin in a letter to Ronald Reagan that he feels like one who sends "a courageous army to Berlin to eliminate Hitler in a bunker." He goes on to say, "we are faithful to our oath that anyone who threatens the Jewish state or the Jewish people will be doomed."[26]

It is not our role to evaluate the appropriateness of the symbols but simply to point up their recurrence in the present crises and the particular problems they create for Israeli public relations when events and personalities evoke one set of symbols for Israelis and another for the rest of the world.

The dissent within Israel over the war in Lebanon points to differences in adherence to the civil religion as well. The degree of opposition to the war tends to correlate with the degree of dissent from the civil religion. The central wing of the Labor party that ruled the state when the new civil religion first evolved has dissented from the war with caution and moderation. Labor's position as an opposition party leads it to seek grounds to criticize the ruling party. But beyond this, we suspect that its leaders' reservations about the war and the government's aims, stem from their less than total commitment to the new civil religion. The civil religion's symbols are not nearly as authoritative to Labor as they are to the Likud and the Labor party's reference groups are less parochial or close to home than are those of Likud. The more radical dissenters to the war, those on the Labor left or many academicians and intellectuals tend to be those who are most marginal to the new civil religion and to the Jewish tradition. It occurs to us that given the association between the new civil religion and Israel's current situation, the eventual outcome of the war may have consequences that either deepen national commitment to the civil religion or shake the faith of many in the efficacy and appropriateness of its symbols.

Notes

1: Traditional Religion and Civil Religion

1. Virtually every textbook in the sociology of religion begins by providing a variety of definitions. The interested reader will have no problem locating such material. Two texts which are themselves contributions to the literature are Susan Budd, *Sociologists and Religion* (London: Macmillan, 1973) and Michal Hill, *A Sociology of Religion* (London: Heinemann Educational Books, 1973). A variety of definitions are offered in a number of different essays in Allan W. Eister, ed., *Changing Perspectives in the Scientific Study of Religion* (New York: Wiley, 1974). For a penetrating essay on the subject of defining religion see Peter L. Berger, "Some Second Thoughts on Substantive versus Functional Definitions of Religion," *Journal for the Scientific Study of Religion*, 13 (June 1974), 125–133.

2. The discussion that follows relies in particular upon Peter Berger, *The Sacred Canopy* (Garden City, N.Y.: Doubleday, 1969); Robert N. Bellah, *Beyond Belief* (New York: Harper and Row, 1970); and Clifford Geertz, *The Interpretation of Cultures* (New York: Basic Books, 1973).

3. Berger, *Sacred Canopy*, develops a conception of man and society into which he builds a need for meaning anchored in a sense of the transcendent. We find this conception appealing but, for our purposes, we are satisfied with a more modest assertion that most men have a need for meaning which can be satisfied by a conscious or unconscious anchoring in the transcendent.

4. This particular function of religion is emphasized by Berger, *Sacred Canopy*, who shares many of the perspectives of Thomas Luckmann, *The Invisible Religion* (New York: Macmillan, 1967).

5. Thomas Fawcett, *The Symbolic Language of Religion* (London: SCM Press, 1970), p. 27.

6. Ibid., p. 31.

7. G. E. Wright, "History and Reality: The Importance of Israel's 'Historical' Symbols for Christian Faith," B. W. Anderson, ed., *The Old Testament and Christian Faith* (London: SCM Press, 1964), p. 183. The citation is taken from Fawcett, *Symbolic Language*.

8. The term civil religion was popularized by Robert Bellah in his now classic essay, "Civil Religion in America," *Daedalus*, 96 (Winter 1967), 1—21. From the vast literature that followed Bellah's essay the reader's attention is called to John F. Wilson, "The Status of 'Civil Religion' in America," Elwyn A. Smith, ed., *The Religion of the Republic* (Philadelphia: Fortress Press, 1971), pp. 1—21; Phillip E. Hammond, "Religious Pluralism and Durkheim's Integration Thesis," in Eister, ed., *Changing Perspectives*, pp. 115—142; and Bellah's elaboration of his concept in *The Broken Covenant* (New York: The Seabury Press, 1975). Bellah does not confine his definition of civil religion to a symbolic system that legitimates the social order; he stresses the crucial element of transcendence that is present in American civil religion. For the description of a religion that serves a purely societal function, which resembles traditional religion morphologically but is nevertheless distinguishable from it, see David Apter, "Political Religions in New Nations," Clifford Geertz, ed., *Old Societies and New States* (New York: Free Press, 1963), pp. 57—104.

9. T. Dunbar Moodie, *The Rise of Afrikanerdom: Power Apartheid and the Afrikaner Civil Religion* (Berkeley, Los Angeles, London: University of California Press, 1975), p. 296.

10. Robert Stouffer, "Civil Religion, Technocracy and the Private Sphere: Further Comments on Cultural Integration in Advanced Societies," *Journal for the Scientific Study of Religion*, 12 (December 1973), 415.

11. See, for example, Leonard Glick, "The Anthropology of Religion: Malinowski and Beyond," Charles Glock and Phillip Hammond, ed., *Beyond the Classics? Essays in the Scientific Study of Religion* (New York: Harper Torchbooks, 1973), p. 208, where a major function of religion is defined as reflecting, sustaining, and legitimating the social order. See also W. S. F. Pickering, *Durkheim On Religion* (London: Routledge and Kegan Paul, 1975), pp. 135, 156.

12. Milton Rokeach, *The Nature of Human Values* (New York: The Free Press, 1973), pp. 6—7.

13. Ibid.

14. Pickering, *Durkheim On Religion*, pp. 88—91.

15. David Bidney, "Myth, Symbol and Truth," Thomas A. Sebeok, ed., *Myth, A Symposium* (Bloomington: University of Indiana Press, 1958), p. 14.

16. Murray Edelman, *Political As Symbolic Action* (Chicago: Markham Publishing Co., 1971), p. 15. For a less constricting typology,

which is not exhaustive, see Henry Tudor, *Political Myth* (London: Macmillan, 1972).

17. This need not necessarily be the case as Henry Tudor demonstrates in his discussion of the Roman foundation myth in *Political Myth*, pp. 65–90.

18. To the best of our understanding this is not the ambivalence or duality described by Claude Levi-Strauss in, for example, "The Structural Study of Myth," William A. Leesa and Evan Z. Vogt, eds., *Reader in Comparative Religion*, second edition (New York: Harper & Row, 1965), pp. 561–574.

19. See, for example, Edelman, *Symbolic Action*; Murray Edelman, *The Symbolic Uses of Politics* (Urbana: University of Illinois Press, 1964); Robert J. Bocock, *Ritual in Industrial Society* (London: George Allen and Unwin, 1974); or Steven Lukes, "Political Ritual and Social Integration," *Sociology*, 9 (May 1975), 289–308 and the extensive bibliography cited therein.

20. Susanne K. Langer, *Philosophy In A New Key: A Study in the Symbolism of Reason, Rite and Art* (New York: Penguin Books, 1942), p. 124. Generally one approaches the holy in a ritualized, that is, formalized manner, but this need not be the case. All societies have religions because all have sacred symbols, all seek for, and relate to, symbols of ultimate meaning, but, as Mary Douglas points out, not all are ritualistic. Mary Douglas, *Natural Symbols* (New York: Random House, Vintage Books, 1973), p. 22.

21. Bocock, *Ritual*, p. 37.

22. Lukes, "Ritual and Integration," p. 291.

23. Bocock, *Ritual*, pp. 64–66. An important monograph with special reference to Israel that also distinguishes religious beliefs and practices from secular beliefs and practices is Ilana Shelach's *Indications Toward Secular Religion in Israel* (Jerusalem: Hebrew University of Jerusalem, Papers in Sociology, 1975, in Hebrew).

24. See Chaim Adler and Reueven Kahana, eds., *Values, Religion and Culture* (Jerusalem: Akadamon, 1975, in Hebrew), pp. 204–209.

25. On postrevolutionary France see Pickering, *Durkheim on Religion*, p. 132. On Germany and Russia see Ernest B. Koenker, *Secular Salvations: The Rites and Symbols of Political Religions* (Philadelphia: Fortress Press, 1965); Jennifer McDowell, "Soviet Civil Ceremonies," *Journal for the Scientific Study of Religion*, 13 (September 1974), 265–280; David E. Powell, *Antireligious Propaganda in the Soviet Union: A Study of Mass Persuasion* (Cambridge, Mass.: The MIT Press, 1975), pp. 66–84; George L. Mosse, *The Nationalization of the Masses* (New York: Fertig, 1975); Uriel Tal, *"Political Faith" of Nazism Prior to the Holocaust* (Tel-Aviv: Tel Aviv University, Diaspora Research Institute, 1978). None of these studies develop the organizational aspect

but it is our impression that those who dictate the specific nature of the cult have little autonomous authority. Perhaps the leaders of the state fear the development of additional centers of authority.

26. Ronald C. Wimberley, "Continuity in the Measurement of Civil Religion," *Sociological Analysis*, 40 (Spring 1979), 59–62. He notes that "civil religion has been discussed often but measured rarely" (p. 59).

27. Unless otherwise noted, public opinion statistics cited here refer to a sample survey conducted by the firm of PORI for the authors. The poll excluded only the kibbutz population who comprise less than 4 percent of the nation's population. The estimated margin of error for a sample this size is 2½ percent.

Confidence in the reliability of the sample is reinforced by comparing two social and demographic variables with figures from the Central Bureau of Statistics. A comparison of gainfully employed heads of households (excluding soldiers) shows the following results:

Occupations of Gainfully Employed Jewish Heads of Households
(in percentages)

Occupation	Sample	Central Bureau (data for 1974)
Manual labor	49.1	50.6
Clerical and sales	28.2	26.2
Professional and managerial	22.7	23.2

Age comparisons are as follows:

Age Distribution of Respondents and of Total Jewish Population

Age	Sample	Central Bureau (data for 1974)
18–29	33.1	34.2
30–39	20.6	16.5
40–49	18.6	15.5
50–59	12.3	14.0
60 and over	15.3	19.8

The sharpest discrepancy between our sample and the Central Bureau's figures was in reported years of formal education. Thirty percent of our sample as opposed to 17 percent of the total Jewish population (according to the Central Bureau of Statistics) had an education of thirteen years or more. This may reflect the desire of respondents to increase their status in the eyes of the interviewer rather than the unrepresentativeness of the sample. It may, however, reflect a disproportionately low number of Oriental Jews in the sample.

28. The argument that modern technologically advanced societies do not require an integrating and legitimating symbol system has been made by Thomas Luckmann, *Invisible Religion*, and Richard Fenn, "Religion and the Legitimation of Social Systems," Eister, *Changing Perspectives*, pp. 143–161. Their points of view are summarized in Robert Stouffer, Cultural Integration in Advanced Societies, pp. 415–425. On the inapplication of this point of view for contemporary Israeli society see Charles S. Liebman, "Toward the Study of Israeli Folk Religion," *Megamot*, 23 (April 1977, in Hebrew), 95–109.

29. The theory of consociational democracy or "the politics of accommodation" was first advanced by Arend Lijphart. He sought to treat Dutch politics in terms of his theory in *The Politics of Accommodation: Pluralism and Democracy in the Netherlands* (Berkeley and Los Angeles: University of California Press, 1968). The model has been applied to Austria, Belgium, and Switzerland by a variety of authors whose work is reviewed in Hans Daalder, "The Consociational Democracy Theme," *World Politics*, 26 (July 1974), 604–621; to South Africa in John Seiler, "Measuring Black Political Support in South Africa," *Politikon*, 1 (December 1974), 19–26; and to Israel in Eliezer Don-Yehiya, "Religion and Coalition: The National Religious Party and Coalition Formation in Israel," Asher Arian, ed., *The Elections in Israel 1973* (Jerusalem: Jerusalem Academic Press, 1975), pp. 255–284.

30. Yehuda Ben-Meir and Peri Kedem, "A Measure of Religiosity for the Jewish Population of Israel," *Megamot*, 24 (February 1979, in Hebrew), 353–362.

31. Hans Kohn traces the disassociation of state and religion in Europe and then notes that although the state "emancipated itself from the church it remained in Europe inseparably united with religion." Hans Kohn, *The Idea of Nationalism* (New York: Macmillan, 1944), p. 191. On the close association of religion and national identity in Latin America, Asia, and Africa see two books edited by Donald Smith, *Religion, Politics and Social Change in the Third World* (New York: Free Press, 1971) and *South Asian Politics and Religion* (Princeton: Princeton University Press, 1966) and Geertz, *Old Societies*. See also Salo Baron, *Religion and Modern Nationalism* (New York: Harper, 1947).

32. Bernard Lewis, "The Return of Islam," *Commentary*, 61 (January 1976), 48. For a similar point with respect to India and Ceylon see Smith, *South Asian Politics*, pp. 24, 25, 28.

33. Smith, *South Asian Politics*, p. 43.

34. Bohdan R. Bocieurkiw and John W. Strong, *Religion and Atheism in the U.S.S.R. and Eastern Europe* (London: Macmillan, 1975)

cited in Thomas Corbishley, "Religion Resilient," *Soviet Jewish Affairs*, 5:2, 111.

35. For some recent summaries and observations on the historical and sociological aspects of the debate see Charles S. Liebman, *The Ambivalent American Jew: Politics, Religion and Family in American Jewish Life* (Philadelphia: Jewish Publication Society, 1973); David Vital, *The Origins of Zionism* (London: Oxford University Press, 1975); and Jacob Katz ed., *The Role of Religion in Modern Jewish History* (Cambridge: Association for Jewish Studies, 1975).

36. The question of whether or not traditional Judaism, Jewish law in particular, can serve as an adequate guide for a modern state is a subject of intense interest to a number of religious Jewish thinkers. A summary of the arguments with some cogent comments is Eliezer Goldman, *Jewish Law and the State* (Tel-Aviv: Kibbutz Dati, 1954, in Hebrew). On the claim that making Jewish law suitable to a modern state would require such revisions that religious leaders themselves have abjured opportunities to expand the role of traditional Judaism see: Moshe Samet, *Religion and State in Israel* (Jerusalem: Hebrew University, Papers in Sociology, 1979, in Hebrew).

37. Ben Meir and Kedem, "A Measure of Religiosity."

38. On the historical background see Emile Marmorstein, "Religious Opposition to Nationalism in the Middle East," *International Affairs* (July 1952), reprinted in J. Milton Yinger, *Religion, Society and the Individual* (New York: Macmillan, 1957), pp. 542−553. For a sociological treatment see Menachem Friedman, "Religious Zealotry in Israeli Society," *On Ethnic and Religious Diversity in Israel* (Ramat-Gan: Bar-Ilan University, 1975), pp. 91−112. For a critical discussion of its ideology see Norman Lamm, "The Ideology of the Neturei Karta—According to the Satmarer Version," *Tradition*, 12 (Fall 1971), 38−53. More sympathetic treatments of the movement are to be found in Emile Marmorstein, *Heaven at Bay* (London: Oxford University Press, 1969) and Yerachmiel Domb, *The Transformation* (London: Hamadpis, 1958).

39. Remarkably little has appeared on the Canaanite movement in English. Its ideology is elaborated upon by one of its major proponents in Yonathan Ratosh, "The New Hebrew Nation," Ehud Ben Ezer, ed., *Unease in Zion* (New York: Quadrangle Books, 1974), pp. 201−234. See also Baruch Kurzweil, "The New 'Canaanites' in Israel," *Judaism*, 2 (January 1953), 3−15.

40. Georges Friedmann, *The End of the Jewish People?* (Garden City, N.Y.: Doubleday, 1967) and Melford Spiro, *Children of the Kibbutz* (Cambridge, Mass.: Harvard University Press, 1958). Simon Herman, *Israelis and Jews: The Continuity of an Identity* (New York: Random House, 1970), showed how inaccurate the prognoses of these

observers were. But the fear that Canaanism would ultimately dominate Israeli society was present within Israel as well. See, for example, Baruch Kurzweil, *Our New Literature—Continuity or Revolution?*
(Jerusalem: Schocken, 1965, in Hebrew), pp. 270—300. (Kurzweil's
essay was originally published in the mid-1950s.) As we note in
chapter six, the fear of Canaanism's spread accounted in part for the
introduction of the Jewish Consciousness Program in 1957. The
question is how does one account for the erroneous conclusions of
very intelligent and able observers? We suggest that three factors are
responsible. First, as already indicated, the Jewish commitment of
the Israeli youth probably has changed in the past 20 years. Second,
the phenomenon of Jewish alienation among Israelis was so shocking
that observers tended to exaggerate its significance. Finally, and most
significantly, the observers measured Judaism and alienation from
Judaism by the standards of traditional Judaism. While Judaism has
been reaffirmed in recent years, it is not quite traditional Judaism.
Rather, it is a nationalized Judaism whose symbol system is,
however, so close to that of traditional Judaism that it is often
misleading.

41. Menachem Friedman, *Society and Religion: The Non-Zionist
Orthodox in Eretz-Israel, 1918—1936* (Jerusalem: Yad Izhak Ben-Zvi,
1977, in Hebrew) and Yehoshua Kaniel, *Continuity and Change: Old
Yishuv and New Yishuv During the First and Second Aliyah* (Jerusalem:
Yad Izhak Ben-Zvi, 1981, in Hebrew).

42. Ali A. Mazuri, "Pluralism and National Integration," Leo
Kuper and M. G. Smith, *Pluralism in Africa* (Berkeley, Los Angeles,
London: University of California Press, 1971), p. 337.

43. Alan Arian, *The Choosing People: Voting Behavior in Israel*
(Cleveland: Case Western Reserve Press, 1974); Erving Birnbaum,
The Politics of Compromise: State and Religion in Israel (Cranbury, N.J.:
Fairleigh Dickinson Press, 1970); Don-Yehiya, "Religion and Coali-
tion"; Emanuel Gutmann, "Religion in Israeli Politics," Jacob Lan-
dau, ed., *Man, State and Society in the Contemporary Middle East* (Lon-
don: Pall Mall Press, 1972); Charles S. Liebman, *Pressure Without
Sanctions: The Influence of World Jewry in Shaping Israel's Public Policies*
(Cranbury, N.J.: Fairleigh Dickinson Press, 1977); Norman L.
Zucker and Naomi F. Zucker, *The Coming Crisis in Israel: Private Faith
and Public Policy* (Cambridge, Mass.: MIT Press, 1973). Exceptions
are: Charles S. Liebman, "Religion and Political Integration in
Israel," *Jewish Journal of Sociology*, 17 (June 1975), 17—27; Eliezer
Don-Yehiya and Charles S. Liebman, "Separation of Religion and
State," *Molad*, 25—26 (August-September 1972, in Hebrew), 159—
171; and Sammy Smooha, *Israel, Pluralism and Conflict* (London:
Routledge and Kegan Paul, 1978).

2: Zionist-Socialism

1. The struggle for, and the eventual achievement of, civil rights by Jews occurred in stages at different times in different parts of Europe. It began in France in the late eighteenth century, but by that time anti-Semitic persecution, after temporary abatement, had begun to again grow severe in some countries. Nevertheless profound psychological changes were wrought by the promise of equality, the impact of victory in one country on the Jews of another country, and by the widely shared belief in the inevitability of emancipation. There is extensive literature on the topic. The most important studies, for our purposes, are Max Wiener, *The Jewish Religion in the Emancipation Period* (Jerusalem: Mossad Bialik, 1974, in Hebrew); Yeḥezkel Kaufman, *Diaspora and Alienation* (Tel Aviv: Dvir, 1932, in Hebrew) vol. 2; Michael A. Meyer, *The Origins of the Modern Jew* (Detroit: Wayne State University, 1967); Jacob Katz, *Out of the Ghetto: The Social Background of Jewish Emancipation, 1770–1870* (Cambridge, Mass.: Harvard University Press, 1973).

2. A classification of the various ideologies in post-emancipation Judaism according to their positions on the question of the relationships between the concepts of religion, nation and country, is to be found in Alain Greilsammer, Eliezer Don-Yehiya and Bernard Susser, "Religion, Nationalisme et état dans le Judaisme," in *International Political Science Association Papers*, vii, 1 (1973), 3.

3. On the early Zionist movement in general and the development of Herzlian political Zionism see David Vital, *The Origins of Zionism* (Oxford: Oxford University Press, 1975). For the later development of political Zionism, see Walter Laqueur, *A History of Zionism* (New York: Holt, Rinehart and Winston, 1972). A study devoted to the concept of normalization and some of the twists it took in Zionist thinking is Amnon Rubinstein, *From Herzl to Gush Emunim and Back Again* (Tel Aviv: Schocken, 1980, in Hebrew).

4. On the conceptions of those Jewish nationalists who denied the validity of any Jewish national spirit or the sanctity, legitimacy, and utility of traditional Jewish culture for national purposes and their relationship to currents in nineteenth-century European nationalism, see Kaufman, *Diaspora and Alienation*, pp. 359–400.

5. Baruch Kurzweil, *Our New Literature: Continuity or Revolution?* (Jerusalem: Schocken, 1965, in Hebrew) p. 137. According to Kurzweil, Brenner felt that "the rejection of our destiny is our sole destiny."

6. Ibid.

7. Ibid., p. 266. Kurzweil discusses the struggle of Hazaz and Tchernichowsky against "religious zealots" as well as against

"modern ideologies and their followers who are working toward secular redemption of humanity."

8. Jacob Katz, *Jewish Nationalism: Essays and Studies* (Jerusalem: The Zionist Library, World Zionist Organization, 1979, in Hebrew), pp. 11–12.

9. On the peculiarity of Zionism among the nationalist movements, see Ben Halpern, *The Idea of the Jewish State* (Cambridge, Mass.: Harvard University Press, 1969), pp. 22–25. Many American Zionists were less sympathetic to this goal which helps account, in part, for the sharp conflicts between Brandeis and Weizmann.

10. On the old yishuv and its relationship to the new yishuv, see Menachem Friedman, *Society and Religion: The Non-Zionist Orthodox in Eretz-Israel, 1918–1936* (Jerusalem: Yad Izhak Ben-Zvi, 1977, in Hebrew). On the yishuv as a sociopolitical system, see Dan Horowitz and Moshe Lissak, *The Origins of the Israeli Polity* (Chicago: University of Chicago Press, 1978) and Binyamin Eliav, ed., *The Jewish National Home* (Jerusalem: Keter, 1976, in Hebrew). The section in Eliav's book by Eliakim Rubinstein, "From Yishuv to State: Institutions and Parties," is of special interest. For a general history in English that includes a description of the five aliyot, see Howard Sachar, *A History of Israel* (New York: Knopf, 1976).

11. Its core membership derived from immigrants of the fourth aliya (predominantly middle-class Polish Jews who came in the 1920s) and the fifth aliya (including many Germans who came in the 1930s). However, the seeds of the ezrahi camp go back to the first Zionist settlers and their children—independent farmers, some of whom accumulated relatively great wealth as land owners and orange growers. The civil camp, probably because it was the least ideologically and politically structured, left the most meager public literature. It is the least well known and has certainly been least studied. A major contribution to the literature on one segment of this camp, the land owners and orange growers, is the recent study by Anita Shapira, *Futile Struggle: The Jewish Labor Controversy 1929–1939* (Tel Aviv: Hakibbutz Hameuchad, 1977, in Hebrew).

12. Numbers, 32:20.

13. Avshalom Reich, "Changes and Developments in the Passover Haggadot of the Kibbutz Movement." (Ph.D. diss., University of Texas, 1972), p. 215. Reich's appendix includes many illustrations from texts of haggadot and we have relied on his study for many of our examples.

14. On the Jewish enlightenment, see Kaufman, *Diaspora and Alienation*. The English language literature on the Eastern European haskala which is of special relevance to the development of Zionism and Zionist thought is quite sparse, especially when contrasted to the literature of the haskala in Central and Western Europe. The classic

study is Simon Dubnov, *History of the Jews in Russia and Poland*, vol. 2, trans. Israel Friedlander, (Philadelphia: Jewish Publications Society, 1918). For a very concise summary, see Vital, *Origins of Zionism*, pp. 43–48. See also Raphael Mahler, *A History of Modern Jewry 1780–1815* (New York: Schocken Books, 1972), pp. 536–601; and Howard Sachar, *The Course of Modern Jewish History* (Cleveland: The World Publishing Co., 1958), pp. 198–220.

15. Avraham Zeitlin, *State and Vision of State* (Tel Aviv: Am Oved, 1956, in Hebrew), pp. 77–88.

16. Reich, "Changes in the Haggadot of the Kibbutz," p. 216.

17. Aharon Gordon, *The Nation and the Labor* (Jerusalem: The Zionist Press, 1952, in Hebrew), p. 126.

18. Deuteronomy, 30:15.

19. Even-Shoshan, *The History of the Labor Movement in the Land of Israel* (Tel Aviv: Am Oved, 1969, in Hebrew), p. 424.

20. Yaacov Fichman, "The Soil Educates," *Davar*, 20 April 1932, in Hebrew.

21. Amos Elon, *The Israelis: Founders and Sons* (New York: Holt, Rinehart & Winston, 1971), pp. 142–143.

22. Gideon Ofrat, *Land, Man, Blood: The Myth of the Halutz and the Ritual of the Land in the Settlement Camps* (Tel Aviv: Tcherikover, 1980, in Hebrew), p. 79.

23. Ibid., p. 26

24. Reich, "Changes in the Haggadot of the Kibbutz," p. 249.

25. Yonina Talmon-Gerber, *Individual and Society in the Kibbutz* (Jerusalem: Magnes Press, 1970, in Hebrew), p. 223.

26. Ibid., p. 224.

27. Ibid., p. 225.

28. Ibid., p. 226.

29. Uri Milstein, *By Blood and Fire Judea* (Tel Aviv: Lewin Epstein, 1973, in Hebrew), pp. 47–48.

30. Reich, "Changes in the Haggadot of the Kibbutz," p. 226.

31. Gordon, *Nation and Labor*, p. 215.

32. There is a formidable literature in Hebrew on the formation of Mapai and its predecessor parties in the yishuv period. Fortunately, two of the best books on the topic have been translated into English: Horowitz and Lissak, *Origins of Israeli Polity*, and Yonathan Shapiro, *The Formative Years of the Israeli Labour Party* (Beverly Hills: Sage, 1976).

33. The attitude of early Zionist immigrants toward religion is the subject of David Knaani, *The Second Worker Aliya and its Attitude Toward Religion and Tradition* (Tel Aviv: Tel Aviv University, 1976, in Hebrew). See also, Muky Tzur, *Doing it the Hard Way* (Tel Aviv: Am Oved, 1976, in Hebrew).

34. Knaani, *The Second Aliya*, pp. 65–70.

35. Berl Katznelson and Yehuda Kaufman, eds., *The Writings of Nachman Syrkin* (Tel Aviv: Davar, 1939, in Hebrew), p. 75.

36. Tzur, *The Hard Way*, pp. 96—97.

37. Knaani, *The Second Aliya*, pp. 89—92.

38. Ber Borochov, *Writings* (Tel Aviv: Sifriyat Poalim V'Hakibbutz Hameuchad, 1960, in Hebrew), 3:334.

39. Reich, "Changes in the Haggadot of the Kibbutz," p. 234.

40. Ibid.

41. Ibid., p. 304.

42. Raphael Weiss, "From Holy to Profane," *L'shonenu L'am*, no. 271 (1977), in Hebrew.

43. Reich, "Changes in the Haggadot of the Kibbutz," p. 234.

44. Ibid., p. 395.

45. Ibid., p. 199.

46. Ibid., p. 387.

47. Moshe Braslavsky, *The Workers' Movement in the Land of Israel* (Tel Aviv: Hotzaat Hakibbutz Hameuchad, 1959, in Hebrew), p. 263.

48. *Education in Israel* (Jerusalem: Hotzaat Misrad Hahinuh, 1973, in Hebrew), p. 22.

49. Eliyahu Biletzky, *Solel Boneh* (Tel Aviv: Am Oved, 1975, in Hebrew), p. 64.

50. Reich, "Changes in the Haggadot of the Kibbutz," p. 197.

51. Ofrat, *Land, Man, Blood*, p. 81.

52. Simon Rawidowicz, *Babylonia and Jerusalem* (London: Ararat, 1975), 2:572—575. It seems to us that contemporary proponents of Zionist-Socialism tend to exaggerate the parallels and blur the contrasts between Zionist-Socialism and traditional Judaism. For example, see Tzur, *The Hard Way*, pp. 95—104; or Alexander Barzel, "Judaism as a Weltanschauung and its Expression in the Labor Movement," *Kivunim*, (May 1980, in Hebrew), pp. 87—106.

53. Yizhak Lamdan, *Masada, Shirim* (Jerusalem: Mossad Bialik, 1973, in Hebrew), 1:27—75.

54. *Encyclopedia Judaica*, 10:1363

55. Lamdan, *Masada, Shirim*, p. 61.

56. Ibid., p. 64.

57. On loneliness, depression, and suicide among the halutzim, see Tzur, *The Hard Way*, pp. 27—44. For an account of the defense of Tel Hai, in which four defenders who became isolated from the rest each reserved a bullet to commit suicide rather than be captured, see Shulamit Laskov, *Yosef Trumpeldor: A Biography* (Haifa: Shikmona, 1972, in Hebrew).

58. Laskov, *Trumpeldor*, includes a letter (p. 234) Tel Hai defender Sara Chizik wrote after a thirteen-hour climb to the battle site a few weeks before the battle, in which she died. Chizik wrote: "The

ascent . . . was particularly difficult but nothing stands before will, for if we did not have a strong will, it would be impossible to walk this long and difficult road."

59. An effort to demythologize the story is Nakdimon Rogel, *Tel Hai* (Tel Aviv: Yariv-Hadar, 1979, in Hebrew). The limited controversy this study generated suggests the Tel Hai story's loss of resonance in recent years.

60. Gershon Rivlin, ed., *The Legacy of Tel Hai* (Tel Aviv: Maarakhot, 1970, in Hebrew), p. 13.

61. Ibid., p. 136.

62. Ibid., pp. 132, 140.

63. Quoted in Even Shoshan, *History of the Labor Movement*, 1:341.

64. Rivlin, *Legacy of Tel Hai*, p. 142.

65. Ibid., pp. 136–137.

66. Ibid., p. 177.

67. Ibid.

68. Gideon Ofrat, "The Arab in Israeli Drama," *The Jerusalem Quarterly* (Spring 1979), pp. 70–92, notes that prior to the period of direct conflict between Jews and Arabs, a romantic conception of Arabs prevailed in much Hebrew writing. The Arab was seen in specific, individual terms and not in general, abstract terms. Ofrat, however, finds this true until the establishment of the State rather than the mid-1930s. Ehud Ben-Ezer, "War and Siege in Hebrew Literature After 1967," *The Jerusalem Quarterly* (Fall 1978), pp. 20–37, also notes that the pre-1948 literature depicts the Arabs between poles of bitter reality and romanticism that refuses to view them as an entity. According to our thesis, this should have changed by the late 1930s.

69. *Davar*, 20 March 1932.

70. Ibid., 16 Dec. 1942; 21 Feb. 1943.

71. Ofrat, *Blood, Man, Land*, p. 40.

72. *Davar*, 27 April 1932.

73. Berl Katznelson, *Writings* (Tel Aviv: Hotzaat Mapai, 1947, in Hebrew), 6:391.

74. *Report on the Education in Immigrant Camps* (Jerusalem, The Knesset, May 9, 1950, in Hebrew), pp. 79–80.

75. Bracha Habas, ed., *The Book of Aliyat Hanoar* (Jerusalem: The Jewish Agency, 1941, in Hebrew), p. 410.

76. Knaani, *The Second Aliya*, pp. 99–104.

77. Ber Borochov, *Writings*, p. 330.

78. Katznelson, *Writings, p. 39*.

79. Reich, "Changes in the Haggadot of the Kibbutz," pp. 5–6.

80. Ibid., pp. 92–188.

81. M. Amitai, "Ma Nishtana on the Kibbutz," Yom Tov Levinski, ed., *The Book of Festivals* (Tel Aviv: Dvir, 1956, in Hebrew), 2:465–466. See also the articles by A. Talmi, pp. 466–468 and Sh.

Reichenstein, pp. 468–469.

82. Daniel Persky, "A Passover Seder for Workers in Tel Aviv," Levinski, *Festivals*, pp. 469–470.

83. Exodus, 34:22.

84. On the Shavuot ceremonies in the kibbutzim, see N. Benari, "The *Bikkurim* Ceremony in the Collective Settlements," Levinski, *Festivals*, 3:209–211.

85. B. Ben-Yehuda, "The Holiday in Memory of the Bringing of the "Bikkurim," Levinski, *Festivals* p. 202.

86. Moshe Gorarli, "The Holiday of the Bikkurim in the Tones of the Homeland," Levinski, *Festivals*, p. 220.

87. Joseph Klausner, "Hanukkah: A Symbol and a Warning," Levinski, *Festivals*, 5:191.

88. Knaani, *The Second Aliya*, p. 101. A penetrating analysis of the Zionist transformation of Hanukkah is Ehud Luz, "On the Maccabean Myth of Rebirth," *Hauma*, 18 (December 1979), 44–52.

89. Benzion Dinur, "The Holiday of Hasmoneans," Levinski, *Festivals*, 5:197.

90. Ibid.

91. "Carrying the Torch from Modiin," Levinski, *Festivals*, p. 212.

92. N. Benari and N. Nisimov, "Sukkot in the Collective Settlement," Levinski, *Festivals*, 4:304–305.

93. B. Ben-Yehuda, "The Tradition of the Flag of Jerusalem on Sukkot," Levinski, *Festivals* pp. 306–307.

94. N. Benari, *Sabbath and Festival* (Tel Aviv: Histadrut, 1946, in Hebrew), p. 33.

95. Quoted in Friedman, *Society and Religion*, p. 299.

96. Moshe Sheinfeld, *The Children of Teheran Accuse* (Jerusalem: Agudat Israel, 1943, in Hebrew), p. 15. For a positive, though atypical, attitude toward *Tisha B'av* among the leading Zionist-socialists, see Katznelson, pp. 366, 393.

97. Benari, *Sabbath and Festival*, p. 50.

98. Borochov, *Writings*, p. 323.

99. Ibid.

100. Ibid.

101. Ibid., p. 324.

102. Our discussion of May Day celebrations relies on a seminar paper by Ruth Movshowitz submitted to the Department of Political Studies of Bar-Ilan University in 1976.

3: Revisionist Zionism As Civil Religion

1. On the history of the revisionist movement, see Joseph B. Schechtman and Yehuda Benari, *History of the Revisionist Movement* (Tel Aviv: Hadar, 1970, in Hebrew). On Jabotinsky, see Joseph B.

Schechtman, *Fighter and Prophet: The Vladimir Jabotinsky Story* (New York: Thomas Yoselof, 1961). For a recent debate over Jabotinsky's thought, see Shlomo Avineri, "The Political Thought of Vladimir Jabotinsky," and Israel Eldad, "Jabotinsky Distorted," *The Jerusalem Quarterly*, 16 (Summer 1980), 3–39.

2. Quoted in Isaac Remba, "Religion and Tradition in His Life and Thought," *Haumah*, 3 (June 1964, in Hebrew), 48.

3. H. Ben-Yeruham, ed., *The Book of Betar—Origins and Sources* (Jerusalem: Havaad L'hotzaat Sefer Betar, 1969, in Hebrew), 1:429.

4. Schechtman, *Fighter and Prophet*, p. 411.

5. Ibid.

6. Schechtman and Benari, *History*, p. 337.

7. Ben-Yeruham, *Book of Betar*, 1:122.

8. Abba Ahimeir, *Revolutionary Zionism* (Tel Aviv: Havaad L'hotzaat Kitvei Abba Ahimeir, 1966, in Hebrew), p. 43.

9. Yaacov Shavit, *From a Majority to a State* (Tel Aviv: Yariv, 1978, in Hebrew), chapters 5 and 6.

10. Moshe Bella, ed., *The World of Jabotinsky* (Tel Aviv: Dfusim, 1975, in Hebrew), p. 245.

11. Ibid., p. 247.

12. Cited in Shavit, *Majority to State*, p. 236.

13. David Niv, *The Battles of the Irgun Zvai Leumi* (Tel Aviv: Mossad Klausner, 1965, in Hebrew), 1:229.

14. See, for example, Bella, *World of Jabotinsky*, pp. 303–306.

15. Ibid., p. 138.

16. Niv, *Battles of the Irgun*, 1:72.

17. Ben-Yeruham, ed., *Book of Betar* (1973), 2:163. Anita Shapira, "The Conflict Within Mapai Over the Use of Violence," *Hazionut*, (Tel Aviv: Hakibbutz Hameuchad, 1978, in Hebrew), vol. 5, points out that the Betar uniform facilitated the symbolic transference, however simpleminded and obtuse it appears in retrospect, between the failure of the German socialists to resist the fascist movement and the necessity of the Zionist-socialists' doing so.

18. Cited in Ben-Yeruham *Book of Betar*, 2:164.

19. Niv, *Battles of the Irgun*, 1:123.

20. Ibid., p. 124.

21. Ze'ev Jabotinsky, *Ze'ev Jabotinsky: The Man and His Doctrines*, ed., w. intro., Joseph Nedava (Tel Aviv: The Ministry of Defense, 1980, in Hebrew), pp. 135–137.

22. Schechtman and Benari, *History*, pp. 338–341.

23. Ahimeir, *Revolutionary Zionism*, p. 58.

24. Ibid., p. 145.

25. Ahimeir, *Revolutionary Zionism*, p. 149. Yehuda Shuster, "A Theoretical Model of Fascist Ideology" (M.A. thesis, Hebrew Uni-

versity, 1976, in Hebrew), discusses fascist influence on Ahimeir. See especially pp. 124–126.

26. Ahimeir, *Revolutionary Zionism*. See the introduction by Joseph Nedava.

27. Shavit, *Majority to State*, pp. 42–45.

28. Ben-Yeruham, *Book of Betar*, 2:984.

29. Cited in Miryam Getter, *The Ideology of Lehi* (M.A. thesis submitted to Tel Aviv University, 1967, in Hebrew), p. 11.

30. Ibid., p. 45.

31. In fact, in the early period, even the revisionists emphasized universalist aspects of their ideology. Jabotinsky expressed his disdain for the generalized hostility of "ghetto Jewry" to the non-Jewish world. He referred to the "dangerous poison with which the soul of the ghetto is filled, the notion that the surrounding world is filled with highway robbers." In his view, "the Gentile has the same sense of justice as we do . . . he also had his prophets . . . and if we are cultured today, then we owe a debt to the Gentile. He created the modern state . . . he freed us from the ghetto—he is our equal, both our student and our teacher." Ze'ev Jabotinsky, *Speeches, 1906–1926* (Jerusalem: Eri Jabotinsky Press, 1947, in Hebrew), p. 322.

32. Ben-Yeruham, ed., *Book of Betar*, 2:527. In the elections to the first congress of the New Zionist Organization the religious list gained 58,000 votes in Poland, compared to 248,000 votes for the general list.

33. Schechtman and Benari, *History*, p. 237.

34. Remba, "Religion and Tradition," p. 147.

35. Ze'ev Jabotinsky, *First Zionist Writings* (Jerusalem: Eri Jabotinsky Press, 1949, in Hebrew), pp. 99–100.

36. Ibid., pp. 137–138.

37. Ibid., p. 118.

38. Ibid., p. 138.

39. Yehoshua Yevin, *Writings* (Tel Aviv: Havaada L'hotzaat Kitvei Yevin, 1969, in Hebrew), pp. 358–364; and Ahimeir, *Revolutionary Zionism*, pp. 235–239.

40. Yevin, *Writings*, pp. 360–361.

41. Ahimeir, *Revolutionary Zionism*, p. 237.

42. Remba, "Religion and Tradition," p. 160.

43. Schechtman and Benari, *History*, p. 238.

44. Ze'ev Jabotinsky, *Speeches, 1927–1940* (Jerusalem: Eri Jabotinsky Press, 1948, in Hebrew), p. 192.

45. Ben Yeruham, *Book of Betar*, 1:149.

46. Cited in Remba, "Religion and Tradition," p. 162.

47. Cited in Schechtman, *Fighter and Prophet*, p. 289.

48. See, for example, M. Madrich, "A National Education,"

Hayarden (August 27, 1937, in Hebrew). In another article, "Critique of Democracy," *Hayarden* (August 27, 1937), M. Giladi argued that "the Hebrew nation, even that part living in the Land of Israel, is still exilic and that is why it is willing to accept the official defeatist policy of the Zionist leaders."

49. Ben-Yeruham, *Book of Betar*, 1:516.

50. On Canaanism, the movement and its ideology see Baruch Kurzweil, *Our New Literature: Continuity or Revolution?* (Jerusalem: Schocken, 1965, in Hebrew); Yonathan Ratosh, ed., *From Victory to Defeat* (Tel Aviv: Hadar, 1976, in Hebrew). Among the limited materials in English, see Yonathan Ratosh, "The New Hebrew Nation," Ehud Ben-Ezer, ed., *Unease in Zion* (New York: Quadrangle Books, 1974), pp. 201−234; and Baruch Kurzweil, "The New 'Canaanites' in Israel," *Judaism*, 2 (January 1953), 3−15.

51. Ratosh's first article appeared July 16, 1937. See Shavit, *Majority to State*, p. 44.

52. Ben-Yeruham, *Book of Betar*, 3:516.

53. In 1928 Ahimeir was appointed editor of Betar's journal, *Tel Hai*. He wrote that he would try to circulate the ideas of Y. L. Gordon, Berdichevski, Bialik, Tchernichowski, Shneur and Y. Kahan. Ben-Yeruham, *Book of Betar*, 1:139. Except for Bialik, these writers were all radical opponents of traditional Judaism. For the comparison with Kurzweil's listing of the spiritual fathers of Canaanism, see Kurzweil, *Our New Literature*, p. 286.

54. Niv, *Battles of the Irgun*, 5:179.

55. Ibid., p. 209. Some thought that the declaration of the Committee was only a propaganda device designed to win the support of American Jews by relieving them of the problem of dual loyalty, but the leader of the Committee, Hillel Kook, who was elected to the first Knesset as a member of Herut, continued to express his Hebrew ideology even after the establishment of Israel. (Herut was the political party established by IZL under Menachem Begin's leadership.) Two other representatives from Herut's fourteen-member Knesset delegation, including Jabotinsky's son, were bitter antagonists of traditional Judaism and all three eventually left the party.

56. Getter, *Ideology of Lehi*, pp. 99−100.

57. Ibid., p. 107.

58. Begin has used religious terminology throughout his career. In the IZL's declaration of revolt in 1944 which he drafted, one goal of the struggle was defined as "rooting the holiness of the Torah in the life of the emancipated nation," and in his speech in honor of the declaration of the State, he prayed, "God of Israel, guard your soldiers. . . ." Menachem Begin, *In The Underground* (Tel Aviv: Hadar, 1978, in Hebrew), I:24; and IV:333.

59. Nathan Yellin-More, *Lohamei Herut Yisrael* (Tel Aviv: Shik-

mona, 1974, in Hebrew), p. 61.

60. Abba Ahimeir, *Brit Habiryonim* (Tel Aviv: Havaad L'hotzaat Kitvei Ahimeir, 1972, in Hebrew), p. 171.

61. Ben-Yeruham, *Book of Betar*, 1:43–45.

62. Ibid., pp. 43–44.

63. Jabotinsky, *The Man and His Doctrines*, p. 117.

64. Ibid., p. 120.

65. Ahimeir, *Brit Habiryonim*, pp. 140–141.

66. Schechtman and Benari, *History*, p. 341.

67. Ben-Yeruham, *Book of Betar*, 3:76.

68. Remba, "Religion and Tradition," p. 159.

69. Yaacov Hurgin, "He Will Come As A Hero," *Haumah*, 3 (June 1964, in Hebrew), 13.

70. Jabotinsky, *The Man and His Doctrines*, pp. 136–137.

71. Schechtman, *Fighter and Prophet*, p. 416.

72. Ibid.

73. Ibid., p. 415.

74. Ben-Yeruham, *Book of Betar*, 1:122.

75. Itamar Even-Zahav, "The Flowering and Crystallization of Local and Native Hebrew Culture in the Land of Israel, 1882–1948," *Catedra*, 16 (July 1980, in Hebrew), 165–189.

76. Ben-Yeruham, *Book of Betar*, 1:209–213.

77. The article by Ahimeir appeared in 1932 and is quoted in *Book of Betar*, 1:259.

78. Cited in Niv, *Battles of the Irgun*, 5:142.

4: Civil Religion of Statism

1. For a full discussion of this phenomenon, see Dan Horowitz and Moshe Lissak, *The Origins of the Israeli Policy: Palestine Under the Mandate* (Chicago: University of Chicago Press, 1978). For a discussion of the breakdown of the system and its reconstitution and relations between the labor and religious camps, 1930–1935, see Dan Vigiser, "The Labor Party of Israel and Mizrahi, Hapoel Hamizrahi: Between Rivalry and Cooperation" (M.A. thesis, Bar-Ilan University, 1978, in Hebrew).

2. Val R. Lorwin, "Segmented Pluralism," Kenneth McRae, ed., *Consociational Democracy* (Toronto: McClelland and Steward, 1974), p. 68, and Daniel J. Elazar, *Israel: From Ideological to Territorial Democracy* (New York: General Learning Press, 1971).

3. Orit Ichilov, "Youth Movements in Israel As Agents for Transition to Adulthood," *Jewish Journal of Sociology*, 19 (June 1977), 25.

4. On the immigrant camp controversy, see Eliezer Don-Yehiya, "Cooperation and Conflict Between Political Camps: The Religious

Camp and the Labor Movement and the Education Crises In Israel"
(Ph.D. diss., Hebrew University, 1977, in Hebrew). See also,
Charles S. Liebman, *Pressure Without Sanctions: The Influence of World
Jewry on Israeli Policy* (Rutherford, N.J.: Fairleigh Dickinson Press,
1977), pp. 64–74.

5. David Ben Gurion, *Vision and Way* (Tel Aviv: Hotzaat Mapai,
2d. ed., 1953, in Hebrew), 3:134. (Unless otherwise noted the quotes
from Ben Gurion are derived from speeches delivered or articles
written before 1956—our approximate date for the decline of statism.
However, since we cite speeches and articles from collections of Ben
Gurion's writings, which were often published after 1956, the date of
publication listed in the footnotes can be misleading.) For other
references expressing the notion that the years just before and immediately following the establishment of the state was a messianic era,
see: David Ben Gurion, *Stars and Dust* (Ramat Gan: Massada, 1976, in
Hebrew), p. 175; *Davar*, 17 July 1948 and an article by the writers
Yehuda Burla and Y. Daniel in *Hapoel Hatzair*, 26 July 1949, p. 12.

6. *Davar*, 3 July 1949.

7. Ben Gurion, *Vision and Way*, p. 134.

8. *Davar*, 3 July 1949.

9. Ben Gurion, *Stars and Dust*, p. 178. See also, *Davar*, 7 October
1957.

10. Ben Gurion, *Stars and Dust*, p. 178.

11. For a similar conception of American civil religion, see Robert
Bellah, "Civil Religion in America," *Dædalus*, 96 (Winter 1967),
1–21.

12. *Divrei Haknesset*, 1951, p. 1339. This is the official record of the
Knesset debates and resolutions.

13. Ibid., 1953, p. 1661.

14. Ibid., 1951, p. 1339. See also *Davar*, 16 August 1949.

15. Moshe Dayan, *Story of My Life* (Jerusalem: Steimatzky, 1976),
p. 129.

16. Avraham Avi-Hai, "Israelocentrism: A Guiding Doctrine of
David Ben Gurion," *Proceedings of the Sixth World Congress for Jewish
Studies, 1973* (Jerusalem: The Jerusalem Academic Press, 1975),
2:355.

17. Ibid., p. 358, and Liebman, *Pressure Without Sanctions*, p. 235.

18. Ben Gurion, *Stars and Dust*, pp. 181, 182.

19. Ibid., p. 183.

20. Ibid., p. 185.

21. *D'var Hashavua*, 5 September 1949.

22. *Davar*, 10 January 1949; 1 February 1949; 2 February 1949; 6
February 1949; 3 July 1949.

23. *Davar*, 3 July 1949.

24. Ibid., 10 October 1949.

25. Ibid., 16 August 1949.

26. Ben Gurion, *Vision and Way*, 1:219. See also 5:253.

27. Ben Gurion, *Uniqueness and Purpose* (Jerusalem: Maarachot, 1971, in Hebrew), p. 193.

28. Ben Gurion, *Vision and Way*, 4:228.

29. Ben Gurion, *Stars and Dust*, p. 104.

30. Ibid., p. 134.

31. Ben Gurion, *Uniqueness and Purpose*, p. 66.

32. Hilb, "Religion and State," *B'terem*, no. 1 (January 1951, in Hebrew), p. 11.

33. *The Report of the Investigation Committee in the Matter of Education in the Immigrant Camps* (Jerusalem: The Knesset, 1950, in Hebrew), p. 34.

34. Ibid., p. 40.

35. Eliezer Don-Yehiya, "Religion and Coalition: The National Religious Party and Coalition Formation," Asher Arian, ed., *The Elections in Israel, 1973* (Jerusalem: The Jerusalem Academic Press, 1975), pp. 255–284.

36. Ben Gurion, *Stars and Dust*, p. 130.

37. The distinguished Jewish philosopher Shmuel Hugo Bergman, citing such examples, cautioned against the dangers of Statism. *Hapoel Hatzair*, 42, 1949.

38. *Davar*, 5 December 1949.

39. "Vision and Independence," *A Play for the Independence Holiday* (Jerusalem: Publications of the Jewish National Fund, 1952, in Hebrew).

40. David Ben Gurion, *The Renewed State of Israel* (Tel Aviv: Am Oved, 1969, in Hebrew), p. 371.

41. Ben Gurion, *Uniqueness and Purpose*, p. 159.

42. *Divrei Haknesset*, 1956, p. 1792.

43. Ibid.

44. Ibid.

45. Ibid.

46. Michael Bar-Zohar, *Ben Gurion: A Political Biography* (Tel Aviv: Am Oved, 1978, in Hebrew), 2:870.

47. Moshe Dayan, *To Live With the Bible* (Jerusalem: Edayim, 1978, in Hebrew), pp. 71, 76.

48. *Hazofe*, 2 June 1950.

49. Ibid.

50. Ibid., 15 July 1951.

51. Bar-Zohar, *Ben Gurion: A Political Biography*, p. 951.

52. See, for example, Ben Gurion, *Stars and Dust*, p. 67.

53. *Divrei Haknesset*, 1949, pp. 1314–1315, 1324, 1330, 1331.

54. Ibid., p. 1359.

55. *Davar*, 17 July 1949.

56. See chapter three.
57. *Divrei Haknesset*, 1949, pp. 1359–1360.
58. *Davar*, 17 August 1949.
59. Amnon Rubinstein, *To Be A Free People* (Jerusalem: Schocken, 1977, in Hebrew). Chapter five is entitled "The Rise and Fall of the Mythological *Sabra.*"
60. Ibid., p. 102.
61. Ibid., p. 103.
62. Dennis Kavanaugh, *Political Culture* (London: Macmillan, 1972), p. 21. See also, Richard R. Fagen, *The Transformation of Political Culture in Cuba* (Stanford: Stanford University Press, 1969), pp. 15, 145–148.
63. Bar-Zohar, *Ben Gurion: A Political Biography*, p. 876.
64. Ibid., p. 876.
65. Ben Gurion, *Uniqueness and Purpose*, pp. 135–136; *Vision and Way*, 3:195.
66. Shabtai Ben-Zvi, *Post-Uganda Zionism in the Crises of the Holocaust* (Tel Aviv: Bronfman, 1977, in Hebrew), p. 55.
67. Even as prominent a writer as Yigal Mosenson, one of the leading figures of Hebrew literature in the late 1940s and early 1950s was criticized for presenting a play, *B'arvot Hanegev*, that was deemed disrespectful to the IDF, *D'var Hashavua*, 3 March 1949, in Hebrew.
68. Ben Gurion, *Vision and Way*, 1:280.
69. Ibid., 4:18.
70. Ben Gurion, *Stars and Dust*, p. 320.
71. Ibid., p. 92.
72. Ibid., p. 320.
73. On the excavations, see Yigal Yadin, *Masada* (New York: Random House, 1968).
74. According to a survey of educational institutions in 1960, about one-quarter of the schools made no mention of the Holocaust either on Holocaust Day (the twenty-seventh of Nissan) or on the tenth of Tevet (which in some religious circles is a remembrance day for Holocaust victims). A substantial portion of the schools devoted no attention whatsoever to teaching about the Holocaust and others assigned it a very small role in their educational program. *Teaching the Holocaust In Schools* (Jerusalem: Ministry of Education, 1961, in Hebrew). The leading Israeli writer, A. B. Yehoshua, "On Hebrew Holocaust Literature," *The Jerusalem Quarterly*, no. 16 (Summer 1980), p. 87, notes that Israeli writers persistently avoided the subject of the Holocaust during the decade after the War of Independence: "Nothing could have been further from the experience of the War."
75. Amos Elon, *The Israelis: Founders and Sons* (New York: Holt, Rinehart and Winston, 1971), p. 199.
76. *Divrei Haknesset*, 1959, p. 1386.

77. Ibid., 1953, pp. 1332, 1340, 2402.

78. Ibid., pp. 1313, 1331, 1336, 1350, and *Davar*, 12 April 1953 and 19 May 1953. In Hebrew.

79. The phrase which was often used in searing criticism of the Holocaust victims. It had special poignancy since it had appeared in the poetry of Haim Nachman Bialik, "the national Hebrew poet" in his "poems of wrath" castigating Jewish victims of the 1904 Russian pogroms because they had not defended themselves against the physical violence inflicted upon them by the Russian peasantry. The phrase evoked a series of negative associations—passive, cowardly, weak, exilic-religious Jews—the opposite of the sabra.

80. Avshalom Reich, "Changes and Developments in the Passover Haggadot of the Kibbutz Movement" (Ph.D. diss. University of Texas, 1972), p. 393.

81. Binyamin Kedar, "The Masada Complex," *Ha'Aretz*, 22 April 1973, in Hebrew.

82. See, for example, the evidence in kibbutz haggadot, Reich, "Changes in the Haggadot of the Kibbutz," pp. 306, 324, 366, 393. Statements such as the following were now inserted into the haggadot: "Synagogues and holy books were set afire. Torah scrolls—symbols of ancient culture that were the fortress of our people in the dispersion—were trampled by coarse feet." and "I abjure our brothers . . . remember your Fathers . . . remember the covenant—the covenant of the Fathers with God. . . . Alas, you have neglected this inheritance of your Fathers, more precious than anything else."

83. Yaacov Maor, "How Is This Haggada Different?" *Yediot Aharonot*, 1 April 1975, in Hebrew.

84. *Davar*, 22 April 1951.

85. *Divrei Haknesset*, 1951, pp. 1310, 1313, 1332, in Hebrew.

86. David Ben Gurion, "Concepts and Values," *Hazut*, 3 (1957, in Hebrew), p. 8.

87. Ben Gurion, *In the Conflict* (Tel Aviv: Hotzaat Mapai, 1949, in Hebrew), 4:12.

88. Yigal Donitz, "Ben Gurion's Fundamental Political-Military Understanding and His Conception of the Israeli Arab Conflict," *Medina Umimshal*, 1 (1971, in Hebrew), pp. 71–73.

89. *Divrei Haknesset*, 1952, p. 910.

90. Ibid., pp. 959–960. See also p. 950.

91. *Davar*, 22 April 1951, in Hebrew.

92. Ben Gurion, *The Eternity of Israel* (Tel Aviv: Eynot, 1964, in Hebrew), p. 307.

93. Harold Fisch, *The Zionist Revolution* (London: Weidenfeld and Nicolson, 1978), p. 110.

94. A brilliant discussion of the meaning of nations' flags and the interpretation of the symbolic import of various types of flags is Sasha

R. Weitman, "National Flags: A Sociological Overview," *Semiatica*, 8 (1973) 327–367.

95. Mordechai Eliav, "Toward a History of the Zionist Flag," *Kivunim*, 3 (June 1979, in Hebrew), 47–59.

96. *The Protocol of the Temporary National Council*, vol. 1, 10th session, in Hebrew, p. 10.

97. Ibid., p. 14.

98. Ibid., vol. 2, 23d session, pp. 43–44.

99. See, for example, ibid., p. 45 and the 24th session, pp. 10, 12, 14.

100. *Divrei Haknesset*, 1953, p. 1486.

101. See, for example, Ben Gurion, *Stars and Dust*, pp. 107–108.

102. Elon, *The Israelis*, p. 280.

103. Ibid., p. 281.

104. Yigal Yadin, *The Message of the Scrolls* (New York: Simon and Schuster, 1957), p. 14.

105. Ibid., p. 57.

106. Elon, *The Israelis*, p. 286.

107. Ibid., p. 289.

108. *Hador*, 25 October 1951.

109. Ben Gurion, *Vision and Way*, 3:239.

110. Ibid., p. 240.

111. The citation is from an article written by Daniel Persky in 1948 and is reprinted in Yom Tov Levinsky, ed., *The Book of Holidays* (Tel Aviv: Dvir, 1957, in Hebrew), 8:465. In a similar vein, see: *Hapoel Hatzair*, 13 May 1948; *D'var Hashavua*, 7 May 1950, in Hebrew; *Davar*, 20 April 1953; and *Divrei Haknesset*, 1949, p. 349.

112. *Davar*, 10 April 1949.

113. *Davar*, 14 April 1950; 20 April 1953; 27 April 1955; and *Hapoel Hatzair*, 3 May 1949.

114. Levinsky, *The Book of Holidays*, vol. 8, p. 505. The term "Torah" referred to scholarship in the arts and humanities and not necessarily to study of sacred scriptures.

115. *Davar*, 17 April 1956.

116. On the presence and meaning of fire in romantic nationalist movements and its origin, see George L. Mosse, *The Nationalization of the Masses* (New York: Fertig, 1975) pp. 40–44.

117. *Davar*, 23 April 1950.

118. Harold Fisch, *Zionist Revolution*, p. 54.

119. Mosse, *Nationalization of the Masses*, p. 41; Robert Bocock, *Ritual in Industrialized Societies* (London: G. Allen and Unwin, 1974), p. 117. According to Bocock these are all phallic symbols of birth and renewal, growth and development.

120. *Davar*, 24 April 1950.

121. *Maariv*, 30 April 1952.

122. The proposal, made in 1949, is reprinted in Levinsky, *The Book of Holidays*, vol. 8, p. 568.

123. *Davar*, 23 April 1950.

124. *Divrei Haknesset*, 1950, p. 1062. See also p. 1068.

125. Ibid., p. 1066.

126. George L. Mosse, "National Cemeteries and National Revival: The Cult of the Fallen Soldiers in Germany," *Journal of Contemporary History*, no. 1 (January 1979), 14:1–17.

127. Ibid., pp. 12–15.

128. *Davar*, 30 April 1953; 3 May 1953.

129. *Davar*, 2 May 1956.

130. We have already discussed the association of the two days above. See also *Davar*, 30 April 1952. On the kibbutz haggadot, see Reich, "Changes in the Haggadot of the Kibbutz," pp. 131–133, 168–169.

131. *Davar*, 16 October 1949.

132. On one such effort among Yemenite immigrants, see *D'var Hashavua*, 21 June 1959, in Hebrew.

5: New Civil Religion

1. David Ben Gurion, *Vision and Way* (Tel Aviv: Hotzaat Mapai, 2d ed., 1953, in Hebrew), 3:104–105.

2. *Divrei Haknesset* (in Hebrew), 1953, p. 1333.

3. Daniel Bell, *The End of Ideology* (New York: The Free Press, 1962), pp. 393–407.

4. David Apter, "Political Religion in the New Nations," Clifford Geertz, ed., *Old Societies and New States* (New York: The Free Press, 1963), pp. 57–104.

5. Ibid., pp. 78, 84, 92, 93.

6. This should be qualified by noting that Ben Gurion did resort to antidemocratic measures in some instances; for example, he imposed a military administration on Israeli Arabs, he did not prevent antireligious coercion in the immigrant camps, he expressed impatience with criticism of the government by the Israeli press. And some of his supporters echoed views of a decidedly totalitarian nature. For example, in a 1949 meeting the labor leader and essayist Shmuel Yavne'el expressed the opinion that writers must be edited and a court of writers should be established to supervise all artistic efforts. Ben Gurion rejected the suggestion and insisted upon complete freedom for the artist. However, he did call upon artists to exhibit national responsibility, to participate in forming the image of the nation and to contribute to national solidarity. Ben Gurion, *Vision and Way*, pp. 83–87.

7. Apter, *Political Religion in New Nations*, p. 63.

8. Ibid., p. 92.

9. This, however, was not true of the religious division of the educational system which retained most of its autonomy and control over its own schools.

10. Apter, *Political Religion in New Nations*, p. 95.

11. Ibid., p. 96.

12. Ibid., p. 97.

13. Ehud ben Ezer, ed., *Unease In Zion* (New York: Quadrangle Books, 1974), p. 66. Amos Elon, *The Israelis: Founders and Sons* (London: Weidenfeld and Nicolson, 1971), pp. 264–279 provides evidence of the moral uneasiness among Israelis over their rights to the Land of Israel, and observes that whereas uneasiness has been present since the very creation of the State, it "rose to the surface in the aftermath of the 1967 war" (p. 267).

14. *Ha'Aretz*, 15 April 1975, in Hebrew.

15. Amos Oz, "Meaning of Homeland," *Who Is the Left?: Zionism Answers Back* (Jerusalem: Hasifriya Hatziburit, 1971, in Hebrew), pp. 158–159.

16. Ibid., p. 159.

17. Misha Louvish, *A People That Dwells Alone: Speeches and Writings of Yaacov Herzog* (London: Weidenfeld and Nicolson, 1975), p. 54.

18. *Ha'Aretz*, 11 January 1976, in Hebrew.

19. "To Be a Jew," *B'Tfutzot Ha'Golah*, 16 (Summer 1974, in Hebrew), 117. The use of the term *Jew* rather than *Israeli* should not go unnoticed.

20. "Society in Protracted Conflict," *Skira Hodshit* (August–September 1975, in Hebrew), pp. 40–58.

21. B.A. seminar paper submitted by Col. (ret.) Zvi Bar to the Political Science Department of Bar-Ilan University, 1975.

22. *Yediot Aharonot*, July 22, 1980, in Hebrew.

23. Virtually all Israelis are convinced that, given the means, their Arab neighbors, the PLO in particular, would kill them. Even the PLO, however, has eschewed public declaration to this effect. Instead, its public demands have been directed toward the dismantling of Israel as a Jewish state.

24. Schweid, *Israel at the Crossroads* (Philadelphia: Jewish Publication Society, 1973), p. 178.

25. Ibid., p. 184.

26. Ibid., p. 185.

27. See, for example, Zvi Lamm, "Imprints of Traditionalism and the Process of Modernization in Judaism," *B'Tfutzot Ha'Golah*, 73/74 (Summer 1975, in Hebrew), 62–72; A. B. Yehoshua, "A Return to Ideology," *B'Tfutzot Ha'Golah*, 75/76 (Winter, 1975, in Hebrew),

28–40, and in the same issue, Yigal Elam, "The Zionist Crises—The Jewish Crises," pp. 52–58. S. Ben-Avraham reflects a far less dogmatic, more questful attitude in an article in the left-wing daily *Al Ha'Mishmar*. He doubts the possibility of a national identity or culture independent of religion, rejects the simple substitution of religious ceremony in the absence of religious belief and asks "how can we believe?" (The article "Religion, Nationality and Secularism" is reprinted in *Hayenu Hadatiyim*, a reprint of all articles appearing in the daily press and published by the Israeli Ministry of Religion. The article appeared in the January 11, 1976, to February 2, 1976, issues of the publication.)

28. Simon Herman, *Jewish Identity: A Social Psychological Perspective* (Beverly Hills: Sage Publications, 1977), pp. 187–188.

29. Ibid. Comparing the 1974 sample of high school youth with data from a 1965 sample leads one to conclude that the decline is accounted for almost entirely by the Oriental population among whom youngsters from religious and traditional homes continue to abandon the tradition. Among non-Orientals, there is, if anything, a return to religion though not in any noticeable quantity. Also of interest is the fact that, among religious non-Oriental youth from religious homes, there is a tendency to be even more observant and religiously zealous than their parents.

30. Educational Office of the Army, "The Day of Memorial for the Holocaust and Bravery," *Informational Guidelines to the Commander*, no. 16 (April, 1976, in Hebrew).

31. Elihu Katz and Michael Gurevitch, *The Secularization of Leisure: Culture and Communication In Israel* (London: Faber and Faber, 1976), pp. 246–248, see also p. 205.

32. Yaacov Manor, "Why Is This *Haggada* Different . . ." *Yediot Aharonot*, April 1, 1975. The subsequent details are also based on this newspaper article.

33. "Israeli Youth and Their Zionist Education," *Dispersion and Unity*, 21/22 (1973/1974), 101.

34. *Maariv*, 22 August 1980.

35. On the day dedicated to those who died in the Holocaust, Tel Aviv's chief rabbi said: "In the year 1975 the gentiles have remained just as they were in the period of the Holocaust, and the eternal hatred of the world against the eternal people . . . still exists." *Maariv*, 8 January 1975, in Hebrew.

36. Misha Louvish, ed., *A People That Dwells Alone*, p. 52.

37. *Jerusalem Post*, 12 January 1976.

38. A sample survey of the adult Jewish population of Israel conducted by the private research organization PORI for the Ministry of Religions in 1975 found, for example, that 38 percent of those

who identified themselves as nonreligious attended synagogue on the High Holidays, 43 percent reported that they kept a kosher home (probably meaning that they bought only kosher meat), 17 percent reported that they observed kashrut outside the home, and 30 percent reported that they celebrated the Sabbath in some way: lighting candles, a festive meal.

39. The proportion of religious is slightly less than is normally found in sample surveys of the population though well within a 2½ percent margin of error. According to the Director of PORI who conducted both our survey, the Ministry of Religions survey, and countless others, the best approximation of the number of Jews in the population over 18 who define themselves as religious is 15 percent.

40. The question was adapted from a similar question posed to Israeli high school students in 1965 and 1974 in the study by Simon Herman reported earlier.

41. *Encyclopedia Judaica*, 11:1091. See also *Encyclopedia of Zionism*, p. 810.

42. See, for example, *Siaḥ Loḥamim* (Conversations of Warriors), a collection of taped interviews with kibbutz members who fought in the Six Day War.

43. For the report of the exchange and an incisive analysis of the Masada story see, Robert Alter, "The Masada Complex," *Commentary*, 56 (July 1973), 19–21.

44. Ibid., p. 20.

45. Ibid., p. 21.

46. Some of the literature is reviewed in Alter and Baila Shargel, "The Evolution of the Masada Myth," *Judaism*, 28 (Summer 1979), 357–371.

47. Alter, "The Masada Complex," p. 22.

48. *Maariv*, 17 October 1980.

49. *Ha'Aretz*, 30 April 1976.

50. *Ha'Aretz*, 2 May 1976.

51. *Maariv*, 18 April 1980.

52. The description of Jerusalem Day is based on Lt. Col. (ret.) Natan Kleinman (B.A. paper, Bar-Ilan University, 1975).

53. *Bamaḥaneh*, 14 April 1976, in Hebrew.

54. S. Clement Leslie, *The Rift in Israel: Religious Authority and Secular Democracy* (New York: Schocken Books, 1971), p. 103.

55. One can find an excellent discussion of the problem and an extensive bibliography in Shalom Lilker, *Kibbutz Judaism: A New Tradition in the Making*, (Ph.D. diss., Hebrew Union College—Jewish Institute of Religion, 1972). See also, Zvi Yaron, "Religion in Israel," in Morris Fine and Milton Himmelfarb, eds. *American Jewish Year Book 1976* (Philadelphia: Jewish Publication Society, 1976).

56. Gideon Krasel, *From Everyone According to His Ability: Stratification Versus Ability on the Kibbutz* (Tel Aviv: Gomeh, 1974, in Hebrew), p. 44.

57. Lilker, *Kibbutz Judaism*, and Yaacov Manor, "Why Is This Haggada Different?" A careful analysis of the changes which documents the steady increment of traditional text was made by David Sorek in a B.A. seminar paper submitted to the Political Science Department of Bar-Ilan University in 1976. See also, Eli Mohar, "If You Wish—This Is A Haggada," in *Bamaḥaneh*, 14 April 1976, 18–19.

58. The material was analyzed by Etty Hirsch as part of a B.A. seminar paper submitted to the Political Science Department of Bar-Ilan University in 1975.

59. A noted non-religious columnist, Heda Boshes, in the militantly secularist daily, *Ha'Aretz*, September 18, 1980, noted that: "Israelis whose parents believed that the 'religion of labor' would replace religion and hoped for a secular state in which Zionism would provide a national identity to the Jewish people wrestle unsuccessfully with their Jewishness . . . and ask themselves . . . what is a Jew and what is the heritage and meaning of Judaism in the State of Israel."

60. *Among Young People* (in Hebrew), a mimeographed booklet of conversations with members of Kibbutz Ein Shemer, a non-religious kibbutz, published in 1969, p. 12.

61. Interview reported by Kewiti Balfor in a B.A. seminar paper submitted to the Political Science Department of Bar-Ilan University in 1976.

62. The statement with appropriate scholarly references is found in David Landes, "Palestine Before the Zionists," *Commentary*, 61 (February 1976), 53.

63. The material is based on a B.A. seminar paper by Lieutenant Colonel (ret.) Gabriel Barshai submitted to the Political Science Department of Bar-Ilan University, 1975.

64. The material on the penetration of Jewish symbols into the Arab village is based on a B.A. seminar paper by Aabed Aabed submitted to the Political Science Department of Bar-Ilan University, 1975.

65. The first four options parallel those suggested by Milton Esman, "The Management of Communal Conflict," *Public Policy*, 21 (Winter 1973), 49–78.

66. See Sammy Smooha, "Control of Minorities in Israel and Northern Ireland," *Comparative Studies In Society and History*, 22 (April 1980), 256–280 and Ian Lustick, *Arabs in the Jewish State* (Austin: University of Texas Press, 1980).

6: Instruments of Socialization

1. The analysis was done by Beny Berkowitz as part of a B.A. seminar paper submitted to the Political Science Department of Bar-Ilan University in 1975.

2. The analysis was done by Naomi Kremnitzer as part of a B.A. seminar paper submitted to the Political Science Department of Bar-Ilan University in 1975.

3. Interviews were conducted by Rachel Avni for a B.A. seminar paper submitted to the Political Science Department of Bar-Ilan University in 1976.

4. *Ha'Aretz*, 20 March 1974.

5. Ibid.

6. Ibid., 16 March 1976.

7. Reprinted in S.N. Eisenstadt, Ch. Adler, R. Kahana and E. Shelach, *Education and Society in Israel* (Jerusalem, Academon, 1968, in Hebrew), p. 29.

8. From a general circular issued by the director general of the ministry of education and culture, September 20, 1957.

9. *Divrei HaKnesset*, 1959, p. 2186; see also p. 2186, in Hebrew.

10. Ibid., pp. 2191−2192.

11. Ibid., p. 2226.

12. Ibid., pp. 2227−2228.

13. Ibid., p. 2224.

14. Ibid., p. 2228.

15. Zvi Adar, *Jewish Education in Israel and the United States* (Tel Aviv: Gomeh, 1969, in Hebrew), p. 70. See also Zvi E. Kurzweil, *Modern Trends in Jewish Education* (New York: Thomas Yoseloff, 1964), pp. 275−303 and J. Schoneveld, *The Bible in Israeli Education* (Assen/Amsterdam: Van Gorcum, 1976), pp. 114−125.

16. Adar, *Jewish Education*, p. 76

17. See, for example, Uzi Ornan, "Jewish Consciousness— Heretical Reservations," *Haḥinuḥ*, 5−6 (July 1976, in Hebrew), 20−26.

18. Simon Herman, *Israelis and Jews; The Continuity of an Identity* (New York: Random House, 1970) and *Jewish Identity: A Social Psychological Perspective* (Beverly Hills: Sage, 1977).

19. Elihu Katz and Michael Gurevitch, *"The Secularization of Leisure: Culture and Communication in Israel* (London: Faber and Faber, 1976).

20. Shlomit Levy and Louis Guttman, *Values and Attitudes of Israeli High School Youth* (Jerusalem: The Israel Institute of Applied Social Research, 1976, in Hebrew).

21. For example, in 1970 sixty high school students sent a letter to Prime Minister Golda Meir protesting the government's refusal to

permit Nahum Goldman to represent it in talks with Egyptian leader
Gamal Abdul Nasser. The episode surrounding a proposed meeting
between Goldman and Nasser is complicated and not relevant to our
study. Without attempting to assess the facts, an impression was
created in Israel that Nasser had indirectly extended an invitation to
Nahum Goldman, a non-Israeli and the most prominent world leader
in organized Jewish life who was known as a dove, to come to Cairo to
discuss Israeli-Egyptian relations, provided that the government of
Israel designated him as an official representative. This the government refused to do. The mass media was filled with denunciations of
the youth and expressions of concern about the failure of Israeli
society in general and the schools in particular to instill proper values
in the youth. In fact, the military censorship originally prohibited the
publication of the letter and it became a topic of discussion by the
Cabinet itself. (Details concerning the episode were gathered by Shai
Mital and presented as a B.A. seminar paper to the Department of
Political Science of Bar-Ilan University in 1975.) The following is the
full text of the letter (our translation) that so excited Israeli society:
"We, a group of high school students about to enter the army, protest
the government's policy with respect to the episode of the Goldman-
Nasser talks. Until now, we believed we were going to fight and serve
for three years because there is no alternative. After this episode it was
demonstrated that even when there is an alternative, *albeit* the very
slightest one, it is ignored. In the light of this we and many others
think—how are we to fight in a continuing war without a future when
our government directs its policy in such a way that opportunities for
peace are missed? We call upon the government to exploit every
opportunity and every chance for peace."

22. Interview schedules were devised and interviews were conducted independently by Shulamit Boneh and Ruth Yanai for B.A.
seminars in the Department of Political Science of Bar-Ilan University in 1975.

23. *Informal Guidelines to the Commander* (April 1980), no. 14. In
fact, this issue is identical with the issues dedicated to Holocaust Day
for the last few years.

24. Material on the officers training school was provided by Col.
(ret.) Zvi Bar, who commanded the school prior to the Yom Kippur
War, and submitted as part of a B.A. seminar paper to the Political
Science Department of Bar-Ilan University in 1975.

25. Gush Etzion comprised four religious settlements prior to
1948. Located about ten miles from Jerusalem, it fell to the Arabs
after a bitter fight. In those settlements which fell to Arab irregulars
rather than the Jordanian Legion everyone was massacred. Gush
Etzion has great emotional meaning to many Israelis, religious Jews in
particular. Immediately after the Six Day War when the area was

retaken, it was resettled by religious Jews. Among the first to return were offspring of the old settlers.

26. The Jew is enjoined to don tephillin during his morning prayers (except for the Sabbath and holidays). The cheapest tephillin cost approximately fifty dollars.

27. The information that follows is based on a B.A. seminar paper by Lt. Col. (ret.) Natan Kleinman submitted to the Department of Political Science of Bar-Ilan University in 1975.

28. Amos Elon, *The Israelis: Founders and Sons* (London: Weidenfeld and Nicolson, 1971), p. 33. Gershon Weiler comments that we live now in the period where "heads of State court Hassidic leaders," *Ha'Aretz*, 19 September 1973.

29. *Hatzofe*, 29 September 1974.

30. *She'arim*, 5 August 1975.

31. *Yediot Aharonot*, 15 August 1975. For a very critical view of Peres's remarks suggesting his particular hypocrisy in posing as a religious Jew by his comments, "I particularly pray when I see the boys in Ramat HaGolan, in Sinai" or that being minister of defense of Israel is "a religious experience," see *Ha'Aretz*, 24 August 1975. To the best of our knowledge, no one commented on what to us seems the worst of Peres's distortions. In the biblical tradition, it is not the Jews who are created in the image of God, but rather all men. Peres's mistake, however, which we suspect was indeed a mistake and not a deliberate effort to distort the text, strongly suggests the impact of the "people that dwell alone" philosophy we described in the previous chapter.

32. A speech given at the dedication of a library in honor of the graduates of a religious high school who died in Israeli wars and reprinted in *Bamahaneh*, 4 February 1976.

33. *Ha'Aretz*, 27 April 1976.

34. Ibid., 28 April 1976.

35. A week later, at the opening Memorial Day ceremonies in honor of those who died in Israel's wars the chief of staff delivered the major televised address in which he stressed the uniqueness of the Jewish people and added: "The world around us did not spare efforts to compel us to deny and abandon our unique and historical faith."

7: Responses of Religious Jews to Civil Religion

1. Charles S. Liebman, "The Rise of Neo-Traditionalism Among Modern Orthodox Jews in Israel," Louis Greenspan and William Shaffir, eds., *Identification and the Revival of the New Religious Orthodoxies* (forthcoming).

2. The group labeled Neo-Orthodoxy is most closely associated with the intellectual and organizational efforts of Samson Raphael

Hirsch (1808—1888) most of whose work has been translated into English. For some secondary literature see Noah N. Rosenbloom, *Tradition In An Age of Reform: The Religious Philosophy of Samson Raphael Hirsch* (Philadelphia: Jewish Publication Society, 1976); Herman Schwab, *The History of Orthodox Jewry in Germany* (London: The Mitre Press, 1950); Eliezer Schweid, "Two Neo-Orthodox Responses to Modernity: Rabbi Samson Raphael Hirsch and Rabbi Abraham Isaac Hacohen Kook" (Imanuel, forthcoming); Norman Lamm, "Two Versions of 'Synthesis,' " Menahem M. Kasher et al., eds., *The Leo Jung Jubilee Volume* (New York: Shulsinger, 1962).

3. On the development of the rejectionist community in the yishuv with special reference to Agudat Israel and their relations to religious Zionism see Menachem Friedman, *Society and Religion: The Non-Zionist Orthodox in Eretz-Israel 1918—1936* (Jerusalem: Yad Izhak Ben-Zvi, 1977, in Hebrew). See also Eliezer Don-Yehiya, "Origins and Development of the Agudah and Mafdal Parties," *Jerusalem Quarterly*, no. 20 (Summer, 1981), pp. 49—64. An uncritical but informative volume is *Yaakov Rosenheim Memorial Anthology: A Concise History of Agudath Israel* (New York: Orthodox Library, 1968). See also Emile Marmorstein, *Heaven at Bay* (London: Oxford University Press, 1969).

4. Friedman, *Society and Religion*. See also his article, "Religious Zealotry in Israeli Society," *On Ethnic and Religious Diversity in Israel* (Ramat-Gan: Bar-Ilan University, 1975), pp. 91—112. For a sympathetic treatment see Emil Marmorstein, "Religious Opposition to Nationalism in the Middle East," J. Milton Yinger, *Religion, Society and the Individual* (New York: Macmillan, 1963), pp. 542—552. On the resistance to and penetration of change in one crucial area see Raphael Schneller, "Continuity and Change in Ultra-Orthodox Education," *Jewish Journal of Sociology*, 22 (June 1980), 35—46.

5. Elhanan Wasserman, *The Footsteps of the Messiah* (B'nei Brak: Histadrut Z'erei Agudat Israel, 3d edition, in Hebrew, first published in 1942), p. 13. The book also appeared in English as *Epoch of the Messiah* (Los Angeles: n.p., n.d.) See also Nathan Birnbaum, *The Nation of God* (B'nei Brak: Nezah, 1977), in Hebrew, first published in German in 1917), p. 60.

6. Ibid., p. 14.

7. The hassidim are religiously observant Jews who are subdivided into a number of groups according to their adherence to one rebbe or another to whom they attribute charismatic qualities. Most, though not all hassidic groups are non-Zionist. This includes the contemporary Lubbavitcher hassidim who support Israel and even oppose its withdrawal from the territories it captured in the Six Day War.

8. "Statement by the Lubbavitcher Rebbe, Rabbi Shulem ben

Schneersohn, on Zionism," Michael Selzer, ed., *Zionism Reconsidered* (New York: The Macmillan Co., 1970), p. 13.

9. Moshe Blau, *Column of Light* (Jerusalem: Homot Yerushalayim, 1968, in Hebrew, first published in 1932), pp. 35–36.

10. Wasserman, *Footsteps of the Messiah*, p. 37.

11. Statement by the Lubbavitcher Rebbe.

12. The statement by Rabbi Grozovsky is found in the Appendix to Wasserman, *Footsteps of the Messiah*, p. 50.

13. Moshe Avigdor Amiel, "Who Are We?" *Hator* (September 28, 1932, in Hebrew), p. 5. *Hator* was a publication of religious Zionism.

14. Ibid., p. 6.

15. Moshe Avigdor Amiel, "Again on the Ideological Foundations of Mizrachi," *Hator*, 24 August 1934, p. 3.

16. Ibid.

17. See, for example, Moshe Avigdor Amiel, "Who Are We?" *Hator*, 2 November 1932, p. 4.

18. See his series of articles in *Hator* from September through December of 1934 under the title "After the Congress and Before the Congress."

19. Isaac Breuer, *Concepts of Judaism*, ed. Jacob Levinger (Jerusalem: Israel Universities Press, 1974).

20. They centered on a group called *El Hamakor* (to the Source) a faction within the religious Zionist party.

21. Isaac Jacob Reines, *A New Light on Zion* (Vilna: R'em, 1902, in Hebrew), p. 276.

22. Isaac Jacob Reines, *The Gates of Light and Joy* (Vilna: R'em, 1890, in Hebrew), p. 25.

23. On the political implications of this stance which led, for example, to Reines's support for Herzl's Uganda proposal and his opposition to cultural Zionism see Eliezer Don-Yehiya, "Ideology and Policy: The Zionist Conception of Rav Reines and the Stance of Mizrachi Under His Leadership on the Uganda Question," *Religion and Zionism: The Relations Between Religious and Secular in the Zionist Movement* (Tel Aviv: Tel Aviv University, Hamachon L'heker Hatziyonut, forthcoming).

24. Essays from both periods are collected in Yeshayahu Leibowitz, *Judaism, the Jewish People and the State of Israel* (Jerusalem: Schocken, 1975, in Hebrew). An excellent summary, which notes the differences between Leibowitz's earlier and later positions, is Eliezer Goldman, "The Jewish Test of the State of Israel," *Amudim*, 24 (Heshvan, Kislev 1975, in Hebrew), 63–68 and 100–105.

25. Leibowitz, *Judaism, The Jewish People*, p. 298.

26. Ibid., p. 246.

27. Ibid., pp. 247–248.

28. Ibid., p. 233.

29. Ibid., p. 234.

30. Ibid., p. 246.

31. Ibid., p. 240.

32. The basic conceptions of Rav Kook from which all the material in this section is drawn are found in a posthumous collection of his writing, *Orot* (Jerusalem: Mossad Harav Kook, 1950, in Hebrew). On Rav Kook's philosophy see Zvi Yaron, *The Philosophy of Rabbi Kook* (Jerusalem, The Department of Torah Education and Culture of the World Zionist Organization, 1974, in Hebrew); Samuel Hugo Berman, *Faith and Reason: An Introduction to Modern Jewish Thought* (New York: Schocken Paperback Books, 1963), pp. 121–141. Neither of these secondary sources reflects our understanding of Rav Kook's thought as it pertains to our topic. Much closer in perspective is Eliezer Schweid's chapter "Secularism From A Religious Perspective," in his book, *Judaism and the Secular Culture* (Tel-Aviv: HaKibbutz Hameuchad, 1981, in Hebrew), pp. 110–142.

33. *Orot*, pp. 63–64.

34. *Letters of Harav Kook*, 2 (Jerusalem: Mossad Harav Kook, 1962), 186–187.

35. Kook, *Orot*, pp. 108–109.

36. Ibid., p. 159.

37. Ibid., p. 84.

38. Ibid., pp. 67–69, 77, 78, 80.

39. Ibid., pp. 57, 59, 77.

40. Ibid., p. 160.

41. Zvi Yehuda Kook, *To The Paths of Israel* (Jerusalem: Zur-Ot, rev. ed., 1969, in Hebrew), 1:159.

42. Ibid.

43. Ibid., p. 160.

44. Ibid., pp. 94–98.

45. Statement by Yochanan Fried, a dedicated follower of Rav Zvi Yehuda who was involved in efforts surrounding the publication of the manifesto. The statement was made at a symposium at Bar-Ilan University, January 14, 1981.

46. Zvi Yehuda Kook, *To The Paths*, pp. 157–158.

47. Ibid., p. 113.

48. Ibid., p. 91.

49. Ibid., pp. 112–113.

50. Gush Emunim is too recent a phenomenon to have been systematically studied though a number of works are now in progress. The only book, Zvi Raanan, *Gush Emunim* (Tel Aviv: Sifriyat Hapoalim, 1980, in Hebrew) is sharply polemical but contains some useful information and transcripts of interviews which are very revealing. One can learn about part of the background to the establishment of Gush Emunim from a study of the Land of Israel Movement, which preceded it, in Rael Jean Isaac, *Israel Divided: Ideological Politics in the Jewish State* (Baltimore: Johns Hopkins University Press, 1976).

Janet O'Dea, "Gush Emunim: Roots and Ambiguities," *Forum* (Fall 1976), pp. 39–50; Lawrence Kaplan, "Education and Ideology in Religious Zionism Today," *Forum* (Fall/Winter 1979), pp. 25–34; and Ehud Sprinzak "Gush Emunim: The Tip of the Iceberg," *Jerusalem Quarterly*, no. 21 (Fall 1981), pp. 28–47.

51. *Yediot Aharonot*, July 13, 1975.

52. Yehuda Amital, *Upward From the Depths* (Jerusalem: Hotzaat Agudat Yeshivat Har Etzion, 1974, in Hebrew), p. 21.

53. Ibid., p. 28.

54. On the young Mafdal Circles and their role in the party, see Eliezer Don-Yehiya, "Stability and Change in a Camp Party," *Medina V'memshal*, no. 14 (November 1979, in Hebrew), pp. 25–52.

55. On the perception of a secularist adherent of Gush Emunim that this group represents the continuation of the original ideals of the Kibbutz founders which their own children had abandoned see the interview with Ephraim Ben-Haim in Raanan, *Gush Emunim*, p. 212–221.

56. The comparison was made by Hanan Porat in a 1979 symposium and is quoted in B'eri Zimmerman, "The Priority of Man Over Soil: A Comparison of Brenner and Hanan Porat," *Shdemot*, no. 72 (Tishrei 1980, in Hebrew), p. 72.

57. The statement by Rabbi Eliezer Waldman appears in an interview with Zvi Raanan in Raanan, *Gush Emunim*, p. 211.

58. Cited by David Schnall, *Radical Dissent in Contemporary Israeli Politics* (New York: Praeger Publishers, 1979), p. 146.

59. Zvi Yehuda Kook, *To The Paths*, 1:239.

60. Ibid., 2:240.

61. On Torah V'avoda see Aryei Fishman, ed., *Hapoel Hamizrachi: 1921–1935* (Tel Aviv: Tel Aviv University, 1979, in Hebrew). On the religious kibbutz movement see Aryei Fishman, "The Religious Kibbutz: A Study in the Interrelationship of Religion and Ideology in the Context of Modernization" (Ph.D. diss., Hebrew University, 1975, in Hebrew).

62. Shabbetai Don-Yehiya, *The Holy Rebellion* (Tel Aviv: Moreshet, 1960, in Hebrew), pp. 70, 90, 91.

63. Cited in Fishman, ed., *Hapoel Hamizrachi*, p. 39.

64. Ibid., p. 59 and see also p. 153.

65. Ibid., p. 49.

66. Ibid., p. 83.

67. Fishman, "The Religious Kibbutz," p. 168.

68. Ibid., p. 157.

69. For some examples of the application of religious terminology to "secular" activity see Fishman, *Hapoel Hamizrachi*, pp. 131, 140 and the biography of the founder of the religious Zionist labor movement by Shabbetai Don-Yehiya, *Holy Rebellion*, p. 122. The term *holy rebellion* used by Torah V'avoda founders is itself of significance.

70. Fishman, ibid., p. 66.
71. Ibid., p. 128, 133 and p. 63 of the footnotes.
72. Ibid., p. 244.
73. Ibid and the footnotes cited on pp. 66, 112 and 113.
74. Ibid., p. 200.
75. Ibid., pp. 205–206.
76. Leibowitz, *Judaism, The Jewish People*, p. 53.
77. Ibid., p. 119.
78. On the rise of expansionism and religious extremism within Israel see Liebman, "The Rise of Neo-Traditionalism."
79. An example is the Hanukkah song "Who Can Retell the Heroism of Israel" which is a conscious transformation of the biblical passage "who can retell the heroism of God." This Zionist song is sung in many religious Zionist schools although recently some of them, consistent with expansionist currents, have rewritten the first verse of the song by substituting the original biblical phrase.
80. *Hazofe*, 25 August 1950, in Hebrew. See also 1 May 1951 and 5 August 1950.
81. Ibid., 4 August 1948; 15 May 1951; and 15 July 1951.
82. Ibid., 18 April 1951.
83. Ibid., 30 March 1951.
84. Ibid., 18 December 1951. See also 13 April 1951; 29 May 1951; and 19 March 1952.
85. An article titled "B'nei Brak Rabbis Call for Volunteering to the Civil Guard" appeared in *Maariv* and was reprinted in *Hayenu Hadatiyim*, vol. 14 (January 13, 1975–February 4, 1975, in Hebrew).
86. *Ma'ariv*, 7 July 1974, in Hebrew. The story quotes Chief Rabbi Goren as saying that using the pill violates the life-saving needs of Israel because Israel needs increased population.
87. *Ha'Aretz*, 19 November 1974, in Hebrew, cites Chief Rabbi Yosef to this effect.
88. *Hazofe*, 15 July 1974, in Hebrew. Chief Rabbi Yosef noted that political isolation and economic difficulty "characterized the Jewish nation in all generations and never shook the foundations of its existence."
89. Simon Herman, *Jewish Identity: A Social Psychological Perspective* (Beverly Hills: Sage, 1977), pp. 183–191.

8: Summary and Conclusions

1. Robert N. Bellah, "Religion and Legitimation in the American Republic," *Society*, 15 (May/June 1978), 19. Bellah calls this notion liberalism and distinguishes it from republicanism which, in our terminology, is a type of moral community. According to Bellah, the purposes or values of republicanism are: political equality, popular government, and the eliciting of ethical commitments from its citizens

(pp. 16–24). In an argument similar to the one we shall present below, Bellah maintains that republicanism requires a civil religion.

2. John Wilson, *Public Religion in American Culture* (Philadelphia: Temple University Press, 1979), p. 152.

3. Ibid., p. 151.

4. Ibid.

5. Ibid.

6. William Cole and Phillip Hammond, "Religious Pluralism, Legal Development, and Societal Complexity: Rudimentary Forms of Civil Religion," *Journal for the Scientific Study of Religion*, 13 (June 1974), 177–189; John Markoff and Daniel Regan, "The Rise and Fall of Civil Religion: Comparative Perspectives," *Sociological Analysis*, 42 (Winter 1981), 333–354.

7. Markoff and Regan, *Rise and Fall of Civil Religion*, p. 348.

8. John Coleman, "Civil Religion," *Sociological Analysis*, 31 (Summer 1970), 67–77 and Markoff and Regan, *Rise and Fall of Civil Religion*, argue that there are three forms of civil religion. Coleman calls one of them church-sponsored civil religion (he cites Israel as an example) and Markoff and Regan call one of their options traditionally dominant religion serving as the civil religion.

9. Contrary to popular opinion, this is even true of Saudi Arabia. James Piscatori, "The Roles of Islam in Saudi Arabia's Political Development," John Esposito, ed., *Islam and Development* (Syracuse: Syracuse University Press, 1980), pp. 123–138. Khomeini's Iran, for a brief period, may be an exception. We concede the point out of our ignorance of the distribution of authority in revolutionary Iran.

10. Jacob Neusner, *The Way of Torah: An Introduction to Judaism* (North Scituate, Mass.: Duxbury Press, 3d ed., 1979), pp. 7–20; Jacob Neusner, *The Rabbinic Traditions About the Pharisees Before 70*, (Leiden: Brill, 1971), 3:301–319; Morton Smith, "Palestinian Judaism in the First Century," Moshe Davis, ed., *Israel: Its Role in Civilization* (New York: The Jewish Theological Seminary of America, 1956), pp. 67–81; Israel Lee Levine, "On the Political Involvement of the Pharisees Under Herod and the Procurators," *Cathedra*, no. 8 (July 1978 in Hebrew), pp. 12–28; and Julius Guttmann, *Philosophies of Judaism* (New York: Holt, Rinehart and Winston, 1964), p. 13.

11. The political implications of this notion are developed in Martin Buber, *Kingship of God* (New York: Harper & Row, 1967). Not surprisingly, Buber was a critic of Israeli civil religion.

12. As we noted in chapter seven, Yeshayahu Leibowitz at one time sought to reformulate Judaism to adapt it to the condition of statehood. This effort, however, stemmed from a religious, not a political, perspective. Unlike the advocates of the new civil religion, Leibowitz never sought to manipulate religious symbols for political purposes.

13. On modern consciousness see, for example, Peter Berger, *The Heretical Imperative* (Garden City, N.Y.: Anchor Press, 1979).

14. On the privatization of religion in a cross-cultural context see, Talcott Parsons, "Christianity," David Sills, ed., *Encyclopedia of the Social Sciences*, 2:425–447; Robert Bellah, *Beyond Belief* (New York: Harper & Row, 1970), pp. 39–44; and Thomas Luckmann, *The Invisible Religion* (New York: The Macmillan Co., 1967).

15. Charles S. Liebman, "The Growth of Neo-Traditionalism Among Israeli Orthodox Jews," Louis Greenspan and William Shafir, eds., *Identification and the Rise of the New Religious Orthodoxies* (forthcoming).

16. Efforts to revitalize Zionist-socialism received special impetus from the 1977 electoral defeat of the Labor party. This effort is likely to fail. The symbols of Zionist-socialism, their ceremonials and especially their myths have already been desacralized and demythologized among the same groups of intellectuals who are the natural bearers of its renewal. See, for example, Gideon Ofrat, *Land, Man, Blood* (Tel-Aviv: Goma, 1980, in Hebrew), pp. 160–199; Muky Tsur, *Doing It the Hard Way* (Tel-Aviv: Am Oved, 1976, in Hebrew); Nakdimon Rogel, *Tel Ḥai* (Tel-Aviv: Yariv-Hadar, 1970, in Hebrew); or Anita Shapira, *Berl* (Tel-Aviv: Am Oved, 1980, in Hebrew).

17. The *Saharane* celebrations of Kurdish Jewry in Israel on a wide scale are too recent to have merited scholarly treatment although a recent article notes that "the Israeli environment has . . . provided an atmosphere for the development and performance of folk Kurdish literature. . . . " (p. 8) in Donna Shai, "Changes in the Oral Tradition Among the Jews of Kurdistan," *Contemporary Jewry*, 5 (Spring/Summer 1980), 2–10. On Georgian Jewry see Yitzchak Elam, *Georgian Immigrants in Israel: Anthropological Observations* (Jerusalem: Papers in Sociology—The Hebrew University, 1980, in Hebrew) and on North African Jewry and their *mimuna* celebrations see Shlomo Deshen and Moshe Shokeid, *Predicament of Homecoming: Cultural and Social Life of North African Immigrants of Israel* (Ithaca: Cornell University Press, 1974).

18. A detailed discussion of ethnicity in Israeli society is found in Sammy Smooha, *Israel: Pluralism and Conflict* (London: Routledge and Kegan Paul, 1978).

19. Baruch Kurzweil, *Our New Literature: Continuity or Revolution?* (Jerusalem: Schocken, 1965, in Hebrew), pp. 31–32.

20. Ibid., p. 203.

21. Ibid., p. 395.

22. Robert Bellah, *Beyond Belief*, pp. 246–247.

23. One can find justification for expelling the Arabs, conceptions of Jewish racial superiority, the idealization of Arab subjugation, raised to the level of religious injunction. For a series of such state-

ments see Amnon Rubinstein, *From Herzl to Gush Emunim and Back* (Jerusalem: Schocken, 1980, in Hebrew), pp. 120–125 and the citations on p. 179. Rubinstein, in our opinion, exaggerates the importance of these pronouncements which in part express the opinions of marginal individuals or hyperbole. What is more significant, however, in our opinion is that the only religious group to interpret traditional Judaism as enjoining a liberal humanist attitude toward the Arabs, a group known as Oz V'Shalom (Strength and Peace) is even more marginal and less influential among religious Zionists.

24. Interestingly, a central charge of civil religions in the past against traditional Judaism was that it was politically passive, lacked national consciousness and was ready to surrender to gentile control. By contrast, religious Zionists and their secularist allies within the new civil religion are now charged with excessive national consciousness and political activism; and the religious tradition is held accountable for this, as well. However, as we already suggested, those who favor policies of national restraint, political tolerance, and a universalist orientation together with the maintenance of Jewish singularity can also cite traditional sources. For a summary discussion of the political implications of the Jewish tradition and differences within the tradition see Bernard Susser and Eliezer Don-Yehiya, "Prolegomena to the Study of Jewish Political Theory," Daniel J. Elazar, ed., *Kinship and Consent: Essays on the Jewish Political Tradition and its Contemporary Uses* (Ramat-Gan: Turtledove, 1981), pp. 91–112.

25. Yehoshafat Harkabi, *Facing Reality: Lessons from Jeremiah, The Destruction of the Second Temple and Bar Kokhba's Rebellion* (Jerusalem: Van Leer Jerusalem Foundation, 1982).

26. *Yediot Aharonot*, 3 August 1982.

Bibliography

Daily and Weekly Newspapers

The following periodicals were reviewed as sources of general information for the period covered by the study. Articles are cited by author when the article reflects opinion and/or analysis rather than only fact.

Bamaḥaneh

Davar

D'var Hashavua

Divrei Haknesset

Hador

Ha'Aretz

Hapoel Hatzair

Hazofe

Jerusalem Post

Ma'ariv

Yediot Aḥaronot

Books and Articles in English

Almond, Gabriel and Powell, G. Bingham. *Comparative Politics.* Boston: Little, Brown, 1966.
Alter, Robert. "The Masada Complex." *Commentary*, 56 (July 1973), 19–24.

Apter, David. "Political Religions in New Nations." *Old Socie*±*ies and New States.* Edited by Clifford Geertz. New York: Free Press, 1963.

Arian, Alan. *The Choosing People: Voting Behavior in Israel.* Cleveland: Case Western Reserve Press, 1974.

Avi-Ḥai, Avraham. "Israelocentrism: A Guiding Doctrine of David Ben Gurion." *Proceedings of the Sixth World Congress for Jewish Studies, 1973.* Jerusalem: The Jerusalem Academic Press, 1975. 2: 355 – 366.

Avineri, Shlomo. "The Political Thought of Vladimir Jabotinsky." *The Jerusalem Quarterly*, no. 16 (Summer 1980), pp. 3 – 22.

Baron, Salo. *Religion and Modern Nationalism.* New York: Harper, 1947.

Bell, Daniel. *The End of Ideology.* New York: The Free Press, 1962.

Bellah, Robert N. *Beyond Belief.* New York: Harper and Row, 1970.

————. *The Broken Covenant.* New York: The Seabury Press, 1975.

————. "Civil Religion in America." *Daedalus*, 96 (Winter 1967), 1 – 21.

————. "Religion and Legitimation in the American Republic." *Society*, 15 (May/June, 1978), 16 – 23.

Ben-Ezer, Ehud. "War and Siege in Hebrew Literature After 1967." *The Jerusalem Quarterly*, no. 9 (Fall 1978), pp. 20 – 37.

Berger, Peter. *The Heretical Imperative.* Garden City, New York: Anchor Press, 1979.

————. *The Sacred Canopy.* Garden City, N.Y.: Doubleday; 1969.

————. "Some Second Thoughts on Substantive versus Functional Definitions of Religion." *Journal for the Scientific Study of Religion*, 13 (June 1974), 125 – 133.

Bergman, Samuel Hugo. *Faith and Reason: An Introduction to Modern Jewish Thought.* New York: Schocken Paperback Books, 1963.

Bickerman, Elias. *From Ezra to the Last of the Maccabees: Foundations of Post-Biblical Judaism.* New York: Schocken, 1962.

Bidney, David. "Myth, Symbol and Truth." *Myth, A Symposium.* Edited by Thomas A. Sebeok. Bloomington: University of Indiana Press, 1958.

Birnbaum, Erving. *The Politics of Compromise: State and Religion in Israel.* Cranbury, N.J.: Fairleigh Dickinson Press, 1970.

Bocieurkiw, Bohdan and Strong, John W. *Religion and Atheism in the U.S.S.R. and Eastern Europe.* London: Macmillan, 1975.

Bocock, Robert J. *Ritual in Industrial Society.* London: George Allen and Unwin, 1974.

Breuer, Isaac. *Concepts of Judaism.* Edited by Jacob Levinger. Jerusalem: Israel Universities Press, 1974.

Buber, Martin. *Kingship of God.* New York: Harper and Row, 1967.

Budd, Susan. *Sociologists and Religion.* London: Heinemann Educational Books, 1973.

Cole, William and Phillip Hammond. "Religious Pluralism, Legal Development and Societal Complexity: Rudimentary Forms of Civil Religion." *Journal for the Scientific Study of Religion,* 13 (June, 1974), 177–189.

Coleman, John. "Civil Religion." *Sociological Analysis,* 31 (Summer, 1970), 67–77.

Corbishley, Thomas. "Religion Resilient." *Soviet Jewish Affairs,* 5, 2:111.

Dayan, Moshe. *Story of My Life.* Jerusalem: Steimatzky, 1976.

Deshen, Shlomo and Shokeid, Moshe. *Predicament of Homecoming. Cultural and Social Life of North African Immigrants of Israel.* Ithaca: Cornell University Press, 1974.

Domb, Yerachmiel. *The Transformation.* London: Hamadpis, 1958.

Don-Yehiya, Eliezer. "Religion and Coalition: The National Religious Party and Coalition Formation in Israel." *The Elections in Israel 1973.* Edited by Asher Arian. Jerusalem: Jerusalem Academic Press, 1975. Pp. 255–284.

———. "Origins and Development of the Agudah and Mafdal Parties." *The Jerusalem Quarterly,* no. 2 (Summer 1981), 49–64.

Douglas, Mary. *Natural Symbols.* New York: Random House, Vintage Books, 1973.

Dubnov, Simon. *History of the Jews in Russia and Poland,* vol. 2. Trans by Israel Friedlander. Philadelphia: Jewish Publication Society, 1918.

Edelman, Murray. *Politics as Symbolic Action.* Chicago: Markham Publishing Co., 1971.

———. *The Symbolic Uses of Politics.* Urbana: University of Illinois Press, 1964.

Eister, Allan, ed. *Changing Perspectives in the Scientific Study of Religion.* New York: Wiley, 1974.

Elam, Yitzchak. *Georgian Immigrants in Israel: Anthropological Observations.* Jerusalem: Papers in Sociology, Hebrew University, 1980.

Elazar, Daniel J. *Israel: From Ideological to Territorial Democracy.* New York: General Learning Press, 1971.

———. "The New Sadducees." *Midstream,* 24 (August/September, 1978), 20–25.

Eldad, Israel. "Jabotinsky Distorted." *The Jerusalem Quarterly*, no. 16 (Summer 1980), pp. 23–39.

Elon, Amos. *The Israelis: Founders and Sons*. New York: Holt, Rinehart and Winston, 1971.

Encyclopedia Judaica, vol. 10, 1963.

Esman, Milton. "The Management of Communal Conflict." *Public Policy*, 21 (Winter 1973), 49–78.

Fagen, Richard R. *The Transformation of Political Culture in Cuba*. Stanford: Stanford University Press, 1969.

Fawcett, Thomas. *The Symbolic Language of Religion*. London: SCM Press, 1970.

Fenn, Richard. "Religion and the Legitimation of Social Systems." *Changing Perspectives in the Scientific Study of Religion*. Edited by Allan Eister. New York: Wiley, 1974. Pp. 143–161.

Fisch, Harold. *The Zionist Revolution*. London: Weidenfeld and Nicolson, 1978.

Friedman, Menachem. "Religious Zealotry in Israeli Society." *On Ethnic and Religious Diversity in Israel*. Edited by Ernest Krausz. Ramat-Gan: Bar-Ilan University, 1975. Pp. 91–112.

Friedmann, Georges. *The End of the Jewish People?* Garden City, N.Y.: Doubleday, 1967.

Geertz, Clifford. *The Interpretation of Cultures*. New York: Basic Books, 1973.

Glick, Leonard. "The Anthropology of Religion: Malinowski and Beyond?" *Beyond the Classics: Essays in the Scientific Study of Religion*. Edited by Charles Glock and Phillip Hammond. New York: Harper Torchbooks, 1973.

Greilsammer, Alain; Don-Yehiya, Eliezer; and Susser, Bernard. "Religion, Nationalisme et etat dans le Judaisme." *International Political Science Association Papers*, No. 1, Vol. VII, 3, 1973.

Gutmann, Emanuel. "Religion in Israeli Politics." *Man, State and Society in the Contemporary Middle East*. Edited by Jacob Landau. London: Pall Mall Press, 1972.

Guttmann, Julius. *Philosophies of Judaism*. New York: Holt, Rinehart and Winston, 1964.

Halpern, Ben. *The Idea of the Jewish State*. Cambridge, Mass.: Harvard University Press, 1969.

Hammond, Phillip E. "Religious Pluralism and Durkheim's Integration Thesis." *Changing Perspectives in the Scientific Study of Religion*. Edited by Allan Eister. New York: Wiley, 1974.

Herman, Simon. *Israelis and Jews: The Continuity of an Identity*. New York: Random House, 1970.

————. *Jewish Identity: A Social Psychological Perspective.* Beverly Hills, Sage Publications, 1977.

Herzog, Yaacov. *A People That Dwells Alone: Speeches and Writings of Yaacov Herzog.* Edited by Misha Louvish. London: Weidenfeld and Nicolson, 1975.

Hill, Michel. *A Sociology of Religion.* London: Heinemann Educational Books, 1973.

Horowitz, Dan and Lissak, Moshe. *The Origins of the Israeli Polity: Palestine Under the Mandate.* Chicago: University of Chicago Press, 1978.

Ichilov, Orit. "Youth Movements in Israel as Agents for Transition to Adulthood." *Jewish Journal of Sociology,* 19 (June 1977). Pp. 21–32.

Isaac, Rael Jean. *Israel Divided: Ideological Politics in the Jewish State.* Baltimore: Johns Hopkins University Press, 1976.

"Israeli Youth and Their Zionist Education." *Dispersion and Unity.* 21/22 (1973/1974). Pp. 91–120.

Kaplan, Lawrence. "Education and Ideology in Religious Zionism Today." *Forum* (Fall/Winter 1979). Pp. 25–34.

Katz, Elihu and Gurevitch, Michael. *The Secularization of Leisure: Culture and Communication in Israel.* London: Faber and Faber, 1976.

Katz, Jacob. *Out of the Ghetto: The Social Background of Jewish Emancipation, 1770–1870.* Cambridge, Mass.: Harvard University Press, 1973.

————. ed. *The Role of Religion in Modern Jewish History.* Cambridge, Mass.: Association for Jewish Studies, 1975.

Kavanagh, Dennis. *Political Culture.* London: Macmillan, 1972.

Koenker, Ernest B. *Secular Salvations: The Rites and Symbols of Political Religions.* Philadelphia: Fortress Press, 1965.

Kohn, Hans. *The Idea of Nationalism.* New York: The Macmillan Co., 1944.

Kurzweil, Baruch. "The New 'Canaanites' in Israel." *Judaism,* 2 (January 1953). Pp. 3–15.

Lamm, Norman. "The Ideology of the Neturei Karta—According to the Satmarer Version." *Tradition,* 12 (Fall 1971), 38–53.

————. "Two Versions of 'Synthesis.' " *The Leo Jung Jubilee Volume.* Edited by Menahem M. Kasher et al. New York: Shulsinger, 1962.

Landes, David. "Palestine Before the Zionists." *Commentary,* 61 (February 1976).

Langer, Susanne K. *Philosophy in a New Key: A Study in the Symbolism of Reason, Rite and Art.* New York: Penguin Books, 1942.

Laqueur, Walter. *A History of Zionism.* New York: Holt, Rinehart and

Winston, 1972.
Leslie, S. Clement. *The Rift in Israel: Religious Authority and Secular Democracy*. New York: Schocken Books, 1971.
Levi-Strauss, Claude. "The Structural Study of Myth." *Reader in Comparative Religion*. Edited by William A. Leesa and Evan Z. Vogt. 2d ed. New York: Harper and Row, 1965. Pp. 561–574.
Lewis, Bernard. "The Return of Islam." *Commentary*, 61 (January 1976), 39–49.
Liebman, Charles S. *The Ambivalent American Jew: Politics, Religion and Family in American Jewish Life*. Philadelphia: Jewish Publication Society, 1973.
————. *Pressure Without Sanctions: The Influence of World Jewry in Shaping Israel's Public Policies*. Cranbury, N.J.: Fairleigh Dickinson Press, 1977.
————. "Religion and Political Integration in Israel." *Jewish Journal of Sociology*, 17 (June 1975), 17–27.
————. "The Rise of Neo-Traditionalism Among Modern Orthodox Jews in Israel." *Identification and the Revival of the New Religious Orthodoxies*. Edited by Louis Greenspan and William Shaffir. Forthcoming.
Lijphart, Arend. *Democracy in Plural Societies: A Comparative Exploration*. New Haven: Yale University Press, 1977.
Lilker, Shalom. "Kibbutz Judaism: A New Tradition in the Making." Doctoral dissertation, Hebrew Union College–Jewish Institute of Religion, 1972.
Lorwin, Val R. "Segmented Pluralism." *Consociational Democracy*. Edited by Kenneth McRae. Toronto: McClelland and Steward, 1974.
Luckmann, Thomas. *The Invisible Religion*. New York: Macmillan, 1967.
Lukes, Steven. "Political Ritual and Social Integration." *Sociology*, 9 (May 1975), 289–308.
Lustick, Ian. *Arabs In the Jewish State*. Austin: University of Texas Press, 1980.
McDowell, Jennifer. "Soviet Civil Ceremonies." *Journal for the Scientific Study of Religion*, 13 (September 1974), 265–280.
McRae, Kenneth, ed. *Consociational Democracy: Political Accommodation in Segmented Societies*. Toronto: McClelland and Stewart, 1974.
Mahler, Raphael. *A History of Modern Jewry, 1780–1815*. New York: Schocken Books, 1972.
Markoff, John and Daniel Regan. "The Rise and Fall of Civil Reli-

gion: Comparative Perspectives." *Sociological Analysis*, 42 (Winter 1981), 333–352.

Marmorstein, Emile. *Heaven at Bay*. London: Oxford University Press, 1969.

――――. "Religious Opposition to Nationalism in the Middle East." *Religion Society and the Individual*. Edited by J. Milton Yinger. New York: Macmillan, 1963. Pp. 542–552.

Mazuri, Ali. "Pluralism and National Integration." *Pluralism in Africa*. Edited by Leo Kuper and M. G. Smith. Berkeley, Los Angeles, London: University of California Press, 1971.

Meyer, Michael. *The Origins of the Modern Jew*. Detroit: Wayne State University, 1967.

Moodie, T. Dunbar. *The Rise of Afrikanerdom: Power Apartheid and the Afrikaner Civil Religion*. Berkeley, Los Angeles, London: University of California Press, 1975.

Mosse, George L. "National Cemeteries and National Revival: The Cult of the Fallen Soldiers in Germany." *Journal of Contemporary History*, 14 (January 1979), 1–20.

――――. *The Nationalization of the Masses*. New York: Fertig, 1975.

Neusner, Jacob. *The Rabbinic Traditions About the Pharisees Before 70*, vol. 3. Leiden: Brill, 1971.

――――. *The Way of Torah: An Introduction to Judaism*. 3d ed. North Scituate, Mass.: Duxbury Press, 1979.

O'Dea, Janet. "Gush Emunim: Roots and Ambiguities." *Forum* (Fall 1976), 38–50.

Ofrat, Gideon. "The Arab in Israeli Drama." *The Jerusalem Quarterly*, no. 11 (Spring 1979), pp. 70–92.

Parsons, Talcott. "Christianity." *Encyclopedia of the Social Sciences*, Vol. II.

Pickering, W. S. F. *Durkheim on Religion*. London: Routledge and Kegan Paul, 1975.

Piscatori, James. "The Role of Islam in Saudi Arabia's Political Development." *Islam and Development*. Edited by John Esposito. Syracuse: Syracuse University Press, 1980. Pp. 123–138.

Powell, David E. *Antireligious Propaganda in the Soviet Union: A Study of Mass Persuasion*. Cambridge, Mass.: The MIT Press, 1975.

Ratosh, Yonathan. "The New Hebrew Nation." *Unease in Zion*. Edited by Ehud Ben Ezer. New York: Quadrangle Books, 1974. Pp. 201–234.

Rawidovicz, Simon. *Babylonia and Jerusalem*, vol. 2. London: Ararat, 1975.

Reich, Avshalom. "Changes and Developments in the Passover Haggadot of the Kibbutz Movement." Ph.D. dissertation. Austin: University of Texas, 1972.

Rokeach, Milton. *The Nature of Human Values*. New York: The Free Press, 1973.

Roof, Wade Clark. "Concepts and Indicators of Religious Commitment: A Critical Review." *The Religious Dimension*. Edited by Robert Wuthnow. New York: Academic Press, 1979.

Rosenbloom, Noah N. *Tradition in an Age of Reform: The Religious Philosophy of Samson Raphael Hirsch*. Philadelphia: Jewish Publication Society, 1976.

Sachar, Howard. *The Course of Modern Jewish History*. Cleveland: The World Publishing Co., 1958.

――――. *A History of Israel*. New York: Knopf, 1976.

Schechtman, Joseph B. *Fighter and Prophet: The Vladimir Jabotinsky Story*. New York: Thomas Yoselof, 1961.

Schnall, David. *Radical Dissent in Contemporary Israeli Politics*. New York: Praeger Publishers, 1979.

Schneersohn, Shulem ben [sic] (Lubbavitcher Rebbe). "Statement by the Lubbavitcher Rebbe, Rabbi Shulem ben [sic] Schneersohn, on Zionism." *Zionism Reconsidered*. Edited by Michael Selzer. New York: The Macmillan Co., 1970. Pp. 11–18.

Schneller, Raphael. "Continuity and Change in Ultra-Orthodox Education." *Jewish Journal of Sociology*, 22 (June 1980). Pp. 35–46.

Schoneveld, J. *The Bible in Israeli Education*. Assen/Amsterdam: Van Gorcum, 1976.

Schwab, Hermann. *The History of Orthodox Jewry in Germany*. London: The Mitre Press, 1950.

Schweid, Eli. *Israel at the Crossroads*. Philadelphia: Jewish Publication Society, 1973.

Shai, Donna. "Changes in the Oral Tradition Among the Jews of Kurdistan." *Contemporary Jewry*, 5 (Spring/Summer 1980), 2–10.

Shapiro, Yonathan. *The Formative Years of the Israeli Labour Party*. Beverly Hills: Sage, 1976.

Shargel, Baila. "The Evolution of the Masada Myth." *Judaism*, 28 (Summer 1979), 357–371.

Smith, Donald, ed. *Religion, Politics and Social Change in the Third World*. New York, Free Press, 1971.

――――. ed. *South Asian Politics and Religion*. Princeton: Princeton University Press, 1966.

Smith, Morton. "Palestinian Judaism in the First Century." *Israel: Its Role in Civilization*. Edited by Moshe Davis. New York: The

Jewish Theological Seminary, 1956.

Smooha, Sammy. *Israel: Pluralism and Conflict*. London: Routledge and Kegan Paul, 1978.

———. "Control of Minorities In Israel and Northern Ireland." *Comparative Studies In Society and History*, 22 (April 1980), 256–280.

Spiro, Melford. *Children of the Kibbutz*. Cambridge: Harvard University Press, 1958.

Sprinzak, Ehud. "Gush Emunim: The Tip of the Iceberg." *The Jerusalem Quarterly*. no. 21 (Fall, 1981), pp. 28–47.

Stouffer, Robert. "Civil Religion, Technocracy and the Private Sphere: Further Comments on Cultural Integration in Advanced Societies." *Journal for the Scientific Study of Religion*, 12 (December 1973).

Susser, Bernard and Don-Yehiya, Eliezer. "Prolegomena to the Study of Jewish Political Theory." *Kinship and Consent: Essays on the Jewish Political Tradition and Its Contemporary Uses*. Edited by Daniel J. Elazar. Ramat-Gan: Turtledove Publishing, 1981.

Tal, Uriel. *"Political Faith" of Nazism Prior to the Holocaust*. Diaspora Research Institute, Tel-Aviv: Tel Aviv University. 1978.

———. *Structures of German "Political Theology" in the Nazi Era*. Diaspora Research Institute, Tel-Aviv: Tel Aviv University, 1979.

Tudor, Henry. *Political Myth*. London: Macmillan, 1972.

Vital, David. *The Origins of Zionism*. London: Oxford University Press, 1975.

Weitman, Sasha R. "National Flags: A Sociological Overview." *Semiatica*, 8 (1973), 327–367.

Wilson, John F. "The Status of 'Civil Religion' in America." *The Religion of the Republic*. Edited by Elwyn A. Smith. Philadelphia: Fortress Press, 1971.

Wilson, John F. *Public Religion In American Culture*. Philadelphia: Temple University Press, 1979.

Wimberley, Ronald C. "Continuity in the Measurement of Civil Religion." *Sociological Analysis*, 40 (Spring 1979), 59–62.

Wright, G. E. "History and Reality: The Importance of Israel's 'Historical' Symbols for Christian Faith." *The Old Testament and Christian Faith*. Edited by B. W. Anderson. London: SCM Press, 1964.

Yadin, Yigael. *Masada*. New York: Random House, 1968.

———. *The Message of the Scrolls*. New York: Simon and Schuster, 1957.

Yaron, Zvi. "Religion in Israel." *American Jewish Year Book 1976*.

Edited by Morris Fine and Milton Himmelfarb. Philadelphia: Jewish Publication Society, 1976.

Yehoshua, A. B. "On Hebrew Holocaust Literature." *The Jerusalem Quarterly*, 16 (Summer 1980), 97.

Zucker, Norman L. and Zucker, Naomi. *The Coming Crisis in Israel: Private Faith and Public Policy*. Cambridge, Mass.: MIT Press, 1973.

Books and Articles in Hebrew

Adar, Zvi. *Jewish Education in Israel and the United States*. Tel Aviv: Gomeh, 1969.

Adler, Chaim and Kahana, Reuven, eds. *Values, Religion and Culture*. Jerusalem: Akadamon, 1975.

Ahimeir, Abba. *Brit Habiryonim*. Tel Aviv: Havaad L'hotzaat Kitvei Abba Ahimeir, 1972.

———. *Revolutionary Zionism*. Tel Aviv: Havaad L'hotzaat Kitvei Abba Ahimeir, 1966.

Amiel, Moshe Avigdor. "After the Congress and Before the Congress." *Hator*. September–December, 1934.

———. "Again on the Ideological Foundations of Mizrachi." *Hator*. 24 August, 1934.

Amiel, Moshe Avigdor. "Who Are We?" *Hator*. September 28, 1932.

Amitai, M. "Ma Nishtana on the Kibbutz." *The Book of Festivals*, vol. 2. Edited by Yom Tov Levinski. Tel Aviv: Dvir, 1956.

Amital, Yehuda. *Upward From the Depths*. Jerusalem: Hotzaat Agudat Yeshivat Har Etzion, 1974.

Among Young People. Mimeographed booklet. Kibbutz Ein Shemer, 1969.

Barzel, Alexander. "Judaism as a *Weltanschauung* and its Expression in the Labor Movement." *Kivunim*, 6 (May 1980), 87–106.

Begin, Menachem. *In the Underground*. Tel Aviv: Hadar, 1978.

Bella, Moshe, ed. *The World of Jabotinsky*. Tel Aviv: Dfusim, 1975.

Benari, N. "The *Bikkurim* Ceremony in the Collective Settlements." *The Book of Festivals*, vol. 3. Edited by Yom Tov Levinski. Tel Aviv: Dvir, 1956.

———. *Sabbath and Festival*. Tel Aviv: Histadrut, 1946.

——— and Nisimov, N. "Sukkot in the Collective Settlement." *The Book of Festivals*, vol. 4. Edited by Yom Tov Levinski. Tel Aviv: Dvir, 1956.

Ben-Avraham, S. "Religion, Nationality and Secularism." *Al Ha'Mishmar*, 11 January–2 February, 1976.

Ben Gurion, David. *The Eternity of Israel.* Tel Aviv: Eynot, 1964.
————. *In the Conflict,* vol. 4. Tel Aviv: Hotzaat Mapai, 1949.
————. *The Renewed State of Israel.* Tel Aviv: Am Oved, 1969.
————. *Stars and Dust.* Ramat Gan: Massada, 1976.
————. *Uniqueness and Purpose.* Jerusalem: Maarachot, 1971.
————. *Vision and Way,* 2d ed. Tel Aviv: Hotzaat Mapai, 1953.
Ben-Meir, Yehuda, and Kedem, Peri. "A Measure of Religiosity for the Jewish Population of Israel." *Megamot,* 24 (February 1979), 353–362.
Ben-Yehuda, Baruch "The Holiday in Memory of the Bringing of the *Bikkurim.*" *The Book of Festivals.* Edited by Yom Tov Levinski. Tel Aviv: Dvir, 1956. 3:202–204.
————. Baruch "The Tradition of the Flag of Jerusalem on Sukkot." *The Book of Festivals.* Edited by Yom Tov Levinski. Tel Aviv: Dvir, 1956. 4:306.
Ben-Yeruham, H., ed. *The Book of Betar—Origins and Sources,* vol. 1. Jerusalem: Havaad L'hotzaat Sefer Betar, 1969.
Ben-Zohar, Michael. *Ben Gurion: A Political Biography,* vol. 2. Tel Aviv: Am Oved, 1978.
Ben-Zvi, Shabtai. *Post-Uganda Zionism in the Crises of the Holocaust.* Tel Aviv: Bronfman, 1977.
Biletsky, Eliyahu. *Solel Boneh.* Tel Aviv: Am Oved, 1975.
Birnbaum, Nathan. *The Nation of God.* Bnei Brak: Nezah, 1977.
Blau, Moshe. *Column of Light.* Jerusalem: Homot Yerushalayim, 1968.
Borochov, Ber. *Writings,* vol. 3. Tel Aviv: Sifriyal Poalim V'Hakibbutz Hameuchad, 1960.
Braslavsky, Moshe. *The Workers' Movement in the Land of Israel.* Tel Aviv: Hakibbutz Hameuchad, 1959.
Dayan, Moshe. *To Live With the Bible.* Jerusalem: Edayim, 1978.
"The Day of Memorial for the Holocaust and Bravery." *Informational Guidelines to the Commander, no. 16.* Educational Office of the Army (April 1976).
Dinur, Benzion. "The Holiday of Hasmoneans." *The Book of Festivals.* Edited by Yom Tov Levinski. Tel Aviv: Dvir, 1956. 5:197–198.
Donitz, Yigal. "Ben Gurion's Fundamental Political-Military Understanding and His Conception of the Israeli Arab Conflict." *Medina Umimshal,* 1 (1971), 60–76.
Don-Yehiya, Eliezer. "Cooperation and Conflict Between Political Camps: The Religious Camp and the Labor Movement and the Education Crises in Israel." Ph.D. dissertation, Hebrew University, 1977.

————. "Ideology and Policy: The Zionist Conception of Rav Reines and the Position of Mizrachi on the Uganda Question." *Religion and Zionism: The Relations Between Religious and Secular in the Zionist Movement*. Tel Aviv: Tel Aviv University, Hamachon L'heker Hatziyonut, forthcoming.

————. "Stability and Change in a Camp Party." *Medina U'memshal*, no. 14 (November, 1979), pp. 25–52.

Don-Yehiya, Eliezer, and Liebman, Charles S. "Separation of Religion and State." *Molad*, 25–26 (August/September 1972), 159–171.

Don-Yehiya, Shabbetai. *The Holy Rebellion*. Tel Aviv: Moreshet, 1960.

Education in Israel. Jerusalem: Hotzaat Misrad Hahinuh, 1973.

Elam, Yigal. "The Zionist Crises—The Jewish Crises." *B'Tfutzot Ha'Golah*, 75/76 (Winter 1975), 52–58.

Eliav, Binyamin, ed. *The Jewish National Home*. Jerusalem: Keter, 1976.

Eliav, Mordechai. "Toward a History of the Zionist Flag." *Kivunim*, 3 (June 1979), 47–59.

Even-Shoshan. *The History of the Labor Movement in the Land of Israel*. Tel Aviv: Am Oved, 1969.

Even-Zahav, Itamar. "The Flowering and Crystallization of Local and Native Hebrew Culture in the Land of Israel, 1882–1948." *Catedra*, no. 16 (July 1980), pp. 165–189.

Fishman, Aryei, ed. *Hapoel Hamizrachi: 1921–1935*. Tel Aviv: Tel Aviv University, 1979.

————. "The Religious Kibbutz: A Study in the Interrelationship of Religion and Ideology in the Context of Modernization." Ph.D. dissertation, Hebrew University, 1975.

Fishman, Yaacov. "The Soil Educates," *Davar*, 20 April 1932.

Friedman, Menachem. *Society and Religion: The Non-Zionist Orthodox in Eretz-Israel, 1918–1936*. Jerusalem: Yad Izhak Ben-Zvi, 1977.

Getter, Miryam. "The Ideology of Lehi." M.A. thesis, Tel Aviv University, 1967.

Giladi, M. "Critique of Democracy." *Hayarden* (August 27, 1937).

Goldman, Eliezer. *Jewish Law and the State*. Tel Aviv: Kibbutz Dati, 1954.

————. "The Jewish Test of the State of Israel." *Amudim*, 24 (Kislev, 1976), 100–105.

Gorarli, Moshe. "The Holiday of the *Bikkurim* in the Tones of the Homeland." *The Book of Festivals*. Edited by Yom Tov Levinski.

Tel Aviv: Dvir, 1956. 3:220.

Gordon, A(haron). *The Nation and the Labor.* Jerusalem: The Zionist Press, 1952.

Habas, Bracha, ed. *The Book of Aliyat Hanoar.* Jerusalem: The Jewish Agency, 1941.

Harkabi, Yehoshafat. *Facing Reality: Lessons From Jeremiah, The Destruction of the Second Temple and Bar Kokhba's Rebellion.* Jerusalem: Van Leer Foundation, 1982.

Hilb, K. "Religion and State." *B'terem*, no. 1 (January 1951), pp. 8–11.

Hurgin, Yaacov. "He Will Come as a Victor." *Haumah*, 3 (June 1964), 7–13.

Jabotinsky, Ze'ev. *First Zionist Writings.* Jerusalem: Eri Jabotinsky Press, 1949.

———. *The Man and His Doctrines.* Tel Aviv: The Ministry of Defense, 1980.

———. *Speeches, 1906–1926.* Jerusalem: Eri Jabotinsky Press, 1947.

———. *Speeches, 1927–1940.* Jerusalem: Eri Jabotinsky Press, 1948.

Kahana, Reuven. "Patterns of National Identity in Israel." *Education and Society in Israel.* Edited by S. N. Eisenstadt, H. Adler, R. Kahana, and I. Shelach. Jerusalem: Akadamon, 1958. Pp. 39–56.

Kaniel, Yehoshua. *Continuity and Change: Old Yishuv and New Yishuv During the First and Second Aliyah.* Yad Izhak Ben Zvi, 1981.

Katz, Jacob. *Jewish Nationalism: Essays and Studies.* Jerusalem: The Zionist Library, World Zionist Organization, 1979.

Katznelson, Berl. *Writings*, vol. 6. Tel Aviv: Hotzaat Mapai, 1947.

Kaufman, Yehezkel. *Diaspora and Alienation*, vol. 2. Tel Aviv: Dvir, 1932.

Kedar, Binyamin. "The Masada Complex." *Ha'Aretz.* 22 April 1973.

Klausner, Joseph. " 'Hanukkah'—A Symbol and a Warning." *The Book of Festivals.* Edited by Yom Tov Levinski. Tel Aviv: Dvir, 1956. 5:189–191.

Knaani, David. *The Second Worker Aliya and its Attitude Toward Religion and Tradition.* Tel Aviv: Tel Aviv University Press, 1976.

Kook, Abraham Isaac. *Orot.* Jerusalem: Mossad Harav Kook, 1950.

———. *Letters of Harav Kook*, vol. 2. Jerusalem: Mossad Harav Kook, 1962.

Kook, Zvi Yehuda. *To the Paths of Israel*, vol. 1. Rev. ed. Jerusalem: Zur-Ot, 1969.

Krasel, Gideon, *From Everyone According to His Ability: Stratification versus Ability on the Kibbutz.* Tel Aviv: Gomeh, 1974.

Kurzweil, Baruch. *Our New Literature—Continuity or Revolution?* Jerusalem: Schocken, 1965.

Madrich, M. "A National Education." *Hayarden* (August 27 1937).

Lamdan, Yizḥak. *Masada, Poems.* Jerusalem: Mossad Bialik, 1973: 27—75.

Lamm, Zvi. "Imprints of Traditionalism and the Process of Modernization in Judaism." *B'Tfutzot Ha'Golah*, 73/74 (Summer 1975), 62—72.

Laskov, Shulamit. *Yosef Trumpeldor: A Biography.* Haifa; Shikmona, 1972.

Leibowitz, Yeshayahu. "In the Absence of Ideological and Spiritual Content the Nation Integrates Around Fascist Values." *Ha'Aretz.* 1 April 1975.

Leibowitz, Yeshayahu. *Judaism, the Jewish People and the State of Israel.* Jerusalem: Schocken, 1975.

Levy, Shlomit and Guttman, Louis. *Values and Attitudes of Israel High School Youth.* Jerusalem: The Israel Institute of Applied Social Research, 1976.

Levine, Israel Lee. "On the Political Involvement of the Pharisees Under Herod and the Procurators." *Cathedra*, no. 8 (July 1978), pp. 12—28.

Liebman, Charles S. "Toward the Study of Israeli Folk Religion." *Megamot*, 23 (April 1977), 95—109.

Maor, Yaacov "How Is This Haggada Different?" *Yediot Aharonot.* 1 April, 1955.

Milstein, Uri. *By Blood and Fire Judea.* Tel Aviv: Lewin Epstein, 1973.

Mohar, Eli. "If You Wish—This Is a Haggada." *Bamaḥaneh.* 14 April 1976.

Niv, David. *The Battles of the Irgun Zvai Leumi*, vol. 1. Tel Aviv: Mossad Klausner, 1965.

Ofrat, Gideon. *Land, Man, Blood: The Myth of the Ḥalutz and the Ritual of the Land in the Settlement Camps.* Tel Aviv: Tcherikover, 1980.

Ornan, Uzi. "Jewish Consciousness—Heretical Reservations." *Haḥinuḥ*, 5/6 (July 1976), 334—339.

Oz, Amos. "Meaning of Homeland." *Who Is the Left? Zionism Answers Back.* Jerusalem: Hasifriya Hatziburit, 1971.

Persky, Daniel. "A Passover Seder for Workers in Tel Aviv." *The Book of Festivals.* Edited by Yom Tov Levinski. Tel Aviv: Dvir, 1956. 2:469—470.

The Protocol of the Temporary National Council, vol. 1, 10th session. Also vol. 2, 23d session.

Raanan, Zvi. *Gush Emunim*. Tel Aviv: Sifriyat Hapoalim, 1980.
Ratosh, Yonathan, ed. *From Victory to Defeat*. Tel Aviv: Hadar, 1976.
Reines, Isaac. *The Gates of Light and Joy*. Vilna: R'em, 1890.
————. *A New Light on Zion*. Vilna: R'em, 1902.
Remba, Isaac. "Religion and Tradition in His Life and Thought," *Haumah*, 3 (June 1964), 145–166.
Report of the Investigation Committee in the Matter of Education in the Immigrant Camps. Jerusalem: The Knesset, May 9, 1950.
Rivlin, Gershon, ed. *The Legacy of Tel Ḥai*. Tel Aviv: Maarachot, 1970.
Rogel, Nakdimon. *Tel Ḥai*. Tel Aviv: Yariv-Hadar, 1979.
Rubinstein, Amnon. *From Herzl to Gush Emunim, and Back Again*. Tel Aviv: Schocken, 1980.
————. *To Be a Free People*. Jerusalem: Schocken, 1977.
Samet, Moshe. *Religion and State in Israel*. Papers in Sociology, Jerusalem: Hebrew University of Jerusalem, 1979.
Schechtman, Joseph B. and Benari, Yehuda. *History of the Revisionist Movement*. Tel Aviv: Hadar, 1970.
Schweid, Eliezer. *Judaism and the Secular Culture*. Tel Aviv: Hakibbutz Hameuchad, 1981.
Shapira, Anita. "The Conflict Within Mapai Over the Use of Violence." *Hazionut*. Tel Aviv: Hakibbutz Hameuchad, 1978. 5: 141–181.
Shapira, Anita. *Berl*. Tel Aviv: Am Oved, 1980.
Shavit, Yaacov. *From a Majority to a State*. Tel Aviv: Yariv, 1978.
Sheinfeld, Moshe. *The Children of Teheran Accuse*. Jerusalem: Agudat Israel, 1943.
Shelah, Ilana. *Indications Toward Secular Religion in Israel*. Papers in Sociology, Jerusalem: Hebrew University of Jerusalem, 1975.
Shuster, Yehuda. "A Theoretical Model of Fascist Ideology." M.A. thesis, Hebrew University, Jerusalem, 1976.
"Society in Protracted Conflict." *Skira Ḥodshit*, (August/September, 1975).
Syrkin, Nachman. *The Writings of Nachman Syrkin*. Edited by Berl Katznelson and Yehuda Kaufman. Tel Aviv: Davar, 1939.
Talmon-Gerber, Yonina. *Individual and Society in the Kibbutz*. Jerusalem: Magnes Press, 1970.
Teaching the Holocaust in Schools. Jerusalem: Ministry of Education, 1961.
"To Be a Jew." *B'Tfutzot Ha'Golah*, 16 (Summer 1974), 117–126.
Tzur, Muky. *Doing It the Hard Way*, Tel Aviv: Am Oved, 1976.

Vigiser, Dan. "The Labor Party of Israel and Mizrachi, Hapoel Hamizrachi: Between Rivalry and Cooperation." M.A. thesis, Bar-Ilan University, 1978.

Vision and Independence. A Play for the Independence Holiday. Jerusalem: Publications of the Jewish National Fund, 1952.

Wasserman, Elhanan. *The Footsteps of the Messiah.* 3d ed. Bnei Brak: Histadrut Z'erei Agudat Israel, n.d. First published in 1942.

Weiss, Raphael. "From Holy to Profane," *L'shonenu L'am*, no. 271 (1977).

Wiener, Max. *The Jewish Religion in the Emancipation Period.* Jerusalem: Mossad Bialik, 1974.

Yaron, Zvi. *The Philosophy of Rabbi Kook.* Jerusalem: The Department of Torah Education and Culture of the World Zionist Organization, 1974.

Yehoshua, A. B. "A Return to Ideology." *B'Tfutzot Ha'Golah*, 75/76 (Winter 1975), 28–40.

Yellin-More, Nathan. *Lohamei Herut Yisrael.* Tel Aviv: Shikmona, 1974.

Yevin, Yehoshua. *Writings.* Tel Aviv: Havaad L'hotzaat Kitvei Yevin, 1969.

Zeitlin, Aharon. *State and Vision of State.* Tel Aviv: Am Oved, 1956.

Zimmerman, B'eri. "The Priority of Man Over Soil: A Comparison of Brenner and Hanan Porat." *Shdemot*, no. 72 (Tishrei 1980), pp. 71–75.

Index

293

Designer: UC Press Staff
Compositor: Trend Western
Printer: Braun-Brumfield
Binder: Braun-Brumfield
Text: 11 point Janson
Display: Janson